Jane Austen's Women

D1596673

Kathleen Anderson

Jane Austen's Women

An Introduction

Published by State University of New York Press, Albany

© 2018 State University of New York

All rights reserved

Printed in the United States of America

No part of this book may be used or reproduced in any manner whatsoever without written permission. No part of this book may be stored in a retrieval system or transmitted in any form or by any means including electronic, electrostatic, magnetic tape, mechanical, photocopying, recording, or otherwise without the prior permission in writing of the publisher.

For information, contact State University of New York Press, Albany, NY
www.sunypress.edu

Library of Congress Cataloging-in-Publication Data

Names: Anderson, Kathleen, 1967– author.
Title: Jane Austen's women : an introduction / Kathleen Anderson.
Description: Albany : State University of New York Press, 2018. | Includes
  bibliographical references and index.
Identifiers: LCCN 2017061602 | ISBN 9781438472256 (hardcover : alk. paper) |
  ISBN 9781438472263 (pbk. : alk. paper) | ISBN 9781438472270 (ebook)
Subjects: LCSH: Austen, Jane, 1775–1817—Characters. | Austen, Jane,
  1775–1817—Criticism and interpretation. | Women in literature.
Classification: LCC PR4038.C47 A63 2018 | DDC 823/.7—dc23
LC record available at https://lccn.loc.gov/2017061602

10 9 8 7 6 5 4 3 2 1

Contents

Part 2
Women's Natures: Mood, Mind, Spirit,
and Female Giftedness

Part 3
Women and Others: The Female Self in Environmental,
Social, and Imaginative Space

Acknowledgments

I am grateful to all the people who have contributed to this book and who have enriched my life in diverse ways.

The dedicated work for many years of librarians Nerolie Ceus and Julia Pichette made this book possible.

I wish to thank Susan E. Jones and Susan Allen Ford for their critical input as well as longtime mentorship and encouragement.

Jordan L. Von Cannon generously co-authored the essay that has become chapter 3.

Thank you to editorial assistants Katie Barriga and C. Dale Girardi Shaw and research assistants Kelsey Satalino and Christopher Jensen for providing valuable feedback and accountability that were instrumental to my completion of this study. Thanks as well to Father Charles Browning for consultation on Anglican history and to him, David Lashbrook, and Carla Yarbrough—former English Department work-study students—for their assistance with the early research stage. Thanks to Jessica Redman for consultation on psychology.

I appreciate the generous support of Palm Beach Atlantic University, the administration, and the Faculty Research Committee for the sabbatical and course load reductions that provided essential time for research and writing.

Thank you to my colleagues for their ongoing support, especially Susan E. Jones and Jenifer Elmore, for helpful and motivating discussions of my work, and Lee Prescott, David Athey, Linda Raeder, and Kimberly Ladd.

The Jane Austen Society of North America (JASNA) has provided numerous opportunities for me to share my scholarship through publication in the society's journals and presentations as a Travel Lecturer and as a Breakout Speaker at Annual General Meetings. Thanks to Joan Klingel Ray, Bobbie Gay, Iris Lutz, and Isa Schaff for their active efforts to make me feel at home in the JASNA community, and to the JASNA-South Florida region for their Austenian comradeship. Thank you to the Massachusetts and Maine regions for inviting me to give the keynote at their super-regional conference, and to the Arizona region for making me a part of their entertaining Jane Austen Day event. The Jane Austen Society of Australia (JASA) and its president, Susannah Fullerton, also gave me a gracious welcome and enthusiastic response as a keynote speaker in Sydney. It is a privilege to be surrounded by so many clever Austen-lovers and to benefit from their insights.

Thank you to Cornel West for his generosity in sharing his time and wisdom with me in multiple phone interviews.

I am grateful to Goucher College for selecting me as the Jane Austen Scholar-in-Residence for 2015–2016, and especially to Juliette Wells, Nancy Magnuson, Tara Olivero, and Deborah Harner for making my experience both productive and enjoyable. Thanks to Susan Allen Ford and Devoney Looser for recommending me, and to Laurie Kaplan for originally encouraging me to apply. This research opportunity helped me to refine chapter 5 and provided material for a new project.

Thanks to Liz Benson Johnson of the University of Minnesota Duluth, and Ellen Marks, Ron Strickland, and Dana Van Kooy of Michigan Technological University for the welcome and library resource access that facilitated my summer of intensive revisions.

The educators in my life also contributed to this book, especially Florence S. Boos, and in grateful memory of Archibald

Coolidge and Richard "Jix" Lloyd-Jones of my doctoral program at the University of Iowa. Alan D. Hodder was a critical positive influence at Harvard. Thanks also to Cathedral High School English teachers Sister Clare Witzman, OSB, and Bob Karn, and youth mentors Larry "Papa" Haws (in memoriam) and Kelly Stark-Haws.

Thank you to my family—Dr. James and Mary Theresa Anderson, Mark Anderson and Sudha Prathikanti, Tim Anderson and Audrey Yang, and Jane Neuhaus and my extended family—for their love and support.

Appreciation to my church family at St. Nicholas Melkite Catholic Church for embracing me as part of the community.

Thanks to the good friends from all the places and phases of my life.

Thanks to my students for being a constant inspiration to me.

Thank you to Marion Donahue for saying that my and Susan E. Jones' Jane Austen class changed her life.

My gratitude to the anonymous reviewers who saw merit in this study.

Thank you to Amanda Lanne-Camilli, Chelsea Miller, Eileen Nizer, and Kate Seburyamo at the State University of New York Press.

Thanks to the editors of the publications credited below for allowing me to incorporate previously published material into this book:

The majority of chapter 1 is an edited version of an article published under the title, "Lounging Ladies and Galloping Girls: Physical Strength and Femininity in *Mansfield Park*," in *Women's Studies: An Interdisciplinary Journal* 38.3 (2009): 342–358. Chapter 1 also contains selected material from an article published under the title, "The Jane Austen Diet: The Weight of Women in Austen's Letters," in *Persuasions: The Jane Austen Journal* 27 (2005): 75–87.

Chapter 3 is an edited version of an article originally titled, "Mrs. Jennings and Mrs. Palmer: The Path to Female Self-Determination in Austen's *Sense and Sensibility*," co-authored with Jordan L. Von Cannon and published in *Persuasions: The Jane Austen Journal* 30 (2008): 135–148.

A portion of chapter 5 was originally published as "The 'Ordination' of Fanny Price: Female Monasticism and Vocation in *Mansfield Park*," in *Persuasions: The Jane Austen Journal On-Line* 35.1 (2014); see *jasna.org*.

Selected material from chapter 6 was published in an article entitled, " 'Every day was adding to the verdure of the early trees': Women, Trees, and the Relationship between Self and Other in Jane Austen's Novels," in *ISLE: Interdisciplinary Studies in Literature and Environment* 25.1 (2018): 80–94.

Selected material was incorporated into chapter 8 from the article, "Jane's 'Wonder Women': Female Heroism the Austenian Way," published in *Sensibilities: The Journal of the Jane Austen Society of Australia* 33 (December, 2006): 20–34.

Abbreviations

The following title abbreviations are used to cite Austen's novels:

E	*Emma*
MP	*Mansfield Park*
NA	*Northanger Abbey*
P	*Persuasion*
PP	*Pride and Prejudice*
SS	*Sense and Sensibility*

Preface

"Nobody doubts her right to have precedence"

Jane Austen's Heroine as Universal Subject

It is an audacious act to produce yet another book about a beloved literary giant. The critical and popular fascination with Jane Austen and her milieu continues unabated, as demonstrated by an endless parade of nonfiction, fiction, media enactments, and novelty gifts that range from the erudite to the profane. Admiration of Austen needs no more explanation than does an enthusiasm for Shakespeare or Mozart, of course, but the intensity of Austen "mania" for over the past two decades in a postmodern culture that actively undercuts many of the values and ideals she endorses renders understandable people's curiosity about the phenomenon. The Regency novelist provokes a prolific creative response in many present-day writers and artisans that manifests their desire to inscribe themselves into her witty world. The magnitude of Austen's literary achievement and the fascination of her novels across the boundaries of time, gender, race, and culture are incontestable.

Among the uninitiated, the uniquely modern practice persists of exoticizing Austen's fiction as "chick lit" and, therefore, inferior.[1] Even seemingly sympathetic media writers sometimes misrepresent the author, her work, and her readers by conflating them with tired female stereotypes that are trotted out like so many dresses at a Regency ball. In coverage of the Annual General Meeting of the Jane Austen Society of North America (JASNA), a penchant for tea, dancing, and parading in historically accurate costume is often equated with triviality rather than good taste and a delightful sense of humor, for example. After conjuring this image of silly girly-chicks playing dress-up, some reporters hasten backhandedly to defend them against the audience's presumed disdain: "These people are not just crazed fans; they're intelligent career women, most of them" ("Oh Mr. Darcy!") whose remarks at the convention proved them to be "not entirely unreceptive to readings that probed underneath the seemingly decorous surfaces of Austen's novels" (Schuessler). The annual "Hemingway Days" events include arm-wrestling and fishing championships, the " 'Papa' Hemingway Look-Alike Contest," and a fake "Running of the Bulls" in which the over one hundred bearded contestants parade through the streets of Key West astride toy bulls on wheels. Yet these entertainments do not seem to necessitate justification of the participants as "intelligent career men," or to call into question the intellectual depth or breadth of appeal of Hemingway's fiction.[2] The wishful insistence on Austen's bonneted benignity betrays its absurdity the moment one opens her novels and confronts the razor-sharp edge of her social satire, just as the caricature of her readers as frivolous air-heads breaks down if one bothers to get to know them. The misogyny behind such attempts to assemble a straw-woman to burn was exposed in an especially malevolent form when the activist who initiated a campaign to feature more women on British currency, a movement many credit for Jane Austen's 2017 appearance on the English ten-pound note, received death threats.[3] However, I will "[l]et other pens dwell on guilt and misery" (*MP* 461).[4] At least the futility of reductionism toward genius, whether female or male in origin, transmutes into farce an otherwise superfluous aggression.

Despite Austen's gender-transcending brilliance, it would be equally absurd to suggest that she does not have special significance for women readers. Her chosen representative of the universal human being in her novels is a woman. Like all male authors whose heroes exemplify humanity as well as a distinctly male subjectivity, Austen depicts heroines as the natural everyperson. Women are the filtering agents in her fiction, and their daily concerns are presented as not only valid, but of chief interest and importance.[5] Her narrator assumes our shared identification with her heroines and invites us into their interior lives—thoughts, convictions, feelings, experiences—while nearly shutting the door on the masculine realm of their consorts. In the process, Austen avoids condescending to her own. Her protagonists are not the angelic "pictures of perfection"[6] she detests; they are multifarious, flawed, mutable. She tests them and they grow before attaining the rewards of that growth as paid in self-knowledge and happy alliances. Though the world belonged to men during Austen's age, at least in the political, economic, and conventional social sense, they occupy a secondary position in her literary imagination. The male characters are relevant only as seen through women's eyes.

The enormity of this contribution becomes clearer when one considers that more than a century after Austen, Virginia Woolf complains of the preponderance of male-centric, female-annihilating narratives in which the first-person point of view becomes an apt metaphor for a masculine egotism fed by privilege. In *A Room of One's Own*, she describes reading a typical male-authored novel by "Mr. A" and being oppressed by the overbearingly self-interested "I" that casts its "shadow . . . across the page":

One began dodging this way and that to catch a glimpse of the landscape behind it. Whether that was indeed a tree or a woman walking I was not quite sure. Back one was always hailed to the letter 'I.' One began to be tired of 'I.' Not but what this 'I' was a most respectable 'I'; honest and logical; as hard as a nut, and polished for centuries by good teaching and good feeding. I respect and admire that 'I' from the bottom of my heart. But—here I turned a page or two, looking for something or other—the worst of it is that in the shadow of the letter 'I' all is shapeless as mist. Is that a tree? No, it is a woman. But . . . she has not a bone in her body, I thought, watching Phoebe, for that was her name, coming across the beach. Then Alan got up and the shadow of Alan at once obliterated Phoebe. (99–100)

This comical critique targets the entitlement that nurtures a male author's perpetuation of his superiority complex in his fictional counterparts, to the detriment of his craft. By contrast, Woolf ranks Austen with Shakespeare, praising her nonreactivity and realization of her talent in the likes of *Pride and Prejudice* despite the social shame imposed on female authorship during her time: "I could not find any signs that her circumstances had harmed her work in the slightest. That, perhaps, was the chief miracle about it. Here was a woman about the year 1800 writing without hate, without bitterness, without fear, without protest, without preaching. That was how Shakespeare wrote" (68). In the mid-twentieth century, Simone de Beauvoir encapsulates the gender bias of her society as one in which "humanity is male and man defines woman not in herself but as relative to him" (xxii). Austen's heroines are the dominant consciousness—the essential sex—of her imaginative world, as well as more psychologically complex and realistic than the heroines depicted by other Regency novelists of both genders. Yet the primacy and multidimensionality of the autonomous female self in her fiction contributes only in lesser part to Austen's abiding significance.

The primary and quite simple reason that Jane Austen and her novels are so popular over two hundred years later, aside from their literary genius, is that she *likes* women. From a conviction of the author's affectionate justice toward them, female readers can indulge in the liberating effect of full imaginative engagement with the novels. No mental energy need be wasted in bracing ourselves to be arbitrarily sullied. Mr. Darcy will not "obliterate" Elizabeth Bennet as Alan does the spineless Phoebe in the novel by "Mr. A," and neither will the narrator demean or nullify female readers along with her. Austen's heroines and the readers they represent will be judged on merit alone. Austen likes herself as well. The voice that emanates from her fiction and letters projects a strong female consciousness characterized by not only comic transcendence, but the self-irony of acknowledged imperfection that preserves her comedy's charm without in the least weakening that core of unquestioning self-worth that comes through in every line of Austen. She allows herself, her narrator, and her heroines the only bearable form of what we now call "self-esteem," built on humility and the resistance of complacence.

It is no surprise that many female readers recognize in Austen, via the voice of her writing, an ideal best friend and mentor who demands of herself and those who aspire to her approval a perpetual striving after personal growth. She functions as a "wiser and better" (Austen-Leigh 16) older sister who, for our own good, will always tell us the truth; according to multiple biographical accounts, this is how the author felt about her sister and lifelong confidante, Cassandra.[7] Austen's readers are the Jane to her Cassandra. The surfeit of guidebooks and articles that purport to glean the author's advice not only on the more predictable topics of dating, marriage, manners, and the moral life, but on writing, thrifty living, sexual harassment, and even care of a loved one with Alzheimer's, further evidences this relationship dynamic.[8] Although we may fantasize ourselves into her heroines at their finest, this is a manifestation of our deeper aspiration to be Austen herself. We assume affinity with her through her narrator or through authorial mimicry and imaginatively circumvent her heroines' growing pains, instead inhabiting the wry omnipotence of the disseminator of novelistic justice who renders her power elegant through self-irony. We recognize the illusoriness of this identification with Austen. Our nagging sense of failure to live up to the perceived superiority of our role model perpetually distances us from her. Yet, paradoxically, our younger-sister complex confirms our resemblance to both Austen and her heroines, as does our common participation in a female universal particular. Jane Austen may be the only great writer in literary history who invites this intimacy with her, as described by Cassandra, as "a treasure, such a Sister, such a friend as never can have been surpassed,—She [is] the sun of [our] li[ves], the gilder of every pleasure, the soother of every sorrow," "a part of" ourselves and we "[love] her only too well" (20 July 1817).[9] The masterpieces of our more knowing big sister will far outlive the cleverest reinterpretation of them.

Austen sustains our fascination through the wittiness and linguistic mastery that distinguish her art and by eluding absolute categorization, whether in a literary or ideological sense. One could describe her canon as neoclassical, realistic, fantastical, moralistic, satiric, conservative, subversive.[10] She is no relativist, yet such terms can be only partial and are insufficient to describe her craft and the persona that directs her pen. Like other greats, Jane Austen gets the last laugh. No matter with what sincerity and conviction we make our truth claims about her work, we are, to varying degrees, remaking her in our own image. Interpreters are always at least partly ventriloquists, channeling ourselves through the author's voice. I do not attempt to escape that subjectivity and can only justify my impudence by quoting the narrator of *Emma*, who declares that "[s]eldom, very seldom, does complete truth belong to any human disclosure" (431). Nonetheless, I herein endeavor to transmit with clarity and candor some insights gained from twenty years of studying Jane Austen.

I am indebted to a number of scholars who have produced incisive readings of women's issues in Austen's fiction from a range of thematic foci, including Alison G. Sulloway, Deborah Kaplan, Claudia L. Johnson, Margaret Kirkham, and Devoney Looser, among others. Their work has provided both inspiration and a valuable critical foundation for my approach, and tends to emphasize the important historical influences on the author. Sulloway explicates the novelist's satire in light of her family upbringing and the philosophical, literary, and educational inheritance she received from an era reactionary to "women in general and women writers in particular" (5), tracing the author's use of the "provinces" of a woman's life as frames for portraying her experiential joys and sorrows. Kaplan contributes a cultural study of the characteristics and effects of a communal "women's culture" on Austen and other women of the period, and of the ways in which her novels reflect the sometimes conflicting values and messages of both the dominant patriarchal gentry ideology and the women's culture that persists within it. Kirkham explores Austen's work as a reflection of and response to its diverse literary-ideological context in eighteenth-century Enlightenment feminism, and Johnson analyzes the author's engagement in "a progressive middle ground" of social criticism through the medium of "conservative fiction" (*Jane* 166). Others offer astute discussions of more focused topics as applied to the author and her epoch, such as women and education, old age, or marriage.

Jane Austen's Women is a general critical introduction to Austen's women that explores the heroines' relationships to body, mind, spirit, environment, and society; how they achieve greatness; and why their stories are still profoundly pertinent to today's readers. That is not to downplay the import of historical-cultural context as a shaper of authors' and readers' divergent meanings or the complexity and flux of the self. This book is a study of the female characters' relationships to their dynamic selves and, simultaneously, a study of the novels as guidebooks on how to live out Austen's vision of the heroinism of everyday life. The chapters are grouped into themed sections accordingly.[11]

In Part 1, "Women and the Body: Strength, Sex, and Austenian Wellness," the first chapter establishes that Austen promulgates women's pursuit of physical health and stamina and the productive, pleasurable life they enable. Women are worthy of feasting and of the literary prominence to which their corporeal wellness subtly alludes. The author explores the associations between physicality and femininity with particular thoroughness in *Mansfield Park*. The heartiness of Maria and Julia Bertram and Mary Crawford suggests an unfeminine sensuality, yet the narrator likewise undercuts Fanny Price's righteous frailty as a manifestation of her initial passivity and social precariousness. Somewhere between the extremes of hyperactive Aunt Norris and slug-like Lady Bertram exists the locus of Austen's ideal, active woman who takes care of herself and has nothing to prove.

Chapter 2 explores the novels' prevalent theme of female sexuality. Austen portrays what I denote "sexual orthodoxy" as a critical strategy of self-protection against male exploitation and domestic violence. Her heroines who not only avoid marrying likely abusers but gain the best husbands are self-respecting women who convey unattainability and require suitors to complete a difficult chivalric test. On their journey of desire, they reject the sensualist male who ultimately betrays his heartless egotism, in favor of the self-disciplined man of duty who demonstrates his fidelity. Even Austen's least intelligent heroine, Catherine Morland of *Northanger Abbey*, soon learns to eschew the company of a man who fantasizes about brutalizing his horse.

Part 2, on "Women's Natures: Mood, Mind, Spirit, and Female Giftedness," opens with an examination of women's emotional lives. Chapter 3 maps out how, in *Sense and Sensibility*, Austen advocates the cultivation of a balanced, autonomous temperament as the key to mental health in an uncontrollable world. She portrays the destructive effects both of Elinor and Marianne Dashwood's emotional co-dependency and of Lady Middleton, Fanny Dashwood, and Lucy Steele's cold-hearted pragmatism. Alternatively, Mrs. Jennings and Charlotte Palmer are celebrated as models of the desirable blend of sensibility with sense; they are "determined to be happy" (*SS* 112) regardless of fickle circumstance and preserve their own psychic stability.

Chapter 4 theorizes about Austen's portrayal of women's "multiple intelligences" and her corresponding views of feminine talents and proclivities.[12] Visual artists Emma Woodhouse (*E*) and Elinor Dashwood (*SS*) draw on their skillset to promote social congruence, and Elinor as well as Eleanor Tilney (*NA*) enlightens less perceptive women through pedagogical illustration. The picturesque-savvy Miss Tilney urges Catherine Morland to reframe her perspective on the value of "embellished" historical narratives. Gifted musicians Anne Elliot (*P*) and Marianne Dashwood (*SS*), in opposite ways, learn to synchronize their needs with the duties of civility. Austen offers clear directives regarding the development, uses, and rewards of the female mind. The paramount consideration is the extent to which a woman employs her intellectual creativity to build community.

Chapter 5 explicates Austen's vision of female spirituality, in the depiction of which she draws on the medieval conception of vocation in women's religious communities. Austen's heroines represent diverse types and degrees of the contemplative and active lives, and must discern and pursue their authentic calling with the help of a spiritual sisterhood of female role models to maximize their vocational efficacy. Influenced by Aunt Norris and Susan Price, introspective "abbess" Fanny Price discovers how to apply her wisdom in productive action as a spiritual director. Busybody Emma Woodhouse must humbly accept Miss Bates's tutelage to ascertain, through observation and reflection, how to extend genuine hospitality to the lowliest guests at her table.

Part 3 is titled "Women and Others: The Female Self in Environmental, Social, and Imaginative Space." As analyzed in chapter 6, conservationist Austen shows the inextricable link between women and nature through her depiction of female characters' eco-affinities. A woman's "place"—her literal occupation of space and how she acts upon and is reflected in it—sheds light on her developing character and relationship to the world. Elizabeth Bennet is a daughter of the soil who connects with the fields and groves she traverses; Marianne Dashwood is like a dying leaf blowing downhill until reunited to the stable family tree; Emma Woodhouse's psyche resembles the shrubbery through which she must know and rebirth her better self; and Anne Elliot's oceanic consciousness requires some bordering for her to seek and find personal happiness.

Yet how do Austen's women find a place for their authentic selves in a patriarchal society that continually thwarts their will, and how do they voice their dissent when thwarted? Chapter 7 explains how Austen employs female fools as mouthpieces for controversial feminist truths. Obnoxious, oblivious, or morally questionable—and, therefore, easily dismissible—characters such as Lady Catherine de Bourgh, Charlotte Lucas (*PP*), Mrs. Elton (*E*), Mary Crawford (*MP*), and especially *Persuasion*'s Mary Musgrove protest against male privilege and female circumscription. Austen's "feminist fools" vehemently expose the logical fallacies and self-aggrandizement in men's practice of gender injustice, while the heroines of their narratives more subtly endorse their views.

The concluding chapter of this study synthesizes Austen's vision of female greatness as epitomized by the individual and collective heroic qualities of her heroines, and theorizes about Austen mania and the applicability of the novelist's principles of personal conduct in an era even more fraught with conflict and change than her own. Growth in self-knowledge is a catalyst for emancipatory self-improvement that produces positive reverberations in the larger community. The preservation of decorum under extreme conditions defines Austen's distinctive heroinism—a decorum that reflects as much a conquest of self as of adversity.

Austen portrays women's acuity, depth, and legitimacy of perspective in the realistic socio-psychological landscape of daily living. The comparative extent to which her fiction pleases and instructs the reader is not my concern in this exposition, though I presuppose that it fulfills both functions and does so effectually because the author eschews heavy didacticism and sentimentality. Her works provide a palatable form of self-help, in which shrewd comedy founded on moral and intellectual substance spurs readers' growth as an effect of their relish for her beautifully expressed convictions about truth, virtue, and the well-lived life. Austen feeds our hunger for higher standards, stricter boundaries. For order. For honor. For elevating humor, enjoyed in soul-expanding laughter that bubbles up from the catharsis of hearing what we need to know from a friend we trust, finding redemptive diversion in our blunders, and resolving to do better. Austen tells us what a woman—and therefore a human being—could and should be, irrespective of time or fashion, to the benefit of self and society. We can consign ourselves to her guidance because we know that she likes women, flaws and all, and has our best interests at heart. In that respect, her heroines are us. Therefore, if we can understand Jane Austen's women, we can begin to understand ourselves and our possibilities.

Part 1

Women and the Body

Strength, Sex, and Austenian Wellness

CHAPTER 1

"I am strong enough now to walk very well"

Vigor and Femininity in Mansfield Park

Jane Austen would be amused at the irony of beginning a women's studies analysis of her work with a focus on the female body. And yet, she wrote embodied narratives about the material world of people, places, mutton chops, and mud, in the materiality of bound print. She encourages her heroines to live in their bodies as her words live on the page because of them, and depicts a human existence in which, as in literature, physicality always points to something beyond itself. The human narrative is grounded in the mud of the material, but communicates through it the more significant realm of the unseen, the mind and spirit, the hand of its Creator. Otherwise, Austen's women (and her readers) would be no more than mutton chops. Perhaps such considerations make more justifiable and interesting beginning our study with such questions as: If we invited Jane Austen to be guest judge at a beauty pageant today, who would be her winner? What image of the female physique would she promote? In her novels, both robust and delicate women are portrayed as beautiful. The athletic Elizabeth Bennet and Marianne Dashwood as well as the more fragile Anne Elliot and Fanny Price are all attractive in their ways, and their relative size does not determine their feminine appeal for either the author or the characters who love them. Similarly, though Harriet Smith lacks heroine status, her charming corpulence equals Emma Woodhouse's "firm and upright figure" (*E* 39) in attractiveness: "She was a very pretty girl, and her beauty happened to be of a sort which Emma particularly admired. She was short, plump and fair, with a fine bloom, blue eyes, light hair, regular features, and a look of great sweetness" (23). Austen communicates a general appreciation for a range of body types and looks in her fiction, yet sketches them in such vague outlines as playfully to foil readers' preoccupation with appearances.[1] She eschews both the reduction of female identity to the sensual and the romanticization of feminine weakness, in favor of encouraging physical health and strength as a signifier of fully embodied, multidimensional selfhood—of woman's worth. Her heroines take a realist literary journey in which corporeality is not merely a requisite vehicle but a catalyst and mirror of figurative forward movement. Thus, Austen is not so interested in the facts themselves of the size, shape, or color of a woman's features as in how those features express her character and its progress—her personal growth curve.

Through numerous comedic epistolary references to her own enthusiasm for good food, the author affirms a woman's right to thrive in body. This message emerges unequivocally, despite the letters' subjectivity as literary constructs intended to entertain the recipients, and is enhanced by exaggeration.[2] Readers love Austen's oft-quoted pronouncement to her sister, Cassandra, "You know how interesting the purchase of a sponge-cake is to me" (15–17 June 1808). She similarly declares that "[g]ood apple pies are a considerable part of our domestic happiness" (17–18 October 1815), relishes "a most comfortable dinner of Soup, Fish, Bouillee, Partridges & an apple Tart" (15–16 September 1813), and praises the merit of Chicken, Asparagus, Lobster, and "Tomatas" [*sic*].[3] Austen's formal capitalization of edibles endows them with the status of proper nouns, of friends. In a letter sent shortly before her return home, Austen tells Cassandra to have a satisfying dinner prepared for herself and their mother: "You must give us something very nice, for we are used to live well" (19 June 1799).[4] On another occasion, she exults, "I always take care to provide such things as please my own appetite, which I consider as the chief merit in housekeeping. I have had some ragout veal, and I mean to have some haricot mutton tomorrow" (17–18 November 1798). Austen catalogs her consumption of objectionably unfeminine meats (ironically framed as rewards for her feminine "housekeeping") and also expresses a penchant for the inessentials of desserts, drinks, and toppings that contribute little nutritional value but add significant enjoyment to one's diet. Austen's emphasis on her gustatory pleasure seems simultaneously a satire on the social expectation of women's abstemiousness and a parody of the other extreme of male-identified self-indulgence, the latter of which was flaunted in the Regency court and elite men's clubs of her day.[5]

Beneath her burlesque of gluttonous decadence, Austen advocates in her letters the same goal she conveys through the portrayal of undernourished and well-nourished heroines in fiction: a balanced lifestyle of health achieved through reasonably pleasurable consumption, exercise, fresh air, rest, and creative enterprise. She encourages women to "live well," by contrast to the admonitory tone of such conduct-book warnings as the negative insistence on "moderation at table, and in the enjoyment of what the world calls pleasures. A young beauty, were she fair as Hebe, and elegant as the Goddess of Love herself, would soon lose these charms by a course of inordinate eating, drinking, and late hours" (*Regency* 33–34).[6] Apparently, the ill-effects to men's charms of gorging on animal flesh and drinking and gambling the night away are not cause for concern. While rejecting the one-sidedness and reactivity of etiquette authors' many injunctions to women, Austen likely agrees with the author identified as "a Lady of Distinction" that either "miserable leanness or shapeless fat" (*Regency* 37) represents an undesirable figural prototype. However, Austen also shares her society's greater anxiety over thinness as connoting sickness and the threat of early mortality.[7] She repeatedly voices concern over loved ones' loss of weight or appetite while praising their increase in either ("Eliza says she is quite well, but she is thinner than when we saw her last, & not in very good looks. I suppose she has not recovered from the effects of her illness in December" [21–22 January 1801]).

In a parallel manner, Austen's narrator bemoans the sickliness of heroines Fanny Price and Anne Elliot while affirming the gusto of her most attractive heroine, hearty hiker Elizabeth Bennet, and her most commanding one, dynamo Emma Woodhouse.[8] Emma's spunky appeal, like Elizabeth's, is associated with her enjoyment of wellness, as Mrs. Weston's burst of admiration indicates: " '[O]h! what a bloom of full health, and such a pretty height and size; such a firm and upright figure. There is health, not merely in her bloom, but in her air, her head, her glance. . . . Emma always gives me the idea of being the complete picture of grown-up health. She is loveliness itself' " (*E* 39). Mrs. Weston implies that Emma's beauty resides in not only her bodily strength, but her strong sense of self, her comfortableness in her own skin. Austen may not allow her heroines the freedom she exercises in letters to parade her gustatory enthusiasms, but she regrets their frailty and celebrates their vitality or restoration thereto—not for appearance's sake, but for themselves and their ability to fulfill their narrative mission. When one compares the developmental trajectories of female characters in Austen's novels, it becomes clear that physical condition and its unfit or fit use often function as a commentary on the merit of the characters portrayed, who fit into one of several categories or shift from one to another.

The over-exuberant women of Lydia Bennet–style "animal spirits" (*PP* 45) whose impulsive activity suggests an over-stimulated body, a dangerous sensuality, and a corresponding lack of mental and spiritual depth include *Pride and Prejudice*'s Lydia and Kitty Bennet; Eliza, her illegitimate daughter Eliza, and the pre-enlightened Marianne Dashwood in *Sense and Sensibility*; Isabella Thorpe in *Northanger Abbey*; *Mansfield Park*'s Aunt Norris, Maria and Julia Bertram, and Mary Crawford; Mrs. Elton in *Emma*; and the Musgrove sisters in *Persuasion*. Of these, Kitty and Julia are rescued from destruction by increased guidance, Henrietta Musgrove by re-alliance with her fiancé, and Louisa Musgrove and Marianne Dashwood by a chastening illness.[9]

On the other extreme from the overactive characters are the chronically sickly ones, such as Anne de Bourgh of *Pride and Prejudice* and Jane Fairfax of *Emma*. *Mansfield Park*'s Fanny Price and *Persuasion*'s Anne Elliot initially reflect this type, until they toughen up and push past being defined as pining victims. We do not learn much about the interior life of Jane Fairfax and especially of Anne de Bourgh, but their ill health seems to suggest mental weakness as manifest in an inability to rise above emotionally detrimental circumstances. Like the overactive characters, they are too self-interested; although we might sympathize with Jane's and Anne's personal challenges, their extreme introversion also proves destructive. The only likeable character in this frail group is Anne Elliot, who leaves behind the category when she becomes hardy enough to contemplate with pleasure being a sailor's wife.

A more gratuitously irresponsible group of female characters includes the dozers and the willful convalescents. The semi-comatose characters include Lady Bertram of *Mansfield Park* and, despite her attractiveness and good nature, somewhat *Emma*'s bovine Harriet Smith.[10] The hypochondriacs include Mrs. Bennet (*Pride and Prejudice*) and Mary Musgrove (*Persuasion*), who are annoying but humorously egocentric in their endless complaints. Some characters in the more credibly sickly group, such as Jane Fairfax, may be hypochondriacs as well, in a psychosomatic enactment of their suffering; however, they do not offset their tediousness by amusing the reader.

The healthy, active women who rarely, if ever, fall ill and generally live lives of moderation, principle, and reflection include Mrs. Croft, Elinor Dashwood, Aunt Gardiner, Mrs. Weston, and, more so post-reform, Elizabeth Bennet and Emma Woodhouse (and somewhat Catherine Morland). These characters do the best they can with what they have, and do not succumb to a life of superfluous hyperactivity, helpless despair, imagined or real ailments, or mind-numbing malaise. In this respect, Mrs. Smith fits the healthy category of female types, because of her mental vigor and courageous buoyancy—she chooses to live as active a life as possible in her circumstances and does not allow her diseased body to "[ruin] her spirits" (*P* 153). She refuses to define herself or to live as a sick person.[11] Admirable women take pride in neither strength nor weakness nor the feigning of either, but demonstrate outward-thinking and inward growth by developing relationships of integrity, gaining in self-knowledge, and turning thought into productive action. They are secure in themselves because they are—or, in Elizabeth's and Emma's case, determinedly become—in moral and emotional balance, as if each is in her own most natural state, neither bubbling over nor fainting away, but fully alive. Fanny Price and Anne Elliot ultimately earn membership in this vibrant group.[12]

A delicate character's increasing weight and energy are intertwined with her improved state of mind as well as lifestyle; as she learns about herself and others, she strengthens in understanding and purpose. Austen acknowledges the tangible selves of women as a semiology of their trajectory toward their rightful place in literature and life: a place of dynamism, fulfillment, and longevity that is epitomized by their wholesome blooming in the flesh. Underlying this paradigm is the author's "deep and instinctive sense of the body as an indispensable signifier" (McMaster, *Reading* 173). She explores the relationship between female corporal strength and womanliness as a central theme in *Mansfield Park*, offering readers an especially illuminating study in the author's prescription of women characters' and readers' pursuit of "fitness" in all senses. Fanny Price's body functions as a symbolic map of her personal and social development, and her increasing activity throughout the novel reinforces her bildungsroman. The Bertram circle's female family members and friends serve as both catalysts for and contrasts to her evolving identity, while the men attempt but fail to impede her self-fortification.[13]

Judging from Austen's epistolary emphasis on the importance of satisfying meals, she empathizes with *Mansfield Park*'s heroine when her neglectful parents deprive her of a farewell breakfast at the end of her Portsmouth visit: "the breakfast table . . . was quite and completely ready as the carriage drove from the door. Fanny's last meal in her father's house was in character with her first; she was dismissed from it as hospitably as she had been welcomed" (*MP* 445). Good food connotes the loving support of family, whereas its dearth conveys the corresponding absence of familial affection. The reader hopes that from this point in the novel, Fanny will never return to the chaotic, impersonal home of her early childhood. As both Austen's letters and fiction stress, bodily nurturance and the symbolic correlative of emotional nurturance are critical contributors to a woman's well-being.

Fanny Price represents the feminine ideal of frailty in some respects, but she is not allowed to rest on this ideal. As a fringe member of the Bertram household, she relies on the chivalry of her cousin Edmund to assist her with prescribed horseback riding exercise, and her corporal weakness functions as a metaphor for her social precariousness in a divergently tyrannous household of assertive women and passive-aggressive men. The narrator emphasizes Fanny's marginal position in the background of scenes, where she often sits and suffers from headaches. The underscoring of her delicacy reinforces her martyrdom by cruel relatives, but does not inherently ennoble her as a character. The repetition of references to Fanny's fragility becomes irritating, renders its realism suspect, and suggests her general lack of agency or impact. One may even feel the sadistic desire for Aunt Norris to slap Fanny out of her righteous torpidity and into concrete action.[14] Austen gently parodies the sentimental tradition's equation of femininity with exaggerated delicacy by implying Fanny's kinship with her Aunt Bertram—a woman who ignores her dysfunctional children in favor of her dog—in extreme passivity. Then the author turns around and undercuts this typecasting by gradually unveiling Fanny's Aunt Norris–like tenacity. Like a wilting woman's ineffectuality, the energetic meddling of Aunt Norris and forceful vitality of Maria and Julia Bertram and Mary Crawford—none of whom ever becomes ill in the novel—can also produce destructive consequences. Maria sacrifices everything to passion and Julia nearly does so; this bodily excess can, at worst, degenerate into an Eliza Brandon–like abandonment to promiscuity and even death. Mary Crawford dazzles Edmund with her more circumscribed vivacity, but he eventually discovers that she is unprincipled at the core, which renders her robustness repulsive and unwomanly, an outgrowth of what Edmund describes to Fanny as "blunted delicacy and a corrupted, vitiated mind" (456). In *Mansfield Park*, as in the other novels, neither bodily weakness (Fanny and Lady Bertram) nor might (Aunt Norris and her uninhibited young affiliates), whether innate or pretended, epitomizes feminine perfection. Austen intermingles and transmutes both the naïve frailty of the virtuous sentimental heroine and the heft of the Chaucerian comic wife, to endorse a healthier median between the two.

Fanny Price's physical being functions as a powerful motif that delineates her struggles and triumphs as her maturing identity emerges among extreme female role models and patriarchal would-be saboteurs. When Fanny first appears at Mansfield Park at the age of ten, she is undersized, which underscores her other disadvantages of timidity, poor education, and social insignificance: "She was small of her age, with no glow of complexion, nor any other striking beauty; exceedingly timid and shy, and shrinking from notice; but her air, though awkward, was not vulgar, her voice was sweet, and when she spoke, her countenance was pretty" (12). Fanny's littleness is a metaphor for her unrealized potential and subtlety of character as well as affectional undernourishment. Her cousins Maria and Julia are insensitive in their self-confidence, displaying a critical detachment toward their vulnerable cousin, whose ignorance they continually expose to their governess and Aunt Norris. They communicate a smug, vulgar superiority that renders their physical development a manifestation of their self-satisfaction. They use Fanny's small stature to demarcate her inferior social status and their figurative, as literal, precedence: "Her elder cousins mortified her by reflections on her size, and abashed her by noticing her shyness; Miss Lee wondered at her ignorance, and the maid-servants sneered at her clothes" (14). Other women exploit Fanny's lesser size to elevate themselves and degrade her to the bottom-rung position on the family social ladder.[15] The narrator's physiological distinctions between Fanny and her cousins are similarly revealing: "the daughters [were] decidedly handsome, and all of them well-grown and forward of their age, which produced as striking a difference between the cousins in person, as education had given to their address; and no one would have supposed the girls so nearly of an age as they really were" (13). Maria and Julia are "forward" both physically and socially; their boldness is shown to be rude, cold, and unfeminine, whereas the delicate

Fanny's "feelings were very acute, and too little understood to be properly attended to" (14). Her petite physique as a child belies her big heart and deep emotions, whereas her cousins' bodily substance belies their shallow minds. Austen is not suggesting that brawny girls are evil and slight ones are angels; rather, she presents a metaphorical commentary on the reverse development of the cousins: Fanny begins with the foundation of a strong character and grows into herself, while her cousins begin with strong selves devoid of character and never grow.

After her initial stage of alienation, Fanny plays an increasingly active role among the Bertrams. She gradually transforms from an anxious recluse on the fringe of her new family, unable to face or interact with others, to its ultimate stronghold. It is not the solicitous, oh-so-kind Edmund who most motivates Fanny to develop her familial role, but her obnoxious aunts and female cousins: "To her cousins she became occasionally an acceptable companion. . . . their pleasures and schemes were sometimes of a nature to make a third very useful, especially when that third was of an obliging, yielding temper" (17). Lady Bertram similarly recruits her niece to be her personal assistant, and "always found her very handy and quick in carrying messages, and fetching, what she wanted" (20). From Fanny's arrival at Mansfield, when Lady Bertram smiled welcomingly and was the least intimidating person at her new home, the two formed a relationship critical to Fanny's development. Her aunt's first act of kindness was to "make her sit on the sofa with herself and pug" (13). While Maria and Julia intermittently spur Fanny to action to further their entertainment, her semi-comatose aunt sticks to her with unexpected dependency. The totally passive Lady Bertram "spent her days in sitting nicely dressed on a sofa, doing some long piece of needlework, of little use and no beauty, thinking more of her pug than her children" (19–20). Because of and by comparison to Lady Bertram, Fanny becomes somewhat useful, busy, and confident. Although she assists her isolated, needy aunt with a pointless task, her own role has meaning as one of affectionate supportiveness. Whether Lady Bertram's reliance on Fanny emanates from motives of selfishness or kindness, it is her only significant, positive function in the novel. She creates a safe place of belonging within the family for her niece. This relative security nurtures Fanny's ability to assert her competence; she grows into a valued contributor by regularly administering to the smiling slug on the couch.

Lady Bertram's abandonment of the London house to remain always on the country estate, "in consequence of a little ill-health, and a great deal of indolence" (20), notably coincides with Fanny's addition to the Bertram family. Lady Bertram withdraws from social life and the limited activity involved in shuttling between homes, to almost no activity at Mansfield in her quiet companionship with Fanny, to whom she transfers most of her needlework and all of the occasional fetching errands. Thus, she simultaneously becomes less present and calls forth more presence in her niece: "Lady Bertram, sunk back in one corner of the sofa . . . was just falling into a gentle doze, while Fanny was getting through the few difficulties of her work for her" (126). Lady Bertram's physical weakness suggests her lack of substance and general apathy toward existence; she is not cruel, but she is usually indifferent. Fanny, however, struggles against physical weakness and strives to contribute to the Bertrams' lives through active good. Lady Bertram chooses a life of extreme retirement and is tolerated in it because of her status; Fanny aspires to justify her dependent position through usefulness and takes small initiatives to help Lady Bertram with her "work." Her aunt's inertia manifests her inconsequentiality, whereas the more Fanny develops socially and intellectually through utility to the Bertram women as well as through the "education and manners" (276) her uncle and Edmund provide, the more she grows physically in an outward manifestation of increasing self-realization.[16]

The primary way that Fanny endeavors to gain strength is through horseback riding. Edmund tells Mary Crawford, " 'Every sort of exercise fatigues her so soon . . . except riding' " (95). The differences in the two women's motivations for and styles of riding dramatize their differences of character. Sensitive Fanny exercises moderately for wholesome self-improvement, and although she finds the activity pleasurable, her subdued method of enjoying it embodies civilized self-restraint, decorum, and sensibility. By contrast, Mary is ceaselessly active and vivacious. She loves to ride and has no wish and little self-discipline to discontinue fulfilling her desire. From the beginning of their acquaintance, it is clear to the reader that Mary possesses more vitality and less virtue than Fanny:

> Miss Crawford's enjoyment of riding was such, that she did not know how to leave off. Active and fearless, and, though rather small, strongly made, she seemed formed for a horsewoman; and to the genuine pleasure of the exercise, something was probably added in Edmund's attendance and instructions, and something more in the conviction of very much surpassing her sex in general by her early progress, to make her unwilling to dismount. (66–67)

While waiting for her mare, Fanny watches Mary's riding triumph from a distance, observing that after she trots in a circle with Edmund, "at *her* apparent suggestion, they rose into a canter; and to Fanny's timid nature it was most astonishing to see how well she sat. . . . he was evidently directing her management of the bridle, he had hold of her hand; she saw it, or the imagination supplied what the eye could not reach" (67). Some scholars identify sexual connotations in *Mansfield Park*'s horseback riding metaphor, in which the female characters' attitudes toward riding correspond to their moral firmness or lassitude.[17] Mary's bold initiation of Edmund's canter with her in this scene adds codified emphasis to her seduction of him—she instigates his ride, leads him astray, coyly directs his direction of her while gesturing toward deferral to his manly prerogative of instruction. She boasts openly, " 'I am very strong. Nothing ever fatigues me, but doing what I do not like' " (68). She attracts Edmund by displaying her willful hardihood while feigning reliance on his guidance—even as she makes clear the pretense of this reliance—and by parading as witty modesty her avowal of selfishness.

Edmund is instinctively drawn to the woman who most resembles his own sisters in her self-assurance of body and mind, and who also embodies in her narcissistic self-conviction a feminine version of himself. Mary Crawford's affiliation with his sisters, centered on a kinship of athleticism, is also central to the narrative's differentiation between Fanny's character and the characters of her female associates. Mary's

> strength and courage [were] fully appreciated by the Miss Bertrams; her delight in riding was like their own; . . . and they had great pleasure in praising it. 'I was sure she would ride well,' said Julia; 'she has the make for it. Her figure is as neat as her brother's.' 'Yes,' added Maria, 'and her spirits are as good, and she has the same energy of character. I cannot but think that good horsemanship has a great deal to do with the mind.' (69)

Although Maria misses the unflattering implications of this ironic remark, she speaks the truth. Mary—like Maria and Julia—exercises as an outlet for her tremendous energy and as a socially acceptable form of exhibitionism. The body, elevated and racing on a horse, with the rider's skillful direction an unpersuasive nod to intellectual involvement, becomes an analogue to the ego. Mary resembles Maria and, to a lesser extent, Julia in expressing an exuberance that masks a shocking preference for self-interest over principle. The fact that Mary and Maria are variants on the same name, an ironic allusion to the counter-Marian sacrilege of their solely materialist values, reinforces the affinity between the characters.[18] Mary's failure to convey moral outrage at Maria's affair with Henry underscores the resemblance, and suggests Mary's capacity for the same temptation. She more effectually camouflages her tendency toward moral deviance in open money-lust, however, and would never sacrifice social position for physical pleasure as Maria does and Julia might have done (although Julia marries Yates, she would have preferred Henry and attains her legitimate marital bond without paternal approval).

Mary is also smaller than the "tall and womanly" Miss Bertrams (20), as if to categorize her as not quite so morally depraved as the stouter and more self-important sisters; she does prove more good-hearted toward Fanny than Fanny's cousins, which enhances her charm for the deluded Edmund. When he finally discovers Mary's true character, he bemoans "how delightful nature had made her, and how excellent she would have been, had she fallen into good hands earlier" (459). Yet Edmund is beguiled by Mary's powerful energy for a long time before facing the truth of the ugliness beneath her "delightful" exterior. He even takes pleasure in promoting her riding at Fanny's expense for four days instead of the one for which he obtained Fanny's permission to use the mare. He pretends to consider his cousin's health while hypocritically encouraging Mary to monopolize the horse, thus inciting her to act in the oblivious pursuit of her own interests, a quality for which he later censures her. In fact, Mary seems not to have known about Fanny's medical need for riding until after her monopoly of the mare, when Edmund chooses to mention it. She immediately chastises him: " 'How abominable in you, then, to let me engross her horse as I did all last week! I am ashamed of you and of myself, but it shall never happen again' " (95). Her use of the word "let" here instead of a more active verb such as "invite" or "urge" hints at a degree of moral honesty lacking in the Bertram sisters in that it suggests her implicit admission of accountability for acting on her own will—Edmund is framed as the abettor, not the instigator. Perhaps Edmund's blind desire for Mary obscures his own self-centered rationalizations and he partially projects his own faults onto her in criticism of her character. Nonetheless, she knew from the first that she was usurping Fanny's horse, and the narrative clearly conveys that Fanny would never behave with such selfishness, whether abetted in doing so or not.

While Edmund abandons his self-sacrificing cousin for four consecutive days, her busybody Aunt Norris makes sure Fanny gets plenty of exercise, challenging her to athletic feats of increasing difficulty and endurance. Aunt Norris's exercise regimen for Fanny consists of stooping and cutting roses in the heat of the sun, followed by two consecutive walking trips to and from her house, and probably innumerable other unspecified tasks. Afterward, Fanny retires quietly to the sofa to nurse a headache, where Edmund finds her when he and Julia return from the last of several pleasure trips. It is a critical commonplace that Fanny's ambiguous illness in this scene emanates from her thwarted love and desire for Edmund, a valid interpretation. John Wiltshire avers that "Fanny Price's body here reproduces social tensions" (*Body* 19) and that "[h]ealth is intimately related to enablement and fulfillment, illness to frustration, anger and defeat" (22). Aunt Norris's harassment, albeit unkind, forces Fanny to strive for strength and prevents her from succumbing to this physical and psychological feebleness, however. Her aunt chastises her before

Edmund: " 'That is a very foolish trick, Fanny, to be idling away all the evening upon a sofa. Why cannot you come and sit here, and employ yourself as *we* do? . . . You should learn to think of other people; and take my word for it, it is a shocking trick for a young person to be always lolling upon a sofa' " (71). This criticism aptly applies to Lady Bertram, whose apathetic stupor is reinforced by her frequent location on sofas. The reader knows it is an absurd accusation to make of Fanny, whom even Julia defends: " 'I must say, ma'am, that Fanny is as little upon the sofa as any body in the house' " (71). In scolding Fanny away from the sofa, however, Aunt Norris inadvertently discourages her from the passive model of femininity represented by Lady Bertram. For this vigorous woman, physical weakness constitutes a moral flaw.

Edmund interrogates his aunt about the tasks she induced Fanny to perform, demanding an explanation for Fanny's second sojourn to her house. Aunt Norris responds, " 'I think nobody can justly accuse me of sparing myself upon any occasion, but really I cannot do every thing at once. And as for Fanny's just stepping down to my house for me, it is not much above a quarter of a mile, I cannot think I was unreasonable to ask it. How often do I pace it three times a-day, early and late, ay and in all weathers too, and say nothing about it' " (73). "Coach Norris" downplays the difficulty level of the athletic regimen she assigns Fanny, challenges her to make intensifying it a goal, and presents herself as an attainable model of female vigor. By contrast, although Edmund responds, " 'I wish Fanny had half your strength, ma'am' " (73), the last thing he desires is for her to have the force of an Aunt Norris. His behavior undercuts his asserted "wish" by denying Fanny the much-needed horseback riding exercise and furthering her dependence on him. Aunt Norris provides Fanny with a diametrically opposite exemplar of womanhood to that represented by Lady Bertram. Aunt Norris is a powerhouse. As Tom remarks, " '[W]hen my aunt has got a fancy in her head, nothing can stop her' " (120). She pursues her ends until she attains them. She is a consummate opportunist and gad-about who sometimes unexpectedly speaks the truth and unintentionally promotes Fanny's interests. Her justification for pushing Fanny to exercise places the guilt of neglect firmly where it belongs—on Edmund's shoulders: " 'If Fanny would be more regular in her exercise, she would not be knocked up so soon. She has not been out on horseback now this long while, and I am persuaded, that when she does not ride, she ought to walk. If she had been riding before, I should not have asked it of her' " (73). Aunt Norris helps to empower Fanny both physically and mentally, while shaming Edmund for neglecting her. This unsympathetic character must be given some credit for simul-taneously absolving herself, promoting self-serving aims, and unknowingly furthering her niece's relationship with Edmund by redirecting his attention toward her.[19] It is arguably Aunt Nor-ris's "training," abetted by Lady Bertram's passivity, that enables Fanny to gain bodily strength.

By contrast, men thwart, stifle, or mandate the cessation of Fanny's physical activity.[20] Not only does Edmund reduce her horseback-riding opportunities as previously described, but he also commands her to remain seated on a bench while he and Mary pursue a flirty walk alone. While the three are out strolling at the Sotherton estate, Mary engages in a kind of deterministic sports competition with Fanny for Edmund's attention and affec-tion. She flaunts her vigor and seeks to distinguish herself as much as possible from her competitor. When Fanny requests of Edmund that " 'if it is not disagreeable to you, I should be glad to sit down for a little while' " and he takes her arm and offers Mary his other, Mary responds smugly, " 'Thank you, but I am not at all tired' " and then does take his arm (94). Edmund complains, " 'You scarcely touch me . . . You do not make me of any use' " as if to invite her to closer physical intimacy (94). Mary wishes to touch Edmund but makes clear that she does not need his help; Edmund desires her to touch and need him, but appears to enjoy the challenge of endeavoring to tease her into dependence. Meanwhile, she continues boasting of her prowess, " 'I am really not tired, which I almost wonder at; for we must have walked at least a mile in this wood' " (94), violating conventions of female decorum by bragging about her stamina.[21]

It is during this conversation that Edmund reveals to Mary that horseback riding is Fanny's only viable form of exercise. However, he then proceeds to stop Fanny from further exercise himself, masquerading as a concerned cousin to achieve a tête-à-tête with Mary. When Mary becomes restless and suggests they proceed with their walk, "Fanny said she was rested, and would have moved too, but this was not suffered. Edmund urged her remaining where she was with an earnestness which she could not resist, and she was left on the bench to think with pleasure of her cousin's care, but with great regret that she was not stronger" (96). Ironically, at this juncture of Fanny's development, she still might have provided Edmund with the delicate, dependent wife that would have maximized his control, but his digressive pursuit of the lively rebel-flirt delays his transfer of desire to Fanny. By the time he converts his full interest to his cousin, he is the one dependent upon her, in a reversal of the romantic and familial power structure.

Henry Crawford's treatment of Fanny parallels Edmund's in significant ways.[22] Though without the influence of family relationship or the success of Fanny's obedience, he likewise voices concern for her health as a mask for his endeavor to usurp control over her both physical and romantic agency:

"If . . . you find yourself growing unwell, and any difficulties arise about your returning to Mansfield . . . if
you feel yourself at all less strong, or comfortable than

usual . . . [my sister] and I will immediately come down, and take you back to Mansfield. . . . I hope you will not be cruelly concealing any tendency to indisposition.—Indeed, you shall *not*, it shall not be in your power, for so long only as you positively say, in every letter to Mary, 'I am well.'—and I know you cannot speak or write a falsehood,—so long only shall you be considered as well." (411)

Henry repeatedly expresses anxiety about Fanny's ill health as the surface rationale for his offer to transport her back to Mansfield, while his remarks of about two pages reveal another agenda. He imposes tremendous pressure on her to hint for a ride home because that would signify her symbolic acceptance of his already rejected marriage proposal. He attempts to set up a moral and linguistic checkmate to remove her power of self-determination, and assumes that control over her bodily movements translates into control over her destiny. In urging Fanny to name for herself the date of her return to Mansfield by traveling there with him at will, Henry also cavalierly disregards Sir Thomas's paternal authority over her and invites her to do the same. Henry's seduction of Maria is based on a related stratagem, in that he challenges her to prove her independence of Mr. Rushworth and, indirectly, of her father, by following him outside the boundaries of the locked gate of her engagement, marriage, and familial ties. He is trying to replace other men as the masked authority over the woman's actions, while offering nothing in return for her obedience.

Sir Thomas's authoritarian behavior toward Fanny provides the model for Edmund's and Henry's encouragement of her passivity and submission to them. On the day of her coming-out ball, she glows with beauty and happiness; she is excited about the big event and Edmund's request that she reserve two dances for him: "She had hardly ever been in a state so nearly approaching high spirits in her life. . . . and was actually practising her steps about the drawing-room as long as she could be safe from the notice of her aunt Norris" (272–273), who had not instigated the activity. This is the first time in the novel that Fanny initiates engaging in physical movement for its own sake, which clearly suggests that her bodily vitality as well as her emotional state has improved, thanks in large part to Aunt Norris's coaching and Lady Bertram's dependence. Fanny dances the night away, and when she begins to show fatigue around 3 a.m., her uncle "gave his orders for her sitting down entirely" (279), and then,

> [s]hortly afterwards, Sir Thomas was again interfering a little with her inclination, by advising her to go immediately to bed. 'Advise' was his word, but it was the advice of absolute power, and she had only to rise and, with Mr. Crawford's very cordial adieus, pass quietly away; . . . In thus sending her away, Sir Thomas perhaps might not be thinking merely of her health. It might occur to him, that Mr. Crawford had been sitting by her long enough, or he might mean to recommend her as a wife by shewing her persuadableness. (280–281)

The narrator suggests that Sir Thomas, Edmund, and Mr. Crawford seek to perpetuate this young woman's weakness and to control her movements and, thereby, her consciousness. This attempt on the part of all three men ultimately fails, and Fanny becomes a self-actualized woman who returns in triumph after her banishment for refusing Henry Crawford, to become the newly styled matriarch of the family.

Several female characters contribute to Fanny's acquisition of the man she loves, increased social and economic status, and fulfillment. Both of Fanny's aunts, in their different modes, challenge her physical and mental strength by inciting her to action and refusing to coddle her. Aunt Norris and Lady Bertram demonstrate different models of femininity, but achieve a shared impact on their niece, reinforcing her position as the fulcrum between the two extremes they represent. When Fanny anticipates her coming-out ball and spending time with Edmund, she thinks to herself, "what was the restlessness of Mrs. Norris? What were the yawns of Lady Bertram?" (273). She will embody neither superfluous energy nor impotent malaise, but will take well-intentioned, productive action.[23]

Mary Crawford shows similarities to Aunt Norris, such as in her restlessness, hardihood, and opportunism. Edmund mistakenly perceives her as the physical, behavioral happy medium between his mother and aunt. In fact, Mary is somewhere between Fanny and the Bertram sisters in body and mind, and the differentiation between her and Fanny must be made symbolically clear through the pattern of body-coding at work in the novel. Edmund senses that Mary possesses the vitality of an Aunt Norris or a Maria or Julia, and the nonthreatening sweetness of a Lady Bertram and active virtue of a Fanny, the ideal combination of the women closest to him. He must be disabused of that misperception. Mary shows more verve than Fanny but less virtue, and is depicted as only a little better than Maria and Julia, as manifested by her smaller physique and less wild ways.[24] The aunts counterbalance Mary's physical superiority to Fanny by exhausting the latter with activity, thereby boosting her endurance while provoking in Edmund a guilty awareness of neglect that recalls him to her. Whereas Fanny rarely voices her most urgent health-related needs, Mary broadcasts her wishes. Fanny's increasing agency often lies in her deliberate patience as circumstances unfold and others' errors and inferiorities are revealed. The ebullience of Aunt Norris, Maria, Julia, and Mary Crawford is often misdirected and wasted. Fanny's patient, long walk through life with intermittent rests creates a sense of her thoughtful deliberateness and determined idealism in holding out for her desired ends. However, she must as resolutely take responsibility and strive for wellness of body and mind.

Many readers consider Fanny Price Austen's least likeable and most exasperating heroine. The narrator continually reminds us of her fragility, her more-feminine-than-thou fatigue, headaches, and prescribed riding excursions. Fanny herself sometimes seems to exaggerate her role as delicate female martyr to garner Edmund's sympathetic attention, like a scheming teen with a crush. She absurdly reassures him, " 'You know I am strong enough now to walk very well' " (70). Her ability to walk merits no boast whatever; she possesses no physical disability. However, clearly, the point is not to ridicule Fanny or even to portray her as weak—she gets everything she wants in the end. Rather, the body-coding on a continuum between rabid hyperactivity and corpse-like immobility creates moral contrasts between Fanny's patient endurance and purity of heart and the mixed motives of other female characters. And yet, those female characters are critical to Fanny's maturation. In her girlhood, she relies on Lady Bertram's reliance on her; her aunt's increased passivity coincides with Fanny's physical growth, increased activity, and improved position in the family. Whereas Maria and Julia's gravitation toward Aunt Norris as an alternative mother figure in response to their mother's neglect proves destructive to them, this aggressive woman's interference in Fanny's life, counterbalanced by Lady Bertram's benign neediness, proves beneficial to Fanny. Aunt Norris challenges her bodily strength and endurance as well as mental toughness in a way that proves essential to her positive development. "That Julia escaped better than Maria was owing . . . [largely] to her having been less the darling of that very aunt, less flattered, and less spoilt" (466), and on the same principle, partly because Aunt Norris is ever demanding rather than indulgent toward her, Fanny "escapes" with a better character than Julia.

The two aunts, cousins Maria and Julia, and Mary Crawford all provide Fanny with diverse opportunities to be active and to feel needed. Fanny gains stature, presence, and self-worth in the course of the novel, becoming a woman who is true to herself. As she gains self-reliance, others depend upon her more and more, and she transforms from a weakling to a bulwark for the Bertrams. Shortly before being recalled to Mansfield during Tom's illness, Fanny envisions the numerous ways that "she must have been of use to all" there, including, significantly, by exerting her physical strength to assist her Aunt Bertram: "how many walks up and down stairs she might have saved her" (432). Edmund transforms from Fanny's controlling instructor, brotherly protector and comforter in her ailments that he sometimes exacerbates, to her sickly, forlorn dependent. When he arrives to retrieve her from Portsmouth, he "pressed [her] to his heart with only these words, just articulate, 'My Fanny—my only sister—my only comfort now.' . . . He looked very ill; evidently suffering under violent emotions" (444–445). In this climax of the two charac- ters' relationship and role-reversal, Edmund expresses physical and emotional frailty and Fanny becomes his succor. The nar- rator insists that Fanny retains her feminine delicacy, however, despite Edmund's declaration of dependency on her as his rock of stability; she must suffer so acutely from empathy with his suffering that she "was ready to sink" as she went to meet him and passively "found herself pressed to his heart" (444). Here, the narrator reassures the reader that Fanny has not become Mary-like—her strength resides firmly in her womanly virtue. Regardless, she does assume the role of Edmund's supporter: "Fanny's friendship was all that he had to cling to" (460).

Lady Bertram's only decisive gesture in the novel is her similarly enacted reaffirmation of her dependence on Fanny.

When Fanny, her sister Susan, and Edmund arrive at Mansfield Park, the narrator tells us, "By one of the suffering party within, they were expected with such impatience as she had never known before. Fanny had scarcely passed the solemn-looking servants, when Lady Bertram came from the drawing room to meet her; came with no indolent step; and, falling on her neck, said, 'Dear Fanny! now I shall be comfortable'" (447). Lady Bertram seems to be transferring to Fanny the role of matriarch in this exchange. In her triumphant return, Fanny is rewarded for her merit and endurance with a new place of consequence in the Bertram family as wife, daughter, and pseudo-matriarch. She is acknowledged as everything that others are not. Edmund "learn[s] to prefer" (470) her to Mary Crawford; Lady Bertram feels restored to consciousness by her restoration to Mansfield; and Sir Thomas, "prizing more and more the sterling good of principle and temper, and chiefly anxious to bind by the strongest securities all that remained to him of domestic felicity" (471), realizes that "Fanny was indeed the daughter that he wanted" (472).

Some scholars question the satisfactoriness of Fanny's triumphal marriage and immersion in comfortable domesticity, claiming, for example, that "[t]his resolution suggests that the exercise of her domestic affections will be enough to get a woman everything she wants—she need not look beyond the family hearth, or admit to impermissible desires" (Pawl 313). This criticism might be made of all of Austen's novels in that they feature courtship plots. The fact remains that Fanny Price gets the life she wanted: the kind of life a Fanny Price—not any woman—would want. Her myriad sufferings in the course of her narrative may also render her ultimate reunion with the Bertrams and marriage to Edmund a relief to some readers, rather than being viewed as a trap.[25] Moreover, the marriages of Austen's heroines always imply more than a future of domesticity. In *Mansfield Park*, Fanny will rewrite the role of matriarch as Edmund's wife; as the stronghold of her husband and the family, she will help the Bertrams to be reborn. She will be stronger because she will be better than Lady Bertram and Aunt Norris, and will live a life of meaningful, active good that redounds to her own and the Bertrams' well-being.

Austen understood and, in all of her novels, promotes the essential role of purposeful activity to psychological as well as physical health: "There is nothing like employment, active, indispensable employment, for relieving sorrow" (*MP* 443).[26] Her women face difficult lives, but that does not justify them in becoming reactionary, self-absorbed, or desperate. The novelist emphasizes not the heroine's body in itself but what its condition can tell us about her mind and character.[27] Fanny Price develops the ability to steel herself against her trials, as do Elinor Dashwood, Elizabeth Bennet, and Emma Woodhouse—women who do not become deathly ill in the face of apparent disappointment in love, but move forward as well as they can, with the conviction of their independent value and duty and faith in the possibility of alternative narratives. When one examines the pattern in Austen's exploration of female physical strength in her novels, it is evident that she does not implicitly extol the robust female constitution or the delicate one but, rather, expects her best characters to make the most of their health and of themselves—to take action—for their own and others' sakes. When they do so, they are amply rewarded.

We are encouraged to admire and aspire to the beauty of the strength that enables a determined, principled woman not only to strive on but to find fulfillment despite any adversities of body, mind, or circumstance. This proven willingness to change, to work with the fluctuations of their plots as if embracing "the warmth of exercise" (*PP* 32), corroborates that Austen's heroines deserve their precedence in her fiction. They become worthy subjects of their lives and the author's pen by choosing to develop. For Fanny Price, physical development coincides with intellectual, emotional, social, and spiritual growth. Austen is not interested in imposing on herself or on other women an artificial, repressive, self-conscious or self-satisfied set of rules for body size, dress, behavior, demeanor, or personality. Indeed, she would be disappointed by the uniform female humanity that would result if everyone followed the prescription promoted in many conduct books of her era. This homogeneity would be counterproductive to her task as a writer. It seems fitting that Austen draws on food metaphors in articulating the writer's struggle for inspiration: "[P]erhaps Breakfast may assist my ideas. I was deceived—my breakfast supplied only two ideas, that the rolls were good, & the butter bad" (19 June 1799). Over a century later, Virginia Woolf draws a similar parallel between food for the body and for the imagination in her critique of male economic as creative privilege, as whimsically epitomized by her bad dinner at the women's college in contrast with male students' habitual feasting: "The lamp in the spine does not light on beef and prunes" (18).

Austen promotes neither obesity nor ultra-thinness, nor does she promote health only for utility, but for the enjoyment of engaged living that yields both pleasure and productivity. We must eat bread with good butter, take frequent walks, visit friends and family, dance, and live in communion and sympathy. The author would be bewildered by our society's obsession with women's body size, especially by its deviant promotion of women's diminution into nothing. For Austen, it would be strangely narcissistic as well as strangely self-destructive to focus on the goal of self-elimination. She does not want women to diet or compete in beauty pageants; she wants us to join in her imaginative banquet. We need not fear her ironic wit. She loves her heroines for their variety, idiosyncrasy, human flawedness, yet ability to change for the better—for their literary substance. Fat, middling, or thin, we can rest assured that we will always be worthy subjects for the skilled author's pen, whether as the target of criticism or praise, as long as we continue to grow.

CHAPTER 2

"I always deserve the best treatment, because I never put up with any other"

Sexual Orthodoxy and the Quest for the Best Mate

As we have seen, Jane Austen conveys in her writing the importance of women thriving in body and mind by eating well, staying active, and engaging in meaningful interaction with the world around them. A natural part of women's physicality, as for men, is their sexuality. Austen portrays the intensity and universality of women's sex drive as a given.[1] Scholars commonly acknowledge that Austen's sexual language is coded in images and words such as "sensations," which some readers would consider "vague and, by current standards, quite prim and primitive" (J. Johnson 53), but which clearly communicate a semiology of desire in her work. That physical intimacy always occurs off-stage, almost always within the narrative privacy of marriage, and is never graphically discussed, should be expected and increases rather than decreases the novels' eroticism. Narrow "conventions which define sex as sexual intercourse and dictate explicitness" (Fergus, "Sex" 66) reflect a contemporary bias that ignores its complexity and undervalues suggestiveness. The sexual content of Austen's novels includes not only the affairs, seductions, and illegitimate offspring, but the sanctioned everyday flirtations, the looking and hinting and rare touching, the electricity of attraction.[2] Austen's courtship plots are not focused on male conquest, but on a critical female choice. The heroine's sexual bildungsroman occurs in a realistic psychic and social landscape littered with disastrous relationships that were founded on looks or economic gain. In this unpropitious context, the heroine nonetheless feels a misplaced magnetism toward—or is coerced into a connection with—the most misogynistic, aggressive suitor in her circle of acquaintance. She must reject or transform this association if she is to find a devoted husband who will best promote her personal and familial happiness.

Throughout Austen's lifetime, both law and custom abetted the man's autocracy in marriage. "[T]he law of femin[ine] *coverture*" still held, conflating the wife's identity with her husband's (Sulloway 36), and adultery laws favored men, protecting their socioeconomic interests in preserving their inheritance through the line of legitimacy. In addition, "English common law . . . ruled that whatever property a woman owned before marriage or might receive thereafter automatically became her husband's" (Swords 77). Men's monopoly of such legal powers and social sovereignty fosters private tyrannies as well and accentuates women's vulnerability and the magnitude of their marital decision in determining their future health, safety, and sanity. Hazel Jones cites correspondence in which wives debate how to respond to unfaithful and sadistic husbands; in one particularly horrifying case, a woman "suffered blows to the head, often delivered unexpectedly, anxieties about being poisoned, imprisonment and starvation" (141). In short, a woman's choice of spouse could mean life, death, or death-in-life.[3] Austen places pragmatic emphasis on the necessity of women's self-protection against abuse or abandonment by men and by the patriarchal society that perpetuates the insuperable sexual double standard that empowers them. She does not excuse either gender for sexual misconduct, but underscores this inequity as a warning to women of the price that would be exacted from them alone: "In this world, the penalty is less equal than could be wished" (*MP* 468).[4]

There is a dark side to the charm of Austen's love stories. The proverbial writing is on the wall for all of her single female characters. They have few or no models of healthy, happy relationships to emulate, and the only two exemplary married couples in the novels consist of fringe characters: the Gardiners of *Pride and Prejudice* and the Crofts of *Persuasion*. The Morlands in *Northanger Abbey*, Westons in *Emma*, and elder Musgroves in *Persuasion* are complacently happy, and the Harvilles co-contribute to a happy family unit, but these marriages are not held up as model-worthy meetings of true minds. In most of the marriages Austen's heroines know about, the wife was or is the target of emotional abuse and neglect, and possibly worse.[5] The deceased Mrs. Tilney and Lady Elliot "had much to bear" (*NA* 197) from respectively tyrannical and vainglorious husbands; Mrs. Bennet, Mrs. Palmer, and Mrs. Price experience habitual verbal abuse; Isabella Knightley's husband vents his temper on her as well as her father; and Lady Bertram and Mary Musgrove are incidental to the lives of their dismissive, often-absent spouses.

Yet despite this disturbing backdrop, even Austen's most intelligent, righteous heroines come terrifyingly close to repeating history. At least five of them consider alliances with men who mask selfish, sadistic, or outright evil natures. Marianne Dashwood, Elizabeth Bennet, and Fanny Price feel the lure of sexual predators Willoughby, Wickham, and Henry Crawford, respectively.[6] Emma enjoys flirting with user Frank Churchill, and the otherwise discerning Anne Elliot is attracted to snaky opportunist Mr. Elliot. In addition, the more genuine and redeemable Mr. Darcy, Mr. Knightley, and Captain Wentworth evince an entitlement that necessitates a thorough ego adjustment for them to become viable husbands.[7] As Mary Bennet declares, a woman " 'cannot be too much guarded in her behaviour towards the undeserving of the other sex' " (*PP* 289). Since all the eligible bachelors start out "undeserving" to varying degrees and the villains often camouflage their deviance, Austen's female protagonists must showcase their self-respect in order to navigate the courtship minefield and find desirable mates. These individuals' collective insistence on men's esteem benefits all women and, thereby, society as a whole.[8]

Austen advocates women's freedom to choose their own husbands and recognizes the desirability of attraction, but underscores how dangerously misleading it can be. Marianne Dashwood is the exception among Austen's female protagonists in that she makes the mistake of falling too hard and too fast for Willoughby, who fails the only major and incidental test of his love—the financial one; she finally obtains a meritorious husband almost in spite of herself.[9] Although by contrast to Austen's "fallen women," her heroines honor the boundaries of virtue, their experiences convey that they should distrust the powerful pull of their sexual attraction to a man unless or until he passes a challenging character test. The author does not view human sexuality as divested from disposition and relationality or suggest that women face an either-or alternative between a good man and a good lover; rather, she advances a careful prioritization and character-vetting process in which male moral growth validates and intensifies female desire and male moral lassitude dispels it.[10] This reduces the corporeal aspect of attraction to a subordinate place in the woman's assessment process, as almost derivative of the amalgamation of higher considerations—virtue, personality, intellect, and social commitment—that compose attraction. In opposition to the Romanticist vision of sublime, fated passion à la Marianne, Austen suggests that, based on demonstrable evidence of these important qualities, one can and should choose whether or not to love someone.

Austen's radicalism emanates from her female-affirming literary departure from the oppressive eighteenth-century seduction plot. Her women are not defined by their bodies or sexual experience or inexperience, but by the personhood that they are accountable to define (Morgan, "Why" 351–352, 355).[11] Austen's heroines express their distinct, self-crafted identities as a means of evaluating men and identifying their own vocations in a treacherous marriage marketplace. Although there were and are no guarantees in marriage, as in life, Austen speaks to fictional and actual women of past and present of the efficacy of holding out as holding on to self in the highest sense, rendering most likely the joyous communion of that self with others and with God, whether through marriage or singlehood.[12]

"Sexual orthodoxy" in this analysis signifies the assertion of personal boundaries that reflect awareness of one's inherent worth in relation to the divine, apart from—as well as within union to—the opposite sex. It goes without saying that the assumption that sex should be circumscribed within marital commitment reflects the devout Anglican author's and her virtuous characters' Christian worldview, as well as her era's social mores for proper female conduct. What requires explication is Austen's illustration of the strategic utility of sexual orthodoxy to women's selection of a spouse. In orthodox Anglicanism, single or married life represents a legitimate female vocation and, in the case of marriage, natural and supernatural coalesce in a sexual union that is mutual and founded upon consent. True consent can occur only from a position of liberty, authenticity, and individual wholeness; "one must possess oneself in order to give oneself" (Giuffre 78). Austen's central heroines recognize their transcendent value, refusing objectification and insisting on truth to themselves as a moral imperative that overrules the pressures of physical passion, socioeconomic considerations, or the male lust for power. In courtship, the women's adherence to their own convictions, even when flawed or false, functions as a crucial test of men's characters. It enables them to distinguish the suitors who are least and most likely to honor their discrete selfhood and partner in a marriage that would be most advantageous to the women's long-term psychological and emotional well-being and, consequently, sexual fulfillment as well.[13]

The Fickle Female Sex Drive

Austen affirms but does not depict as easy her heroines' exercise of moral-intellectual control over their physical passions. For example, even Jane and Elizabeth of *Pride and Prejudice*—the good Bennet sisters—show kinship to their scandalous sister Lydia and her "animal spirits" (*PP* 45) in their strong, sometimes blindly irrational interest in handsome men. Modest, shy Jane Bennet has apparently "liked" enough men to merit teasing by her sister, even if one assumes that Elizabeth exaggerates for the sake of jest. When Jane circumspectly praises Bingley's good sense and sociability, Elizabeth cuts right through to his sex appeal: " 'He is also handsome . . . which a young man ought likewise to be, if he possibly can. His character is thereby complete. . . . he certainly is very agreeable, and I give you leave to like him. You have liked many a stupider person' " (14). This passage, in combination with Mrs. Bennet's anecdote of the poetry-writing admirer, suggests a reading of "dear Jane" that complicates her image of perfect docility. If her sister's quip contains at least a grain of truth, Jane has a hankering for hunks and is too quick to assume—like her supposedly smarter sister—that a striking exterior must house a heart of gold. Perhaps none of her previous connections came to fruition not merely because of her lack of fortune but because many of the dashing suitors to whom Jane is drawn turn out to be fools or jerks. Her immediate infatuation with the nice-looking Bingley further evidences that she easily develops crushes on cute boys and is following the pattern of past romantic folly. The gentleman who Mrs. Bennet claims " 'wrote some verses on her, and very pretty they were' " was sufficiently pointed in his attentions to Jane that even sensible Aunt Gardiner " 'was sure he would make her an offer' " (44) that never came, as if foreshadowing Jane's experience with Bingley, who shows marked partiality and then vanishes.

Jane resembles Lydia in having had many "favourites" (285) and in her naïve attitude of overlooking an appealing man's possible possession of serious and even dangerous flaws. Her principles and propriety preserve her from Lydia's fate, but her attraction to spineless, indecisive men causes her much stress and makes her ultimate engagement to Bingley a mixed blessing. In addition, Jane's defenses of Darcy, Wickham, and even Bingley may reveal more than good nature, but also her identification with the traditionally male-identified weakness for physical attraction. She easily imagines a susceptibility to the magnetic power of sex appeal that could lead a " 'poor Mr. Darcy' " (225) to bitter disappointment when rejected, a Bingley to such liveliness that he projects more serious interest in a woman than he feels, and even a Wickham to a moral lapse that he later regrets. Jane holds true to her values and complications happen to resolve in her interests, but her passivity magnifies her vulnerability to outside factors, to being forsaken.

Elizabeth does not initially scrutinize the character of dashing Wickham or his promise as a lifelong partner, nor hold him to the same standard she does Darcy. She simply feels sexually attracted to him, as Lydia, Mary King, and many other women do—an unthinking passion that requires the cautionary intervention of her Aunt Gardiner to awaken her to a more rational analysis of his marriage potential.[14] As Elizabeth later, self-referentially remarks in the wake of Lydia's elopement with him, " 'we all know that Wickham has every charm of person and address that can captivate a woman' " (284). Until she knows his true character, she instinctively views his physical appeal as itself a virtue; thus, when Wickham performs the forbearance of an honorable gentleman betrayed by an ignoble Darcy, "Elizabeth honoured him for such feelings, and thought him handsomer than ever as he expressed them" (80). She mistakes surface for substance: "Whatever he said, was said well; and whatever he did, done gracefully" (84). Sharp-witted Elizabeth's interlude of poor judgment and Darwinian reliance on the merit of Wickham's fancy feathers discomfits us; we admire her spirited individuality and transcendent ideals and may overlook that she is as capable of being duped by a man's sex appeal as her ditzy sister Lydia. The difference is that she chooses not to succumb to mere lust, and thus takes more time to discover his true nature. Once Elizabeth comprehends Wickham's falseness, she finds his company irksome and his striking surface offensive for the ugliness it masks, "resolving within herself, to draw no limits in future to the impudence of an impudent man" (316).

At some point in every Austen novel, the heroine realizes or receives reinforcement of her belief that genuine goodness is essential to a man's lasting sex appeal and no degree of physical charm can compensate for his lack thereof. That Elizabeth is a sexual being who is drawn to handsome men illustrates her normalcy—Austen implies that sexuality constitutes part of woman's nature and does not condemn it. However, she emphasizes that although chemistry matters, character matters more and must take precedence in a woman's monumental selection of a spouse. Elizabeth evinces her conviction of this principle when striving to delude herself that her interest in Wickham emanates from admiration of his integrity; after she learns his true character, she recognizes Lydia's case as a warning to women of the dangers of being led by their sex drive: "how little of permanent happiness could belong to a couple who were only brought together because their passions were stronger than their virtue, she could easily conjecture" (312). Lydia's fling with Wickham quickly fizzles and they lead separate lives.

Pride and Prejudice illustrates a sliding scale of female conquests and corresponding outcomes, in which the more a woman challenges a man's honor in courtship, the more desirable he becomes as a future husband. Thus, Lydia Bennet presents no challenge to Wickham and gets a seducer and unwilling spouse who is quick to neglect her. Nice but passive Jane maintains her virtue and feminine propriety—she refuses to chase Bingley—but she also neglects to test him. Thus, she gets a nice but passive husband who has yet to prove that he can act for himself or place loyalty to her above the influence of a male friend. After the singeing of her pride by Wickham, Elizabeth pushes Darcy the hardest and gets the most devoted husband in the end.[15] A woman must assert moral and social boundaries that display her strong sense of self-worth and insistence on a man's deference if she is to weed out the louts and find a supportive life partner. Her sexuality is a real and potent dimension of her identity, but often leads her toward the worst prospective husband. Her physical attraction to others cannot be her primary influence in her relationship choices—it objectifies both her and the men she contemplates.

Resisting Objectification

Austen's works underscore as a fundamental principle that in a successful marriage, the woman does not function as an object for the man.[16] Appropriately, the degree of her bodily freedom or confinement in interactions with a potential suitor foretells her likely level of agency in the relationship. A heroine's communication of her sexual orthodoxy, as her right to preserve her physical and ideological boundaries and to direct her movements according to her conscience, often triggers a retaliatory or supportive response in the man that reveals his level of regard for her personhood. Austen's female protagonists thereby expose men's worst proclivities in their treatment of women, on a scale from murderous misogyny to the subtlest symptoms of unconscious phallocentrism. The data heroines generate through this experiment enables them to make educated decisions about their future lives.

Of all of Austen's suitors, *Northanger Abbey*'s oafish villain, John Thorpe, exposes the most palpable signs of his total objectification of women and his likelihood to inflict violence on his future wife. The naïve Catherine Morland must discern and provoke enough of these indicators to reject his company and to better assess her chosen love interest. Thorpe swiftly strives to take possession of Catherine. Within four pages of their being introduced, and without asking her, he has announced that he "will drive [her] out" in his curricle daily and repeated twice more that he will do so on the morrow (*NA* 47–48), after which he critiques the appearance of "every woman they [meet]" (48), including telling his mother she "look[s] like an old witch" and his two younger sisters that "they both [look] very ugly" (49). He tries to direct the movements of a woman he has just met, insults his female family members in her presence, and judges women's looks, despite being quite homely himself as "a stout young man of middling height . . . with a plain face and ungraceful form" (45). Moreover, although his awkward behavior toward Catherine implies his sexual innocence, his obsession with horses and equipage hints at his brutishness.

Thorpe's preoccupation with buying and selling horses, his pleasure in whipping them, and his fantasies of driving them into a frenzy and curbing them into obedience at will convey disturbing connotations for his relationship to women and sex. He channels his sexual frustration into visions of domination, and seeks to corral Catherine as he imagines he does his horses. He engages her for the first two dances at a ball and then appears late, forcing her to wait for him and reject Mr. Tilney's invitation to dance. The first time he takes her out in his carriage, he warns her of the horse's spirits but adds that the horse " 'will soon know his master' " (62). Thorpe calls on Catherine with Freudian suggestiveness to admire "the merits of his own equipage" (64) and driving; menaces her by predicting the collapse of her brother's gig; and boasts of heavy drinking, bird killing, and "the boldness of his riding" in the hunt, which "had been constantly leading others into difficulties, which he calmly concluded had broken the necks of many" (66). His relish for conjuring up violent scenes, often featuring himself as the perpetrator of carnage, does not impress Catherine, who boldly decides "that John Thorpe . . . was quite disagreeable" (69).

Thorpe's controlling behavior toward Catherine intensifies in the course of their acquaintance. At another assembly, she avoids him to be free to dance with Mr. Tilney; as their dance commences, Thorpe interposes to accuse her of reneging on a nonexistent prior commitment to him and delays her with pompous chatter. The next day, he hoodwinks her into going out with him instead of the Tilneys by lying that he'd seen "the man [she] danced with last night" drive away with "a smart-looking girl" (85), as if to punish her for socializing with another man. When Catherine spots the Tilneys walking and realizes Thorpe's deception, she repeatedly insists he stop the carriage and liberate her, but he "only lashed his horse into a brisker trot; . . . laughed, smacked his whip, encouraged his horse, made odd noises, and drove on" (87). He revels in the opportunity to control her body, taking pleasure in actively thwarting her wishes as an assertion of power that is presented as subhuman—he "ma[kes] odd noises" like an animal rather than speaking to Catherine coherently, and twice whips the horse in response to her urgent requests for liberty, as if it functions as a symbolic substitute for her.[17] This suggests he would treat sex as no more than a physical satisfaction of his primal power lust on another body, an act devoid of mutuality or any hint of sacramentalism.

Yet, because of his very commodification of women, John Thorpe will be a sexual failure. He drives and drives but does not seem to arrive at a destination, which evokes an image of sexual impotence. He never succeeds in bringing Catherine to the much-anticipated Blaize Castle, because he cannot bring himself or her to "blaze"—the fire of true passion that emanates from joint attraction, admiration, and liberty of choice. Thorpe also demonstrates his linguistic impotence in his five-minute conversation with Catherine in which he obliquely refers to matrimony; he later claims this was a clear declaration that she understood and reciprocated. While Catherine may or may not suspect that John Thorpe would be both sexually sadistic and impotent, his compulsive cursing, falsehoods, and manipulations soon provoke her to claim her independence.

The climax of Catherine's self-assertion occurs when she directly counters Thorpe's will and insists on keeping her appointment with the Tilneys. The previous time he had thwarted her plans, she was trapped in his carriage "with no power of getting away" and forced to "submit" (87) until she could go apologize to the Tilneys. This time, after her repeated refusals to capitulate and Thorpe's audacious rescheduling of her engagement behind her back, she declares, " 'I cannot submit to this' " (100) and refuses to be cajoled or bullied into acquiescence. When John and Isabella each "caught hold of one hand" (100) to prevent her from going to the Tilneys, she delivers two forceful speeches against his social tyranny, concluding, " 'If I could not be persuaded into doing what I thought wrong, I never will be tricked into it'" and then "broke away and hurried off" (101). Thorpe's instinct is to pursue Catherine; when her brother deters him, he offers a glimpse of his likely reaction to a wife's opposition: "'She is as obstinate as—' Thorpe never finished the simile, for it could hardly have been a proper one" (101). If Thorpe had not been stopped by James Morland, he would have chased and restrained Catherine against her will, in public.[18] He craves complete control and is intent on forcing the woman into his will, moving from flattery to lies and coercion to the impulse to stalk and entrap—stages along a continuum of worsening treatment. Thorpe's violent temper nearly erupts in this scene, in which he feels free to make an insulting remark about Catherine to her own brother, one which, though uncompleted, equates her with a mule. He views her as yet another of his beasts of burden, a commodity to be used. One can assume that he would behave worse toward his legal wife in private, even possibly inflicting on her a realization of his sadistic fantasies of horse-whipping dominion (which would likely be multiplied in compensatory savagery by every reminder of his sexual or social impotence). Thorpe's behavior reinforces today's common-knowledge understanding that abusers tend to segregate their targets from their supportive social circle and to inflict maltreatment of an incrementally increasing brutality.[19]

Confirmed in her dislike of John Thorpe and more confident in her own voice and perceptions, Catherine has awakened to the symptoms of male despotism and tests General Tilney and his son through the filter of her experience, observing the latter's benevolence by contrast to the two brutes. The General and John Thorpe are kindred spirits in their hot tempers and derogatory view of women as their emotional punching bags and pawns in mercenary schemes of self-aggrandizement. Despite the parodic Gothicism of Catherine's speculations regarding General Tilney, she accurately discerns his cruel character as an oppressive patriarch through her border-crossings—by being late to a meal, and especially by entering spaces in the abbey that he prohibits. His open rage at catching Eleanor about to let Catherine into the apartment where Mrs. Tilney died suggests that Eleanor parallels her mother in being subject to the same abuse—he shouts her name "in his loudest tone," evoking in Catherine "terror upon terror" and the instinct to run and hide in her locked room as soon as Eleanor "disappeared" with him, "deeply commiserating the state of her poor friend" (192). Catherine fears for both her own and Eleanor's safety in a situation charged with implications of domestic violence. That Eleanor afterward tries to explain away the roaring-father incident with the understated claim that "My father only wanted me to answer a note" does not produce a comedic counterpoint to Catherine's imaginings, because the emotional imprint of his ire is too visceral and convincing in its magnitude (192). This scene effectively portrays the severity of emotional abuse, regardless of whether physical violence accompanies it, and the vulnerability of women in even the domestic sphere. General Tilney models as a patriarchal right the habitual bullying of women, including his wife before her decease, his daughter, and his daughter's guest. This example at least partially explains heir Captain Tilney's misogyny; Henry's sardonic wit that occasionally borders on aggressive toward women; and Eleanor's depression. As Gretchen Cohenour argues, "While marketed as a space where women are generally sheltered from harm, the home offered little actual protection from the male owner's anger and lust. Women's behavior could be controlled by the threat of violence alone" (20). This discomfiting reality renders the heroines' study and push-back test of men even more critical during singlehood, as it may be their only socially safeguarded opportunity for investigative research into prospective husbands' tendencies, particularly regarding how they would respond to challenges to their monocracy.

Catherine responds to the General's prohibition by circumventing his control, sneaking back to "the forbidden door" (192) alone. As soon as she has explored the room and re-shut the door, Henry appears and confronts her in a counter-scene to his father's. Rather than shouting, he makes polite conversation while insistently questioning her motives and conjectures; acknowledges his mother's suffering from his father's temper while also defending the General's honor; and treats Catherine with greater kindness rather than resentment after the humiliating revelation of her suspicions. Except during Henry's gentle but firm interrogation, in which he reasons with rather than threatens her, Catherine seeks his proximity and finds pleasure in his company. By subverting General Tilney's authority over his domestic space and then candidly revealing her perception of his murderous misogyny to his son, she prompts Henry further to demonstrate his contrasting regard for women. In addition to showing sensitivity to Catherine when he might be justified in expressing anger, Henry also refuses to join his father and Thorpe in treating her as a monetary acquisition. He places his principles and love for her above pleasing a greedy patriarch and, thus, above his own social and economic prosperity, defying the General by considering himself "bound as much in honour as in affection to Miss Morland" (247) and proposing to her before his father is persuaded to approve the relationship. Henry passes Catherine's test with flying colors, and amply justifies her choice.

Other Austen heroines similarly read their relative physical liberty or bondage in a man's company as a gauge of his attitude toward them. Fanny Price accurately perceives Henry Crawford's importunate suit as an imperialistic invasion. The reader is privy to his insidious plan to conquer her heart as a transient, gratuitous ego-boost, as boasted to a sister whose dispassionate reaction shifts all real concern for Fanny's protection to the helpless reader. Henry obtains a thrill from assuming his power to make

Fanny blush, as a foretaste of his imagined ability to awaken her to orgasmic pleasure—to be the one to give her something "'to express'" in her cheeks, "'eyes and mouth'" (*MP* 230). His calculated scheme to emotionally seduce the protagonist unexpectedly becomes a marriage proposal, but even then it remains a desire for possession of an unconquered virgin consciousness: "It would be something to be loved by such a girl, to excite the first ardours of her young, unsophisticated mind!" (235–236).

Fanny abstains from anything of which she disapproves, including Henry's address: "'No, no, no,' she cried, hiding her face. 'This is all nonsense. Do not distress me. I can hear no more of this. . . . I do not want, I cannot bear, I must not listen to such—No, no, don't think of me. But you are *not* thinking of me. I know it is all nothing'" (301–302). Fanny reasserts her virginal inaccessibility in covering her face, and her many linguistic negations here—as when the Bertrams attempt to hound her into acting as well as into accepting Henry—showcase her primary method of expressing her sexual orthodoxy. Fanny's unremitting abstemiousness at length exposes the slick actor's core depravity. She thwarts "the brutal power-politics of [Henry's] sexual quest" while manifesting a deeper sexiness than the shallow Crawford variety: "a type of sexuality bound up closely with an integrated sense of self" (Giuffre 78).

Confident of his irresistible magnetism and true to his rakish persona, Henry relishes pursuing his resistive object, anticipating "the glory, as well as the felicity, of forcing her to love him" (*MP* 326). Fanny views his uninvited "close neighbourhood" (342) and touch as a violation that heightens her skepticism of his character. He continually worms his way into her proximity and speaks to her in excessive language of praise and overfamiliarity, such that she finds relief in the servant's entrance with refreshments, which "delivered her from a grievous imprisonment of body and mind" (344). Henry takes advantage of the very propriety that amplifies the difficulty of courting a shy woman, adroitly crossing her boundaries through the asserted freedom of honorable intentions that checkmate her from a forceful rebuff. His physical liberties with Fanny are always taken rather than given, a usurpation of her will and the chastity of her personal space: "he would take her hand, he would not be denied it" (365).

Henry's imposed courtship of Fanny as epitomized by his unwelcome physical contact accentuates for her the impulsive sensuality and underlying lack of self-discipline that would most endanger her marital happiness with him, and foreshadows his irredeemable loss of her potential love. Fanny consistently communicates her refusal, while Henry continues to stalk her by extending his stay and attentions at Mansfield, visiting her in Portsmouth, and using his sister Mary to harangue her with allusions to his devotion. His improved conduct and persistence through her discouragements begin to suggest to her the possibility of his genuine fidelity, and the narrator even hints that his continuation in this more estimable, actual courtship would have won her over in the end (assuming Edmund married Mary). Fanny resists Henry's intensive wooing efforts long enough, however, to unearth his fatal inability to resist instant gratification. Instead of earning the wife he wanted by gaining her hard-won respect, he succumbs to his own weakness and elopes with the already-married Maria. Fanny's determined denial outlives both his lust for power and his insufficient best intentions. Her firm boundaries expose his own lack thereof, a lack that causes his avoidable self-destruction as it ensures her self-protection from a feckless cheater for a husband.

As observed in chapter 1, the immature Edmund displays a tendency to impose control over Fanny's physical movements; he also betrays a growing sexual attraction to Fanny—praising her beauty and figure beneath the guise of quoting her uncle (*MP* 198)—while pursuing another woman. Both of these Henry-like behaviors indicate Edmund's like need for testing and character growth to become husband material. Fanny's only notable challenge to Edmund is her staunch insistence on her power of choice—" 'I think it ought not to be set down as certain, that a man must be acceptable to every woman he may happen to like himself' " (353)—and obdurate waiting for him to align his choice with hers. Fanny's truth to herself takes precedence over the outcome of her courtship plot; she loves Edmund and refuses to consider anyone else, despite her own conviction that he will never reciprocate her feelings. She would rather "risk" remaining single on her terms than attain a profitable marriage to someone she neither loves nor respects. Fanny patiently observes as Edmund neglects and takes advantage of her while working through his misplaced infatuation with Mary and then matures through suffering. Without being calculating, she persists in his vicinity until he awakens to desire for her; she makes herself available to be his rebound, and it works. Like *Sense and Sensibility*'s Edward Ferrars, Edmund experiences a character reformation when he discovers the heedlessness of his attraction to a pretty but perverted woman and tastes the misery attending an incompatible relationship. Fanny gets her man at a time when he can best appreciate her virtues as a woman who is "of course only too good for him" (471), a man who discovers the beauty of her eyes only after long recognizing her moral worth.

Whereas Henry fails Fanny's test of his reformation, thus confirming her conviction of his physical and moral weakness as manifested in his continual efforts to possess her, Edmund is prepared to win her voluntary love through conscientious effort over time (though this proves unnecessary), aware of her strong sense of self and nearly immutable feelings. Having developed his capacity for reciprocity in a relationship, Edmund is no longer an insensitive user, but a devotee.[20] Fanny's obduracy while under continual pressure both masks and manifests her sexual energy.

While others cede to weakness and fall away from even their own intentions, she insists on the fulfillment of her desire in her own way and endures to make it so.

Just as Fanny Price repulses the encroaching Henry Crawford, Emma Woodhouse experiences a similar aversion to the invasion of her space by an unwelcome suitor and countermands this transgression in reinforcing the boundaries of her personhood. She finds herself trapped alone in a carriage with Mr. Elton after the Westons' party, and has just begun a dignified conversation when "she found her subject cut up—her hand seized—her attention demanded, and Mr. Elton actually making violent love to her" (*E* 129), a narrative description reminiscent of Mr. Collins's assertion of "the violence of [his] affection" in his unsuccessful proposal to Elizabeth Bennet (*PP* 106). In both cases, the man's forcing of intimacy and use of clichéd language to describe his sentiments expose the artifice as well as intrusiveness of his masqueraded feelings. Even after Emma has communicated her shock and disdain for his attentions as properly belonging to Harriet, Mr. Elton attempts "to take her hand again" (*E* 131) and they have an additional exchange in which she creates emotional distance between them with her emphatic, formal rejection. She categorizes him as a casual social connection, not even a friend, and stresses that any particular attention she gave him was only as the "admirer" of Harriet; " 'In no other light could you have been more to me than a common acquaintance' " (132). Emma perceives Mr. Elton's gold-digging motivation "to aggrandize and enrich himself; and if Miss Woodhouse of Hartfield, the heiress of thirty thousand pounds, were not quite so easily obtained as he had fancied, he would soon try for Miss Somebody else with twenty, or with ten" (135). She satirically assumes his mercenary point of view here—as commodities, all women are interchangeable to him and defined by sums, as Catherine Morland was for John Thorpe and General Tilney. By contrast to this objectifying attitude toward women symbolized by Mr. Elton's greedy seizure of Emma's hand, Mr. Knightley consistently shows disinterested consideration for women, and Emma's growing passion for him is encapsulated in her wish that he would not be so restrained in his touch.

However, Mr. Knightley must prove the purity of his intentions toward Emma before she actively pursues a romantic relationship with him. Emma employs Harriet as her courtship surrogate, not, as many critics believe, to evaluate other men's husband potential for herself or to play vicarious powerful male, but to test Mr. Knightley's desirability. All three of the single men courting Emma's attention instinctively view Harriet as her representative and their medium in the communication of their interest in Emma. At first, the proud heroine declares her intention of remaining single (to which Harriet expresses doubt as if seeing her double's future), but repeatedly uses Harriet to assess Mr. Knightley's devotion to herself. Emma has known her future spouse since childhood, which is problematic due to the age difference and necessitates her careful assessment of his ability to treat her in an egalitarian manner. She marries him only after he has fulfilled the equalizing humbling process that marks his shift from the role of fraternal mentor to that of attentive lover.

Ironically, Emma must first establish that Mr. Knightley does not see her as a sex object. He dislikes her friendship with Harriet because he senses it represents a barrier between her and himself. When Emma jokingly dares him to love Harriet—symbolic of her sexual self—she conducts a Cartesian test of his attitude toward women, whether as bodies or minds, and of his attitude toward their right to choose their own spouses.[21] She encourages Harriet to delay marriage, to "pick and choose" and "have time to look about her" (64)—an indirect message to herself; Emma's matchmaking functions as both the mirror and means of postponing her own marriage until she is sure of her choice. Just as the narrator describes in detail Emma's admiration of Harriet's beauty as "a very pretty girl" (23), Mrs. Weston catalogs Emma's beautiful features and forces Mr. Knightley to admit that he " 'love[s] to look at her' " and considers her " 'very handsome' " (39); he was focused on her character until a woman redirected his attention to her physicality.[22] Emma senses the chemistry between herself and Mr. Knightley and subtly reveals her romantic interest in him through her methods of testing his motives. She projects her own sexual desirability onto Harriet and experimentally offers her to him, claiming that " 'Harriet is exactly what every man delights in—what at once bewitches his senses and satisfies his judgment. . . . Were you, yourself, ever to marry, she is the very woman for you. And is she, at seventeen, just entering into life, just beginning to be known, to be wondered at because she does not accept the first offer she receives?' " (64).

Emma subconsciously speaks of herself with reference to Mr. Knightley here, as he is subconsciously aware. His anger at her arguments and interference with Harriet and Mr. Martin represents his own frustrated desire for her, as if the two of them are speaking in code of their feelings about each other. When Mr. Knightley promotes the marriage between Emma's connection and his, Mr. Martin functions as his corresponding surrogate in their debate. Emma resents Mr. Knightley's assumption of the role of arbiter of Harriet's (as of her own) life, challenging his patriarchal attitude toward women's self-determination as she tests the basis of his attraction to herself and the extent of its foundation on appearances. His anger stems from being thwarted in his own passion for Emma as well as in his male privilege of dictating to others, a privilege that he proves himself unprepared to forfeit at this stage.[23] He does pass one of Emma's tests, however—he denies being an objectifier mindlessly led by lust, declaring that Mr. Martin (and by extension he himself) is not motivated by " 'selfish passion' " (63) and that " 'Men of sense . . . do not want silly wives' " (64).

Although Emma and Mr. Knightley have multiple arguments in the course of the novel, in which she proves as stubborn as he is by maintaining her position despite the force of his arguments and anger, they always reconcile because he always accepts her ultimate independence of his will. He scrupulously defers to her on the all-important issue of her choice of mate. Emma seeks complete control over her own romance plot and enjoys narrating it. She resents Mr. Elton when he intrudes himself as the presumptive hero of her story, and later resents Frank Churchill for not only refusing to follow her storyline but appropriating her as surface heroine to cover his actual romance plot.[24] By contrast, Mr. Knightley refuses to use Emma and exhibits the true gentility that inspires both her regard and her notice of his sex appeal. At the Westons' ball at Randalls, she wishes he would dance, admiring "[h]is tall, firm, upright figure, among the bulky forms and stooping shoulders of the elderly men . . . He moved a few steps nearer, and those few steps were enough to prove in how gentlemanlike a manner, with what natural grace, he must have danced, would he but take the trouble.—Whenever she caught his eye, she forced him to smile" (326). Although dancing with Frank, Emma is absorbed in observing Mr. Knightley's phallic virility and fluidity of movement and drawing his notice to herself. By "forc[ing] him to smile" while she dances with another man whom he views as competition, she insists that he acknowledge her social and sexual liberty. Emma uses Frank as a reciprocal screen for her own subconscious romantic subtext—her love for Mr. Knightley—and insists on the chastity of choice. She will discover her own vocation, whether the single or married life and, if the latter, with whom to share it. During the second-to-last dance before supper, Emma witnesses Mr. Elton rudely refusing to dance with the partnerless Harriet to exact revenge against herself, but then "a happier sight caught her;—Mr. Knightley leading Harriet to the set!—Never had she been more surprised, seldom more delighted, than at that instant. She was all pleasure and gratitude, both for Harriet and herself, and longed to be thanking him; . . . her countenance said much, as soon as she could catch his eye again" (328). Mr. Knightley declares his love to Emma through attentiveness toward Harriet, her project and avatar, and she intuits his behavior as such.

Convinced of Mr. Knightley's honorable intentions toward women and, more specifically, toward herself, Emma feels free to act on her physical attraction to him and to invite his attraction to her. She surveils his sexy physique, "extremely good" dancing (328), and gallant treatment of Harriet, and unwittingly chooses him for herself. Harriet serves as a love messenger between Emma and Mr. Knightley, a mediator of their growing passion and esteem. They exchange looks while Mr. Knightley dances with Harriet; they converse about her superiority to Mr. Elton in an intimate chat; and, later the same evening, Emma initiates their first dance together by inviting Mr. Knightley to ask her. This represents their first romantic social ritual as eligible adult singles. Emma's sexual interest in Mr. Knightley is further suggested by their brief, spontaneous hand-holding in the aftermath of her rudeness at Box Hill, when he learns of her conciliatory visit to Miss Bates. He makes "a little movement of more than common friendliness on his part.—He took her hand;—whether she had not herself made the first motion, she could not say—she might, perhaps, have rather offered it—but he took her hand, pressed it, and certainly was on the point of carrying it to his lips—when, from some fancy or other, he suddenly let it go" (385–386). The ambiguity in Emma's mind over who initiated the touch reflects the improved mutuality of the relationship, and Mr. Knightley's forestalled completion of the gesture indicates his increased humility toward her. She is disappointed when he does not complete the impulsive near-kiss of her hand, and her reaction is described in sexually charged terms: "He would have judged better, she thought, if he had not stopped" (386). However, Mr. Knightley reveals not only his uncertainty of Emma's heart, but more importantly his recognition that he must "let [her] go"—she must be the one to initiate their courtship.

Harriet's unexpected interest in Mr. Knightley enlightens Emma to her own love for him, thus rendering obsolete her proxy's substitutionary role. Once Emma frees herself to fulfill her desire for Mr. Knightley, her double breaks free and marries her first love as well, Mr. Martin. Mr. Knightley learns to defer to Emma with the patience and devotion of Mr. Martin; he awaits her signal to propose and has become worthier of her because he now views her as his equal. Like Darcy's second, successful proposal, Mr. Knightley's proposal is part confession; he apologizes for his presumptuous lecturing and superior attitude. Although Harriet embodies a sexuality that is dangerous if undisciplined (as with her parents, who produced an illegitimate child), Austen also cautions against a woman being prematurely and unequally yoked, as Emma would have been with the unreformed Mr. Knightley. Once Emma's union with him is dictated by her will, not his, it succeeds. She puts him through multiple tests and chooses him in her own time when confident of his worthiness. In the course of their indirect courtship, he has learned to respect her agency as an autonomous being; his "abandonment of his paternalism" inspires the increased "fervour and openness of Emma's love" (L. Smith 152). Rather than continuing to act as lord over Emma, Mr. Knightley concedes to her will, awaits her invitation to love, and voluntarily moves into her father's house.[25] She asserts her desire for a man who surrenders his social prerogative of power to love of her, thereby freeing her to be giving in return. Emma seeks and finds a love that will not cost her her own nature.

Resisting Emotional Abuse

Emma pointedly tests Mr. Knightley for his capacity to tolerate differences of opinion from his future wife, who insists on the freedom of her mind. Mental and emotional liberty proves critical to the success of relationships in Austen's novels. Elizabeth Bennet famously dislikes her future husband at first, partly because she overhears his insult to her desirability, when he describes her as a woman who is " 'not handsome enough to tempt' " him to dance and is " 'slighted by other men' " (*PP* 12). Elizabeth thoroughly pushes back against Darcy's every presumption of superiority. After hearing his affront, she twice rejects his offers to dance—both the one initiated by Sir William Lucas and Darcy's spontaneous invitation to dance a reel at Netherfield. In response to his overture, she is openly rude, pretending not to hear him; when he repeats the request, she soundly rebuffs him, claiming that she " 'always delight[s] in . . . cheating a person of their premeditated contempt . . . now despise me if you dare' " (52). She dares him to despise her, not for her taste in dances but for her reckless tongue, her independent voice, her blatant freedom to oppose him. The unexpected "gallantry" (52) of his reaction to what would likely appear an arbitrary insolence (considering his unawareness that she overheard his unflattering remarks about her), manifests his potential for reform and marriageability.

During Darcy's first proposal, Elizabeth must repulse him again and more vigorously to inspire the introspection and motivation essential to his self-improvement and her corresponding increase of regard. His arrogant entitlement would have rendered him an unbearable husband who would expect her to perform the role of grateful subject rather than partner in life, a sure groundwork for the proliferation of inequities throughout their marriage. Darcy's rudeness in expressing qualms about "her inferiority—of its being a degradation—of the family obstacles that judgment had always opposed to inclination" (189) provokes Elizabeth to be more personal in retaliation. She volunteers several, expansive explanations for her refusal; declares, "You could not have made me the offer of your hand in any possible way that would have tempted me to accept it"; itemizes Darcy's character flaws; and concludes with the punchline, ". . . I had not known you a month before I felt that you were the last man in the world whom I could ever be prevailed on to marry" (192-193).

This famous disquisition is often quoted and quite satisfying from a female point of view. Darcy's stunned disbelief in Elizabeth's rejection reveals how much he needed humbling. She refuses to be slapped with one hand and embraced with the other, rejecting Darcy's profound sense of his own desirability and assumed freedom to step on her feelings while claiming to love her.[26] Through her collective acts of reacting and overreacting to Darcy's liberties, Elizabeth reverses the dynamic between the two of them, establishing herself as the unattainable one and him as the petitioner. Moreover, his "love" for her cannot consist in a giving over to his irrepressible "feelings" against his principles—this motive too closely resembles the objectifying drive of lust (189). Elizabeth asserts her right of self-determination and conveys to Darcy her uncompromising insistence on real love or nothing. As Maureen Sabine observes, "Elizabeth's behaviour is a reminder that romantic love derives its power from the sexual politics of chastity, from the virgin's insistence that she will exercise control over her own body, that she will not submit to marriage without love like Charlotte Lucas, or to sex before marriage like Lydia Bennet" (sec. 43).

Darcy becomes Elizabeth's choice only after demonstrating a true transformation that includes the deflation of his enormous ego. He must genuinely respect her (and, therefore, treat her family with respect, no matter how obnoxious they may be) and view marriage to her as a privilege rather than a social sacrifice in order to render possible a long-term egalitarian friendship. Elizabeth and Darcy show sparks early on in Beatrice-and-Benedick style, engaging in a contest of minds and wills that signals a physical attraction as well, but Elizabeth requires that her man prove his change of heart before she commits herself. She asserts as an inalienable " 'right' " a woman's freedom " 'to determine and direct in what manner [she is] to be happy' " (185–186).[27] Elizabeth will not admit her attraction to Darcy—either to herself or to him—until she is convinced of his eligibility as a lifelong companion. After he reforms and performs noble deeds that go beyond her husband-worthy test requirements, she accepts him. His social and financial rescue of her family from Wickham's perfidy, anonymously and without any guarantee of a return, demonstrates his moral enlightenment and the intensity of his persistent passion for her. In Austen's novels, a suitor's exercise of authentic virtue becomes a courtship ritual, a language of love.

A woman can experience emotional violation by a man indirectly as well as through cutting words. Seemingly sweet, benign Edward Ferrars in *Sense and Sensibility* does not criticize Elinor Dashwood's looks or family, but knowingly engages her feelings and draws her into an implied relationship that cannot come to fruition.[28] Like Darcy, Edward must reform his character to become a desirable husband, but he behaves even worse than Darcy by being deceptively rather than frankly hurtful, thus necessitating a harsher corresponding punishment. Not unlike Elizabeth's father, Mr. Bennet, Edward had been led by physical attraction to choose the wrong mate, conflating Lucy Steele's looks with her presumed temperament.[29] As he later explains to Elinor, she " 'appeared everything that was amiable and obliging. She was pretty too—at least I thought so *then*, and I had seen so little of other women, that I could make no comparisons, and see no defects' " (*SS* 362). Edward bitterly regrets his poor judgment in having prematurely committed himself to what reveals itself to be a counterfeit relationship with an ignorant woman. However, he then commits a more egregious act by becoming attached to Elinor, leading her on while emotionally betraying his secret fiancée, which causes Elinor much suffering. Edward must repent his unfairness to her and prove his trustworthiness, ironically, by being true to the woman he no longer even likes. He prepares to be chained to Lucy for life as a fitting penance for his errors; in so doing, he demonstrates to Elinor his honorability and that he is no longer the sexually led man he was. He acknowledges not only the absurdity of his naïve young lust for Lucy, but his culpability in deceiving Elinor by pursuing a forbidden, futile relationship with her. He becomes the righteous, self-disciplined man who can truly make her happy.

When Edward is finally freed of Lucy's shackles, he proposes and confesses all to Elinor, and she lectures him as Elizabeth does Darcy when he first proposes, as if to cement his reform and establish her expectations of her future husband's conduct: " 'Your behaviour was certainly very wrong,' said she, 'because— to say nothing of my own conviction, our relations were all led away by it to fancy and expect *what*, as you were *then* situated, could never be' " (368). He respects Elinor's judgment, and when she explains Lucy's likely reasons for her contradictory behavior, "Edward was of course immediately convinced that nothing could have been more natural than Lucy's conduct, nor more self-evident than the motive of it" (367). His deference to Elinor's discernment foreshadows his reliance on her wisdom throughout their companionate, egalitarian marriage.

Chastity as Truth to Self

The twenty-seven-year-old Anne Elliot of Austen's last completed novel learns through her heartbreak what Elinor Dashwood and Fanny Price knew well before theirs—to follow her own certitude of feeling and judgment above all else, regardless of outcome. In the course of the over eight years following her broken engagement, despite her "early loss of bloom" (*P* 28) and ticking biological clock, Anne refuses to "settle." She will not compromise her desire to socioeconomic considerations and, until Wentworth's reform, is the only one to honor herself. Like Fanny Price, Anne always knows who she wants, but she must endure a much longer period of suffering and the intervention of two successive rivals for her own affection as well as two seeming rivals for her beloved's affection before her longstanding desire can be consummated. In the process, Captain Wentworth, like nearly all the male protagonists, must be fully awakened to his true love's shining merit.

We cannot blame Lady Russell for pressuring Anne to break with Wentworth when they are first engaged; in fact, she is correct about the unacceptability of his then-temperament. Although the couple's young love seems idyllic, he exhibits the same edge of arrogant overconfidence from which characters like Darcy and Mr. Knightley must be purged to merit the love of self-respecting women. The narrator remarks that "[h]e was, at that time, a remarkably fine young man, with a great deal of intelligence, spirit and brilliancy; and Anne an extremely pretty girl, with gentleness, modesty, taste, and feeling" (26), emphasizing Wentworth's abilities as a "man," but only Anne's physical appeal and virtues as "an extremely pretty girl" who would suit his pleasure, comfort, and convenience. The narrator successively assumes each of the two lovers' subject positions in this description, which reveals that Anne admires Wentworth for himself, independently of her, whereas Wentworth admires her for her benefits to him as a physically attractive and compliant woman. He had "spen[t] freely, what had come freely" and rather than saving, "had realized nothing. But, he was confident that he should soon be rich" and displays "fearlessness of mind" and a "headstrong" nature, all of which suggests he was too preoccupied with his own abilities and insufficiently aware of Anne's to be capable of mutuality in their marriage (27). Anne's sacrificial motivation for breaking off with him as well as her youthful malleability in being persuaded to do so further confirms the likelihood of a one-sided relationship: "Had she not imagined herself consulting his good, even more than her own, she could hardly have given him up.—The belief of being prudent, and self-denying principally for *his* advantage, was her chief consolation" (28).

Anne's romantic detour includes two men who are even more preoccupied than Wentworth with the physical at the expense of the intellectual and spiritual. Charles Musgrove proposes to Anne when she is twenty-two and represents a more benign version of John Thorpe, in that "he did nothing with much zeal, but sport; and his time was otherwise trifled away, without benefit from books, or any thing else" (43). Like Thorpe and *Sense and Sensibility*'s Sir John Middleton and Willoughby, Charles Musgrove is risibly portrayed as a man lacking substance or depth who is preoccupied with stereotyped masculine entertainment—hunting and its accompaniments in guns and animals. Although Anne suspects that "a more equal match might have greatly improved him" (43), she has already once sacrificed her happiness for mistaken ideals of another's best interests and will not do so again. She rejects Charles because she does not love him as well as because she loves Wentworth. By contrast, when Wentworth returns from naval service, he cavalierly pursues the interchangeable Musgrove sisters. He displays his immature reactivity to Anne's now years-old refusal in his frivolous and even cruelly vengeful pursuit of Louisa before Anne's eyes, thus showcasing his unworthiness of his former beloved.

However, Wentworth's experimental pseudo-courtship of Louisa, discovery of Charles Musgrove's failed suit, and competition from the "conversing and smiling" (244) Mr. William Walter Elliot bring him to his senses and humble him into an Edmund-like awareness of the preeminence of the woman he loves, as a "[t]oo good, too excellent creature!" (237). He has learned to see Anne as far more than a sweet, "pretty girl" like a Louisa or a Henrietta.[30] The couple's mutual physical attraction reawakens as an outgrowth of his deeper awakening to her merit as a human being; the now twenty-eight-year-old Anne herself recognizes Wentworth's "homage"—summed up in his declaration that " 'to my eye you could never alter' "—as "the result, not the cause of a revival of his warm attachment" (P 243). Scholars underscore the sensuality of the couple's subtle interactions, such as Anne's tremulous response to sitting on the couch with only Mrs. Musgrove between herself and Wentworth, his handing her into the Crofts' carriage, or his removal of her nephew from her back, but this undercurrent of touch and sensation is symptomatic of their mutual study of one another's characters and feelings.[31] Anne stands by her decisions; following Lady Russell's advice in her youth enables Captain Wentworth's ultimate growth into the best husband, just as following her own distrust of unprincipled Mr. Elliot's slick image protects her from the worst prospective spouse. A female mentor's intervention; time; and expanded self-knowledge and self-appreciation prove her greatest allies in testing potential mates. Though older and wiser in some respects, Anne becomes more like Fanny Price, Elizabeth Bennet, and Elinor Dashwood by learning to act on truth to herself as the ultimate consideration, regardless of circumstances. After unwillingly breaking her first engagement, she passes up at least two other marriage prospects, disregarding social pressures and willfully preserving what she believes to be a futile, unrequited love. She will honor her authentic feelings and principles, with or without a man, so she can live with herself.

The collective example of Austen's heroines conveys that women must assert their sexual orthodoxy by drawing a bold, insurmountable line for men that underscores their moral absolutes—their non-negotiable boundaries of conduct, sentiment, and conviction. Women must exercise their freedom of choice in marriage by carefully testing men over time for insight into their true characters and motivations. It is better to be honorably single, regardless of poverty or social disapproval, than to become a Charlotte Lucas, much less a used and discarded Eliza, Lydia, or Maria. A self-respecting person recognizes a higher purpose in either married or celibate single life. In addition, as Margaret Kirkham points out, Austen's protagonists cannot "get married at all until the heroes have provided convincing evidence of appreciating their powers of rational judgement, as well as their good hearts" (31). A man's reaction to a woman's resistance of his attempts to penetrate her physical and psychic space tells her all she needs to know. Her refusal of objectification, emotional abuse, or cooptation of any kind separates the users from the lovers who show accountability to a higher power than their flawed selves. By tenaciously asserting her subjective will, the heroine avoids the fate of cast-off woman—whether as spinster, fallen woman, or wife. By disinterestedly living her life according to her values and dictates, she does what is right while employing her suitor-testing filtration system until only her most suitable hero remains.

Austen suggests that sexual attraction enhances a romantic relationship founded on friendship and esteem, but cannot replace those foundational elements. After a successful courtship trial, sexual expression in a loving marriage works to preserve what is best in both the men who have proven their integrity and the women who necessarily exacted it. Sparks fly among authentic couples who share an intelligent passion fueled by mutuality and tempered by self-control. Moreover, these committed lovers' recognition that the body and sexual intercourse are more than their material reality—as they are themselves more than themselves, whether as one, two, or two-become-one—necessarily dissolves any presumptive power hierarchy between mortals in the sacramental communion of the human with the divine. Whether Austen's heroines establish their apartness of worth via deliberate, subconscious, taught, or instinctive tactics, those tactics accentuate their boundaries of selfhood and distinguish the good men from the would-be tyrants or "squeamish" weaklings who, in Mr. Bennet's words, "are not worth a regret" (*PP* 231). Austen speaks to us of the life-affirming efficacy of truth to one's sexual orthodoxy.

Part 2

Women's Natures

Mood, Mind, Spirit, and Female Giftedness

CHAPTER 3

"Determined to Be Happy"

The Path to Emotional Health in
Sense and Sensibility

CO-AUTHORED WITH JORDAN L. VON CANNON,
FLORIDA GULF COAST UNIVERSITY

We have examined Austen's thoughts about the role of the body in the lives and identities of women, and ways in which their corporal condition and sexuality communicate their degree of inward wellness. As argued in the previous chapter, a heroine's establishment of firm physical, moral, and psychological boundaries with men emanates from and reaffirms her self-worth. She honors her significance as the offspring of an omnipotent Creator by acting upon the values that relationship engenders over any consideration of material gain or even personal happiness. In return, she secures both, as if the recipient of an almost fantastical reward for righteousness. And yet, Jane Austen's novels are not fantasies; their female protagonists must square off with adversity and face down the reality of disappointment, deferral, dearth, and death, but still accept responsibility for their own emotions and actions. Regardless of the plot twists out of their control, they must exercise and strengthen their hearts, minds, and spirits. As part of this endeavor, Austen insists, they can create their own happiness, or they should at least try.

Both men and women are vulnerable to potentially overwhelming feelings and attachments that can lead to co-dependency. In *Sense and Sensibility*, Colonel Brandon's and Edward Ferrars's acute melancholia over their romantic disasters illustrates this—the Colonel's still-raw heartbreak is of fourteen years' standing. Likewise, both genders reveal an equal capacity for the polar opposite in coldblooded opportunism, as the well-matched Lucy Steele and Robert Ferrars demonstrate. However, Regency women face social, economic, and cultural disadvantages—along with far fewer resources or protections with which to face them—and, consequently, possess less emotional insurance.[1] In addition, Austen presents as a distinctly female problem the question of how to cope with limited control over one's quotidian life. As Anne Elliot explains to Captain Harville, " 'We live at home, quiet, confined, and our feelings prey upon us. You are forced on exertion. You have always a profession, pursuits, business of some sort or other, to take you back into the world immediately, and continual occupation and change soon weaken impressions' " (*P* 232). Thus, Austen targets women with her message of self-determined mental stability. Pairs of female characters who represent the respective extremes of romantic feeling or calculating detachment appear in all the novels—Jane Bennet versus Charlotte Lucas (*PP*), Catherine Morland versus Isabella Thorpe (*NA*), Fanny Price versus Mary Crawford (*MP*), Harriet Smith and Emma versus Mrs. Elton (*E*), Anne Elliot versus her sister Elizabeth and Mrs. Clay (*P*). The novelist deprecates the extremes of emotionalism or impassivity and advocates a self-help program of willful positivity as the key to women's long-term psychological wellness.

Austen does not encourage the forced hysteria of wishful joy that today's self-help industry often seems to understand by "positive thinking"—which can produce even greater self-displacement in people who are already at rock bottom—but the steely, teeth-gritting mental toughness bred of the decision to survive in the best spirit one can. Our ancestors probably shared and better understood this attitude that steadfast grace amidst hardship is an obligatory duty to God and society. Virtuous behavior also tends to produce the gratifications of "self-approbation" and joy in aiding others' joy (Dadlez 61), though these benefits do not noticeably ease Elinor Dashwood's veiled desolation. Austen expects her heroines to be strong, no matter what, and has little tolerance for whiners and hypochondriacs. And yet, while undercutting hedonistic self-absorption as a threat to the health of individuals and civilization, she also validates women's proactive preservation of their psyches for their own flourishing.[2]

In *Sense and Sensibility*, as in all of Austen's novels, the courtship plot of love lost and love found is secondary to the protagonists' simultaneous personal development. As in *Pride and Prejudice* and *Persuasion*, this female bildungsroman is more nuanced than the seeming absolutism of its archetypes. The coalescence of the qualities of sense *and* sensibility in the novel's title indicates its ultimate message to women, which Austen propounds through the collective impact of her several subgroups of female character types: those with excessive sensibility, those with too much "sense" and no apparent sensibility, and those with an optimal blend of both qualities. Despite Elinor Dashwood's practicality and Marianne Dashwood's dramatic self-expression, both heroines manifest the dangers of heightened feeling. Their true foils are not each other but characters such as Lucy Steele and her role models, Lady Middleton and Mrs. John Dashwood, who portray a self-serving, distorted "sense."[3] Two commonly overlooked characters—Mrs. Jennings and her younger daughter, Charlotte Palmer—embody the blend of sense with sensibility that the novel depicts as most advantageous to a woman's mental health. Through her delineation of the worst and best female attitudinal prototypes, Austen endorses these unlikely role models for their assumption of a deliberate stance of psychic self-reliance in their allegiance to an emotional median.[4]

The elder Dashwood sisters both possess sense and sensibility, and their conduct becomes more parallel in the course of their development. Marianne's melodramatic affect begins as self-centered and theatrical, while Elinor experiences intense emotions but suppresses them; Marianne learns duty, restraint, and compassion, while Elinor learns to express herself more openly.[5] The two also share in common various traits, attitudes, and circumstantial challenges, such as their "distinctive intellectual qualities, perceptions, and resistance to commonplace conversation" (Folsom 32) in the mundane social world they occupy (35). A detrimental commonality is that the sisters are emotionally dependent on men and are traumatized by betrayal and assuaged by marriage and its consequential emotional restoration. Despite their divergent temperaments and trajectories of personal growth, Austen portrays both women as heroines of sensibility whose tender hearts render them too vulnerable to the vicissitudes of a realistic social universe.[6]

Marianne's excessive sensibility is well-covered (probably wet-leaf-covered) ground in criticism of the novel, so the first section of this chapter will focus on extrapolating how the seemingly rational Elinor reveals a dangerous level of lovelorn emotionalism. The eldest Dashwood sister and family leader always "had an excellent heart;—her disposition was affectionate, and her feelings were strong; but she knew how to govern them" (*SS* 6). That the narrator first praises her "strength of understanding" and "coolness of judgment" (6) before offering this tribute to her sensibilities does not negate them. While Elinor demonstrates her adherence to social responsibility over personal passion, she nonetheless exposes to the reader her keen feelings for Edward. She falls as deeply in love and feels as devastated when thwarted in the object of her desire as Marianne—perhaps more so, considering her interiorization of concentrated emotion. In private, Elinor indulges her "disappointed heart" (198) and endures racking suffering, without the relief of open purgation.[7]

Neither Elinor nor Marianne is capable of creating her own contentment, as emphasized not only each time Marianne is indisposed for company or everyday living while nursing a broken heart, but also each time Elinor throws herself into duties to family and friends to distract herself from such consuming emotions as the "distress beyond any thing she had ever felt before" (135) evoked by the revelation of Edward's engagement to Lucy. Despite the rationalism of Elinor's asserted philosophies, such as her pronouncement regarding the impossibility " 'of one's happiness depending entirely on any particular person' " (263), her happiness does depend on her union with Edward Ferrars. This is nowhere more apparent than when the news of his unforeseen release by Lucy triggers Elinor's spontaneous release of long-suppressed emotion: "She almost ran out of the room, and as soon as the door was closed, burst into tears of joy, which at first she thought would never cease" (360), and "it required several hours to give sedateness to her spirits, or any degree of tranquillity to her heart" (363).

These descriptions sound like Marianne, who ironically relinquishes her original convictions regarding romantic felicity to discover a new kind of love in a "second attachment" (56). Although many readers are dissatisfied with Marianne's marriage, she *needs* to be passionately in love and transfers that need to a new object in the form of a better man. "Marianne could never love by halves; and her whole heart became, in time, as much devoted to her husband, as it had once been to Willoughby" (379)—or more so, because she can respect and admire the Colonel's genuine sensibility. Although one might argue that if Edward had married Lucy Steele, Elinor, likewise, would have managed to live a joyful life with someone else, the narrator offers no assurance that this is possible. Elinor resembles Jane Bennet, who, without her man, "was not happy. . . . so fervently did she value his remembrance, and prefer him to every other man, that all her good sense, and all her attention to the feelings of her friends, were requisite to check the indulgence of those regrets, which must have been injurious to her own health and their tranquillity" (*PP* 227). That unhappiness and those regrets persist—though Jane and Elinor rightly suppress them to avoid cresting the cliff of sadness into despair—and are overcome only by the fortuitous outcomes that restore the women's co-dependent bliss. Fortunately for Elinor, she glimpses but is never required to experience the full consequences of her philosophy of the primacy of duty over all other claims, including those of love.

Elinor and Marianne exemplify an unhealthy degree of sensibility, demonstrating absorption in and emotional reliance upon extrinsic sources of fulfillment. Their perpetual entertainment of romantic notions—Elinor's assumption that the lock of hair in Edward's ring must be her own (*SS* 98), or Marianne's belief that Willoughby has shown her Allenham because it will one day be hers (68–69), for example—threatens their ability to develop independent identities. During the sisters' London visit with Mrs. Jennings, though they have faced ample evidence that their loves are unlikely to be consummated, Elinor continues her secret submersion in sorrow (198) while Marianne impulsively sends correspondence to Willoughby (161). The more mature sister's "behavior has turned out to differ from Marianne's only in degree and not in kind" (C. Johnson, *Jane* 63). In their acute sensibility, they both remain romantic heroines throughout the novel, though they prove fortunate enough to attain loving marriages by the end. By beginning the plot with their father's death and their ejection from Norland and then depicting Marianne's loss and Elinor's near-loss of her first love, Austen elucidates the strong likelihood that one's narrative will not follow one's desired path and, therefore, that an attachment to particular outcomes—which often depend on forces beyond one's control—will lead to devastation. One can and should be prepared to adapt one's vision to encompass inevitable plot twists.[8]

While Austen does not endorse women's immersion in a sensibility that produces an emotionally precarious position, neither does she propound the kind of callous, egocentric determinism that somewhat protects women from the whims of fate or circumstance but diminishes their humanity. Austen approves and recognizes the necessity for a distinctly female "sense," defined as the resourcefulness to further one's survival in a patriarchal material and social landscape without compromising one's conscience or social citizenship. However, Lucy Steele and her role models, Lady Middleton and Fanny Dashwood, function as representations of overblown sense; they embrace a materialistic vision of life in which self-aggrandizement is the only goal. These female characters possess decidedly unromantic ideals—those of wealth and social status—upon which "all [their] happiness depends" (*SS* 131).

Lucy Steele arguably functions as the chief villain in the novel, given the obstructive role she plays in Edward and Elinor's relationship. Although ignorant and unprincipled, she proves herself extremely clever in securing her future prosperity. She represents over-pragmatism in her focus on self-preservation in the deterministic jungle of English social life. She perceives that her best protection in such a society lies in marrying well, and she achieves this aim through tactical toadying as a "sycophant to wealth and power" (C. Johnson, *Jane* 50). Lucy makes the decision early on to "steel" herself emotionally, avoiding the vulnerability of a tender heart by approaching marriage as a business agreement. She demonstrates a worldly detachment in stepping outside of herself and controlling the only aspects of her life she can. A resourceful strategist, she abstracts herself from all true feeling throughout her interactions with possible suitors, secretly making and breaking engagements until she settles on the richest man she can manipulate into marriage. Once Mrs. Ferrars replaces Edward as heir with his younger brother Robert, Lucy as easily replaces Edward with the "great coxcomb" in her sham affections (*SS* 148). The narrator satirically praises her heartless pragmatism as an object lesson in "what an earnest, an unceasing attention to self-interest . . . will do in securing every advantage of fortune, with no other sacrifice than that of time and conscience" (376). Lucy's steely determination to attain affluence at all costs also includes the sacrifice of her own emotional life, genuine relationships, and worth, leading to her self-dehumanization.

Austen's portrayal of Lucy's role models, Fanny Dashwood and Lady Middleton, accentuates her narrative condemnation of living for social and financial gain. The two women prove "equally pleased with" one another because "[t]here was a kind of cold hearted selfishness on both sides, which mutually attracted them" (229). Recognizing that Mrs. Dashwood and Lady Middleton possess the riches and consequence she desires, Lucy lavishes obsequious attention on both, flattering their vanity with false compliments and pretended adoration of their unruly children: "Her flattery had already subdued the pride of Lady Middleton, and made an entry into the close heart of Mrs. John Dashwood" (254).

Lady Middleton substantiates for Lucy that wealth and title provide sufficient fulfillment to one with an empty head and luxurious habits; she appears not in the least discomfited by the fact that she and her spouse are "dissimilar in temper and outward behaviour" (32). Her pleasures consist of "spoil[ing] her children all the year round" and displaying "the elegance of her table, and of all her domestic arrangements; and from this kind of vanity was her greatest enjoyment in any of their parties" (32). Lady Middleton defines herself only by her offspring and her manipulation of domestic interiors; her mental interior is vacant: "She had nothing to say one day that she had not said the day before. Her insipidity was invariable, for even her spirits were always the same" (55). Her disapproval of her mother, Mrs. Jennings, underscores her choice of empty elegance over benignly boisterous substance. Lady Middleton has chosen to be middling, surrendering selfhood to surface appearances and becoming robotically repetitive in her intellectual and affective stasis.

Fanny Dashwood is the queen of self-interest in the novel, "a caricature of sense" (Lauber, *Jane* 28). Like Lady Middleton, she proves herself to be devoid of substance, in inverse proportion to her choice of material power over cultivation of character or the joy of human connection. Fanny's selfishness also manifests itself in active cruelty. Her main preoccupation is securing and proliferating her nuclear family's wealth and social éclat, at the expense of her sisters-in-law and anyone else she considers inferior. Early in the novel, we see this obsession burlesqued in her affected fear that any gift from John to his half-sisters would lead "to [the] ruin [of] himself, and their poor little Harry" (*SS* 8). The narrator conveys that a lifestyle focused on money and status degrades one's humanity, rendering one mentally and temperamentally bereft:

> John Dashwood had not much to say for himself that was worth hearing, and his wife had still less. But there was no peculiar disgrace in this, for it was very much the case with the chief of their visitors, who almost all laboured under one or other of these disqualifications for being agreeable—Want of sense, either natural or improved—want of elegance—want of spirits—or want of temper. (233)

Stone-hearted Fanny, Lady Middleton, and their protégée, Lucy, all choose narcissistic self-absorption over genuine community, eschewing the suffering that arises from give-and-take relationships. In so doing, however, they also limit themselves to petty satisfactions that leave their "spirits" and "temper" lacking and their isolated selves insatiable, no matter how many worldly riches they accumulate. By contrast, Elinor and Marianne depend too much on others for their happiness, as we are reminded when even the matter-of-fact eldest daughter, who efficiently manages her mother's household and finances, is unable to protect her sensitive heart from the anguish she experiences each time it appears that Edward does not return her love.

And yet, the steely women of distorted "sense" are not so different from the women of distorted sensibility; although their aloofness spares them the inner turmoil the Dashwood sisters endure, they likewise rely on factors outside themselves for what paltry gratification they are able to feel. One's financial and social stability can alter as swiftly as an engagement can be broken or the character of an inconstant man be revealed.

In a world in which romantic and monetary prosperity are elusive, Mrs. Jennings and her daughter Charlotte Palmer are the two women whose happiness does not depend on anything or anyone other than themselves. Neither overly sensitive nor emotionless, they also remain consistent in their benignity. Because the mother and daughter appear sporadically and do not play a direct role in the pivotal plot conflicts, their significance is easy to overlook. Readers may associate them with other characters' disregard or denigration of them as silly, clueless women. The narrator describes even the sensitive Colonel Brandon as "probably . . . perfectly indifferent" to Mrs. Jennings's "raillery" (36). Similarly, Mr. Palmer disregards his voluble wife or goes further and flaunts his lack of respect for her through cutting rejoinders (Dinkler). The assumption that both Charlotte's and Mrs. Jennings's good spirits result from deficient perception and ignorance of others' true opinions of them downplays the characters' importance as exemplars of mental health and social magnanimity.[9]

The minimal textual presence of the mother-daughter duo does not negate their efficacy as models for Austen's heroines and readers. Mrs. Jennings and her daughter embody the perfect measure of sense and sensibility in the novel: they are emotive without being melodramatic and sensible without being opportunistic. They preserve their good spirits, never overwrought by the mini-dramas occurring around them. Charlotte and Mrs. Jennings invest in others' lives without letting external complications affect their individual well-being. Moreover, neither appears to need men, luxury, or society to find contentment. Although both women are often belittled or dismissed, they have achieved what no one else has: they have discovered how to be happy in themselves. Other people cannot conceive of this emotional autonomy and, perceiving no tangible justification for the women's joy, cynically misinterpret it as insensibility.

The narrator introduces Mrs. Jennings as "a good-humoured, merry, fat, elderly woman, who talked a great deal, seemed very happy, and . . . was full of jokes and laughter" (*SS* 34). And yet, her life has not been perfect. Unlike the Dashwood women, Mrs. Jennings is well provided for as "a widow, with an ample jointure" (36) whose husband "had traded with success in a less elegant part of" London (153), but she knows grief as well. She still recalls "all the particulars of Mr. Jennings's last illness, and what he said to his wife a few minutes before he died" (54). On a smaller scale, she also discerns her older daughter's and friends' disapproval of her vulgar jokes and topics of conversation, but is unfazed and continues to be herself. She pries into the personal concerns of others, as when Colonel Brandon is unexpectedly called away the morning of the excursion to Whitwell and she is the only one who interrogates him on the nature of his urgent business in town (63–66). Mrs. Jennings evinces no anxiety at violating decorum with her queries, which might reasonably be judged insensitive, but she acts on warmhearted authenticity rather than hurtfulness in her frankness. She does not care that family and friends such as Mr. Palmer and Marianne underappreciate her humor and sometimes treat her with outright rudeness. Her joie de vivre springs from within. She even enjoys joking at her own expense, which offsets her occasional insensitivity, as when she cites as her rationale for inviting both Elinor and Marianne to London that " 'if they [get] tired of me, they might talk to one another, and laugh at my odd ways behind my back' " (154). She feels secure enough to make herself a joke while being immune to ridicule.

In addition, "Mrs. Jennings's well-meant but ill-judged attentions" (193) give the recipients and Austen's readers food for thought as evidence of not only her emotional and social independence but her desire to encourage that same independence in those she loves. Regardless of the delight she takes in company, she does not rely on it to preserve her buoyancy and always socializes on her own terms, as implied by the fact that "[t]hough Mrs. Jennings was in the habit of spending a large portion of the year at the houses of her children and friends, she was not without a settled habitation of her own" (153). Mrs. Jennings's kindness sometimes reveals a bluff crust of hard realism that produces dark comedy while suggesting her subconscious effort to propel others to face life's exigencies from a wider view, thereby reducing the scale of a seeming crisis to its proper proportions. For example, Elinor observes Mrs. Jennings's lack of perception when she assumes that Willoughby's cruel rejection letter delivered to Marianne must be a love letter, "which appeared to her a very good joke," and she "hop[ed], with a laugh, that [Marianne] would find it to her liking" (181). Mrs. Jennings later bursts in on the Dashwood sisters upon hearing the news of Willoughby's engagement to Miss Grey, expressing outrage at his dishonorable behavior and offering the sobbing Marianne "comfort" with the observation that " 'he is not the only young man in the world worth having; and with your pretty face you will never want admirers' " (192). Her simple, earthy methods of striving to assuage Marianne's agony are comical but instructive: "She treated her . . . with all the indulgent fondness of a parent towards a favourite child on the last day of its holidays" and attempted "to cure a disappointment in love, by a variety of sweetmeats and olives, and a good fire" (193). She plans to have friends over to play games with her house guests, asking Elinor which game Marianne prefers. These gestures may all seem hurtful, condescending, or at least absurd, but they may also be what the childish Marianne needs.

Mrs. Jennings models for her immature friend and the reader a transcendent, life-affirming perspective that acknowledges not only present pain but also the possibilities of present and future pleasure. As Beth Lau observes, Marianne must realize her misery's transience, and she "recovers from her depression by learning . . . to substitute temporary and local thinking habits for permanent and pervasive ones" (48). As fatuous in its simplicity as Mrs. Jennings's treatment of Marianne appears, it reflects emotional sense, a psychologically healthier alternative to the surrender to hysteria. A similar example occurs in *Northanger Abbey*, in which the down-to-earth Mrs. Morland tries to impress upon the secretly lovelorn Catherine the truism that " 'Wherever you are you should always be contented' " and assigns her to read a didactic novel about " 'young girls that have been spoilt for home by great acquaintance' " (241). While her mother goes in search of the book, fortunately for Catherine, Henry Tilney arrives at Fullerton to propose. Austen comically and compassionately admits the difficulty of achieving the kind of courageous, thankful vision urged by the likes of Mrs. Morland

and Mrs. Jennings; *Northanger Abbey*'s narrator accedes that "there are some situations of the human mind in which good sense has very little power" (239).

Mrs. Jennings has much more "good sense" and is far more penetrating than others realize. She immediately perceives Fanny Dashwood's ugly character: "to *her* she appeared nothing more than a little proud-looking woman of uncordial address, who met her husband's sisters without any affection, and almost without having any thing to say to them; for of the quarter of an hour bestowed on Berkeley-street, she sat at least seven minutes and a half in silence" (*SS* 229). Mrs. Jennings's awareness of Fanny's coldness is reflected in humorously precise detail as to both the duration and the spirit of her bad behavior. Though her efforts are sometimes misplaced, Mrs. Jennings consistently shows kindness, generosity, and compassion toward the Dashwood sisters as well as many others. After the revelation of Willoughby's betrayal, she and Charlotte refrain from speaking of him in Marianne's presence (214), but she also expresses her moral integrity "with blunt sincerity" on such subjects as Edward's virtue in remaining loyal to Lucy (267) and the absurdity of Mrs. Ferrars's decision " 'to make one son independent, because another had plagued' " her (269). Mrs. Jennings early discerns Elinor's being in love and accurately predicts Marianne's marital future with Colonel Brandon. As Eva Brann remarks, "No one would argue for Mrs. Jennings's tact, but who can deny her a species of sense, superior in its quickness to Elinor?" (131). She is an empathetic truth-speaker with solid principles who cares for others without becoming distraught over their concerns. Overall, while Mrs. Jennings demonstrates sense in her ability to recognize that she is the only one responsible for her happiness, she also maintains a moderated but sincere sensibility to the joys and sufferings of those around her. She proves to be an excellent role model for her younger daughter, Charlotte.

Although typecast as inane, Mrs. Palmer radiates a joviality that offsets the novel's sedate characters and dark themes. She "had a very pretty face, and the finest expression of good humour in it that could possibly be. . . . She came in with a smile, smiled all the time of her visit, except when she laughed, and smiled when she went away" (106). Charlotte's pleasantness remains intact beside her stoic husband's artful contemptuousness throughout the Palmers' visit with the Dashwoods. Every time the Palmers make an appearance in the novel, the reader is keenly aware of Mr. Palmer's apparent disregard for his wife. He habitually separates himself from conversation with her and ignores the questions she directs to him. This marital relationship is not enviable, yet Mrs. Palmer seems perfectly content. Although some critics cite Mr. and Mrs. Palmer's interactions as intentional burlesque, one cannot ignore the hurtful element in Mr. Palmer's treatment of his wife. How would Elinor or Marianne react to such open disrespect? However, in response to Mrs. Jennings's joke that Mr. Palmer is stuck with her daughter, "Charlotte laughed heartily to think that her husband could not get rid of her. . . . The studied indifference, insolence, and discontent of her husband gave her no pain: and when he scolded or abused her, she was highly diverted" (112). She has made a conscious attitudinal decision, as indicated by her "exultingly sa[ying], she did not care how cross he was to her, as they must live together" (112).

Furthermore, this marriage is more complex than appears on the surface. Though Elinor "wonder[s] at Charlotte's being so happy without a cause" (118), she begins to suspect Mr. Palmer of role-playing; she "was not inclined, after a little observation, to give him credit for being so genuinely and unaffectedly ill-natured or ill-bred as he wished to appear. . . . It was rather a wish of distinction she believed, which produced his contemptuous treatment of every body, and his general abuse of every thing before him" (112). On the visit to Cleveland, Elinor "found him very capable of being a pleasant companion" (304) and "liked him . . . much better than she had expected" (305). He also reveals his better nature when he helps the Dashwoods during Marianne's illness. Charlotte, like her mother, is more discerning than she appears. She knows better than Elinor her husband's true identity in private, enjoying his charade even and especially when it is at her expense. Such an interpretation of Charlotte's marriage adds even more comic tension through the irony of her asseveration that " 'Mr. Palmer is just the kind of man I like' " (117).

Like her mother, Charlotte does not depend on man or circumstance for her well-being; she has chosen to be joyous and is authentically so: "It was impossible for any one to be more thoroughly good-natured, or more determined to be happy than Mrs. Palmer" (112). She is sensible enough not to place the responsibility for her contentment on anyone or anything outside of herself.[10] Charlotte is prosperous but not mercenary. Her unconcern toward money or society's perception of her sets her apart from women of either too much sensibility or too much frigid "sense." Elinor, for example, in addition to being highly attuned to others' feelings, worries over her family's social image; she goes to great lengths to make amends for her sister's improper conduct. Charlotte shows cognizance of her husband's behavior, amusedly asking him, " 'Do you know that you are quite rude?' " (112), and goes about her self-reliantly pleasant day. She is happier than susceptible women like Elinor and Marianne or cold fish like Lucy Steele, Fanny Dashwood, and her own sister, Lady Middleton. She delights in the comradeship of others and loves them freely, though without neediness, and enjoys being alive. Upon seeing the Dashwoods, "She took them all most affectionately by the hand, and expressed great delight in seeing them again" (110). Like her mother, Charlotte expresses her loyalty through outrage over Willoughby's bad behavior, which she voices only in Marianne's absence: "she hated him so much that she was resolved never to mention his name again, and she should tell everybody she saw, how good-for-nothing he was" (215). That benevolence is often dressed in comic or ironic garb in the novel does not lessen its sweetness, and both Mrs. Jennings and Charlotte Palmer function as salves to others' pain without themselves being exposed to the sharp edge of others' wickedness.

In *Sense and Sensibility*, Austen presents readers with three subgroups of female characters that divergently illuminate these two titular concepts. Both Elinor and Marianne Dashwood embody a form of sensibility that illustrates their dependence on romantic love for happiness. Lucy Steele and her mentors demonstrate unfeeling pragmatism in their focus on monetary and social elevation. Austen dissuades readers from emulating either of these groups' psychological patterns, though she inspires our admiration for Elinor and empathy for her and Marianne. We do not aspire to the struggles they have endured, whether through martyr-like fortitude or juvenile histrionics. It is in the characters of only Mrs. Jennings and Charlotte Palmer that the reader finds exemplars of the healthiest blend of sense with sensibility. These two feel for others without dysfunctional emotional embroilment. Comfortable with and successful in taking their fulfillment into their own hands, they might be forbearers of the best of the modern women to come. They gain their happiness without stepping on or envying other people and while actively seeking others' good. Mrs. Jennings and Mrs. Palmer demonstrate independence of the whims of circumstance even as they reach out with empathetic benevolence toward others—an attribute essential to self-preservation in an erratic world.

Our heroines, on the other hand, betray their common possession of a shattering co-dependency, which leads Marianne to near-suicide and Elinor to a depth of inner melancholy that we might now term clinical depression.[11] Other Austen heroines, including Jane Bennet, Fanny Price, and Anne Elliot, evince this dangerous tendency as well. The near total self-investment of these creatures of habit in their unlikely hopes and persistent loves accentuates the almost-inevitability of their despair, which is prevented only through their rescue by a compassionate author who chooses to spare them and the reader this outcome by granting their wishes at last.

Austen acknowledges but does not grant women the excuse of gender injustice or other adversities as absolution from seeking emotional as well as physical and marital self-determination. Some of her characters seem more naturally predisposed to succeed in this quest than others—Miss Bates overflows with joy despite her scarcity of personal, material, or social advantages, and Anne Elliot enviously views the buoyancy of poor, sickly Mrs. Smith as "the choicest gift of Heaven" as well as the outgrowth of her "fortitude" and "resignation" (*P* 154). Nonetheless, all women have the choice to make the best or worst of their lives under the conditions they face. Despite her apparent naïveté, sensitive but sagacious Jane Bennet recognizes this, responding to her sister's misanthropic rant, " 'My dear Lizzy, do not give way to such feelings as these. They will ruin your happiness' " (*PP* 135). Her rare moments of bitterness aside, Elizabeth agrees; the narrator affirms that "to fret over unavoidable evils, or augment them by anxiety, was no part of her disposition" (232). Although Elizabeth is somewhat like Elinor with respect to Edward in that she feels sharp regret when she believes her relationship with Darcy can never be, she seems more successful than Jane in rising above disappointment. Like Charlotte Palmer, Mrs. Jennings, and Mrs. Smith, women of all temperaments must be "determined to be happy" (*SS* 112), come what may. Mrs. Smith earns accolades for the fact that "neither sickness nor sorrow seemed to have closed her heart or ruined her spirits" (*P* 153), and Austen encourages Anne Elliot and her readers to emulate this transcendence of life's exigencies. The author does not force her worthy heroines permanently to live out this principle of resilience irrespective of circumstance, doling out marital bliss at the end of their courtship journeys.

Other challenges will inevitably come in the futurity of a realist-grounded narrative, however. One hopes that Austen's heroines have learned to prepare for them with stronger heads and hearts and the courage "to act in that manner, which will, in [their] own opinion, constitute [their] happiness" (*PP* 358). Moreover, even getting what one wants can prove an obstacle to fulfillment, owing to the perversity of human nature. *Persuasion*'s narrator encapsulates this phenomenon in her satirical quip regarding Mrs. Smith's material and social gains:

> Mrs. Smith's enjoyments were not spoiled by this improvement of income, with some improvement of health, and the acquisition of such friends to be often with, for her cheerfulness and mental alacrity did not fail her; and while these prime supplies of good remained, she might have bid defiance even to greater accessions of worldly prosperity. She might have been absolutely rich and perfectly healthy, and yet be happy. (252)

Human beings have such trouble finding contentment, and especially women often face so many obstacles to it, that it makes special sense for Austen to use marginalized female characters as models of mental health. The comic Mrs. Jennings and Charlotte Palmer have separated their inner lives from dependence on particular individuals or conditions while maintaining their humanitarian spirit. These women's unique balance of sense and sensibility serves them and Austen's readers well; as the only characters to remain happy of their own accord throughout the novel, they impart persuasive and edifying guidance.

CHAPTER 4

"Ingenious or Stupid?"

Women's Intelligences, according to
"the most unlearned and uninformed female
who ever dared to be an authoress"

" 'I have frequently detected myself . . . in a total misapprehension of character in some point or other: fancying people so much more gay or grave, or ingenious or stupid than they really are, and I can hardly tell why, or in what the deception originated' " (*SS* 93), reflects Elinor Dashwood. As demonstrated in the previous chapter, Austen implies that women can choose to be "gay or grave" and should emulate the former spirit; through the examples of Mrs. Jennings and Charlotte Palmer, she exhorts women to take control of their emotional lives with compassionate but transcendent optimism. Is it similarly possible to control one's intellectual endowments—the extent to which one is "ingenious or stupid"? The narrator of *Northanger Abbey* quips that to most men, "imbecility in females is a great enhancement of their personal charms" (111), but Austen seldom portrays imbecilic females in her fiction. Through such narratorial tongue-in-cheek, she satirizes men's expectation of mental inferiority in women and pleasure in indoctrinating them.

The author's downplaying of her own mind, as in her self-designation as "the most unlearned, & uninformed Female who ever dared to be an Authoress" (11 December 1815), likewise manifests her playful mockery of patriarchal condescension by exaggerating the trope of feminine modesty that both masks and parades her complacent genius.[1] Jane Austen proliferated in talents. In addition to being a great writer, she was the "great reader" that Elizabeth Bennet denied being, an informed theatergoer, and an effective dramatic reader, all of which assisted her novel writing.[2] She was likely "a fine amateur pianist" as well, like Marianne Dashwood or Anne Elliot, judging from her music collection of "nearly 1,500 pages" (Wood 367). Austen's niece Caroline suggests that her aunt's daily habit of morning practice, away from the family, was for her own enjoyment (Wells, "In music" 103). The novelist also demonstrated a gift for both utilitarian and decorative needlework, as corroborated by her preserved presents to loved ones.[3] Committed pursuit of such diverse activities stimulates facility in all of them and in realizing their common object: an evocative thought life that invigorates one's companionship with self and others. In addition, everyone has a tacit obligation to be a proficient conversationalist, each apt expression a stitch reinforcing the social fabric. Austen understands that wit is dialogic; we must live with each other, so we might as well do so to our reciprocal enjoyment. She gilded others' pleasures through exercise of every ability, as she continues to gild our pleasures through a legacy of communications—novels, juvenilia, letters—that engaged her self.

The range of male and female character types in Austen's canon communicates the author's rejection of any gender-specific assumptions regarding intelligence; she evidences no interest in exercising the literary equivalent of gender phrenology. Even confident Henry Tilney, a devoted brother to an equally intellectually gifted sister, deigns to acknowledge that " '[i]n every power, of which taste is the foundation, excellence is pretty fairly divided between the sexes' " (NA 28).[4] At least as many male as female idiots blunder across Austen's pages, with less excuse for their "imbecility."

The descriptor "intelligent" is more often applied to women than to men—characters as diverse as Aunt Gardiner, Charlotte Lucas, and Mrs. Reynolds merit the appellation. Darcy early earns some credit for discovering that Elizabeth Bennet's "face . . . was rendered uncommonly intelligent by the beautiful expression of her dark eyes" (*PP* 23)—he feels attracted, not by her facial features as such, but by the vital intellect they project. Anne Elliot admires Mrs. Croft for "looking as intelligent and keen as any of the officers around her" while the Crofts hobnob with the Admiral's naval buddies (*P* 168). Women pronounced "clever" in narratorial exposition include Emma Woodhouse, Marianne Dashwood, Lucy Steele, and Mrs. Clay. In addition, others consider the Bertram sisters, Bennet sisters, and Lady Catherine to be clever, and numerous female characters consider themselves so. The Bingley sisters manifest sharp minds—"Their powers of conversation were considerable" (*PP* 54)—and Mary Crawford sparkles with sassy wit. And of course, Elinor Dashwood "possesse[s] a strength of understanding, and coolness of judgment" (*SS* 6) far beyond her nineteen years. This conglomeration of examples conveys a sense of the intrigue and charisma of intelligent women in Austen's eyes and makes a large part of her fiction's appeal for modern-day readers. Whether devious or virtuous, these women are always interesting. As a popular magazine headline of today might reductively put it, "Smart has never been so sexy!"

Austen never absolves women of responsibility for their own self-making. The social and financial limitations imposed on her female characters result in the channeling of their intellectual energy into the few available modes of expression, and some of them allow this to distort their potential. Manipulative flatterer Lucy Steele seems "naturally clever . . . but her powers had received no aid from education, she was ignorant and illiterate . . . Elinor saw, and pitied her for, the neglect of abilities which education might have rendered so respectable" (*SS* 127). All Lucy has to offer is the temporary resource of her middling physical attractiveness—or what Wollstonecraft derides in *A Vindication of the Rights of Woman* as "barren blooming" (23)—and her feigned social charm. Austen also recognizes the role of genetics in determining one's gifts, as in such absolutist statements as the narratorial declaration that "Elinor was neither musical, nor affecting to be so" (*SS* 250) or that Anne Elliot possesses "no voice" (*P* 47) for singing, though a talented pianist. The author examines women's given mental capacities and how they direct their potentiality. As Elizabeth Bennet admits to Lady Catherine, " 'such of us as wished to learn, never wanted the means. We were always encouraged to read, and had all the masters that were necessary. Those who chose to be idle, certainly might' " (*PP* 165). Though offered far fewer opportunities than men of their class, most of Austen's female characters possess ample resources to further their enlightenment, and all of them possess the ability to develop "all the excellencies of . . . character" (*NA* 243) that matter most. The author bestows on both major and minor characters distinctive combinations of aptitudes and ineptitudes that assume women's equal capacity to men for intellectual and creative achievement, even as they suggest more particularized implications for the role of women's minds in their self-concepts, employments, relationships, and worth.

The premises underlying Austen's portrayals of her heroines' talents reflect a futuristic understanding of brain function—the novelist presupposes the intersectivity of thought processes, the breadth of creditable abilities, and the ambiguously coinherent roles of nature and nurture in the development of specific gifts. As Antonina Harbus summarizes, Austen views "the human subject as product both of innate qualities and of education and experience, which in turn determine the mental life" (776).

Today, although the subject of brain cognition is still characterized by much debate and mystery, there has been a general movement away from narrow standardized definitions of IQ and from the concept of right- and left-brain lateralization, toward a view of the brain as an interactive network of cross-hemispheric interconnections that produce a diversity of mental competencies that should be described rather than evaluated.[5] Austen is prophetic in recognizing such qualities as physical and social grace, self-knowledge, and appreciation of nature as modes of intelligence, and in refusing to typecast her heroines as either creative or rationalist.[6] Thus, for example, her visual artists are both skilled in logical argumentation and socially outgoing; her most talented musicians are also sensitive to the expressive language of love, poetry, and letters; and her most jolly, hospitable characters are her least existential but sometimes most intuitive.

Austen's sketches of her heroines' talent profiles reveal more about their characters than about the relative merit of their individual proficiencies. The significance of women's physical activity in Austen's vision has already been considered, and their spirituality and relationship to nature will be examined separately as well. This chapter will explicate the novelist's illustration of how women's intellects and their expression in such media as music and visual art can and should function in the performer's relationship to her self, her medium, and her audience. When she applies her gifts with purity of intent and disciplined intuition, she enriches herself and society in beautiful ways. Her "accomplishment" becomes the performance of herself.

"Independent Resources": Mind and Self

Women's intelligence should benefit them; engaging in activities that rely on and enhance that intelligence enriches their own consciousness. Even modest Anne Elliot recognizes and appreciates her intellectual ascendancy over the Musgrove sisters: "saved as we all are by some comfortable feeling of superiority from wishing for the possibility of exchange, she would not have given up her own more elegant and cultivated mind for all their enjoyments" (*P* 41). Anne's approbation of Henrietta and Louisa's loving sororal relationship forms the context of this reflection— not a competitive comparison—but it nonetheless underscores the irreplaceable value of a "cultivated mind" to its possessor, especially to a heroine as isolated and underappreciated as Anne. "[W]hen she played" the piano, she assumed "she was giving pleasure only to herself" (47), but recognizes that her mental superiority to the Musgrove sisters enables her to enjoy a deep interior life of which they are incapable.[7]

Despite her self-deluding determination that "[w]armth and tenderness of heart . . . will beat all the clearness of head in the world, for attraction" (*E* 269), Emma Woodhouse, likewise, would never exchange her smart self for a sweet but softheaded Harriet Smith. Emma delights in her imaginative brain and the freedom to direct it to manifold ends. As she explains when assuring Harriet that her life as a single woman would be just as full as a wife's, "mine is an active, busy mind, with a great many independent resources. . . . If I draw less, I shall read more; if I give up music, I shall take to carpet-work" (85). Emma's longest speech in the novel consists of an energetic commentary on her portfolio of portraits—spoken as if to herself rather than to Harriet or the sycophantic Mr. Elton—in which she details her subjects' relative cooperativeness and difficulty of depiction and evaluates her degree of success, making self-congratulatory remarks on several likenesses. Her zest for drawing stems from its versatility, which invites experimentation. As the narrator catalogues, "Miniatures, half-lengths, whole-lengths, pencil, crayon, and water-colours had been all tried in turn. She had always wanted to do everything. . . . There was merit in every drawing—in the least finished, perhaps the most; her style was spirited . . ." (44–45). Home-bound in the dull community of Highbury as the companion to an obsessively anxious father, an oft-cited factor in her zealous matchmaking, Emma has done "everything" within the exploratory world of her portraiture, reveling in the inventive acts of a porous mind that leaves every image incomplete, an open-ended possibility. This open-endedness of Emma's portraits mimics her author's suggestive literary style.[8]

Whereas a woman should invest in and thrive on her talents, her inability to enjoy them lessens their beauty and may indicate either excessive or insufficient emotional engagement with the medium and a corresponding psychological imbalance. On one extreme, Marianne Dashwood unleashes her emotions through the piano, sometimes at the expense of her art. After Willoughby's betrayal, she commandeers the keyboard and her vocal chords exclusively as an outlet for her "indulgence of feeling. . . . She spent whole hours at the pianoforté alternately singing and crying; her voice often totally suspended by her tears" (*SS* 83). She degenerates from a talented musician "who sang very well" (35) when she applied her mind to her craft, to a hysteric who parodies her own achievement. Marianne's abuse of piano and voice as a venting mechanism parallels her behavior toward other people as mere instruments for her purgative display of egocentric moods and opinions. The logical counterpoint in this symbology—though comparably extreme—is her eventual determination to rediscipline her musical passion as part of a program of intensive study; she asserts "with firmness . . . that she should in future practise much" (342) and spend each day "divid[ing] every moment between music and reading" (343).[9] Marianne's successive, opposed attitudes toward the appropriate use of her talents neutralize each other. Although she never institutes her program of austerity, her resolution to pursue it foreshadows her psychological healing. Marianne's revelation of her need for wisdom, that " 'I shall gain . . . a great deal of instruction which I now feel myself to want' " (343), facilitates the restorative equanimity that makes possible the higher mindfulness she has learned to covet.

Anne Elliot suffers even more acute grief over the longer-standing loss of her beloved, but in a reverse trajectory, sometimes strives to conceal it with the distracting façade of the piano rather than infusing her technical skill with authentic feeling to produce music that resonates with her. The depth of Anne's depression is signaled by the loss of her private pleasure in performing, such that "her fingers were mechanically at work, proceeding for half an hour together, equally without error, and without consciousness" (P 72). Though also a considerate use of her talent, her robotic accompaniment of others' dancing in this scene shows a utilitarian self-displacement that violates the nature of the medium and the woman's right to full creative consciousness.[10] Anne hides behind rather than speaking through the piano, unnaturally disconnected from her gift when "her eyes would sometimes fill with tears as she sat at the instrument . . . glad to be employed, and desir[ing] nothing in return but to be unobserved" (71).

Both the suppression and the expulsion of emotions through the instrument represent unhealthy misappropriations of musical ability and its medium of expression, but so, too, does emotional detachment. This sterile approach undermines the performance for both musician and audience. For example, the mediocre piano playing of Elizabeth and Mary Bennet reflects their lack of personal investment in their performances, Elizabeth because of underapplication and Mary because of overinvestment in the cerebral skills of execution excised from affect. Though Elizabeth's performance pleases her audience more than "pedantic" (PP 25) Mary's, their second-rate playing emblematizes the same weakness of character—the evasion of their true feelings toward key relationships and events in their lives.[11]

Outstanding musicians Jane Fairfax and Georgiana Darcy seem to succeed in balancing "taste" and "execution" (*E* 232), or self-expression and technique, respectively, to produce powerful music that feeds their minds and solaces their secretly aching hearts while entertaining others. Both of these private characters infuse their passion into masterful method to produce virtuoso performances, though they repress themselves in social life, thereby neglecting other gratifying intellectual competences such as interpersonal and communication skills. However, both young women also reveal glimpses of their yearning to rectify this neglect that presage their future growth. By contrast, Lady Middleton and Mrs. Elton desert the prospect of personal growth altogether, as signaled by their renunciation of their beloved music once married. Lady Middleton had "played extremely well" (*SS* 35), and Mrs. Elton alludes to her playing and her crayons as if to imply a facility in fine arts that we never witness and a sacrificial merit in foregoing these endeavors that the text undercuts as arbitrary and absurd. Both characters use marriage as an excuse to forsake the laborious challenges of self-cultivation in favor of illusory roles: Lady Middleton plays elegant cipher, and Mrs. Elton plays self-appointed village manager in the teeth-grating style of Aunt Norris.

For Austen, women's deliberate or subconscious underuse or misuse of their minds constitutes a form of self-abandonment. Women should explore a range of modes of thought and activity to enhance their mental thriving throughout their lives, "hav[ing] pleasure in many things" (*PP* 37). They will attain the greatest skill and satisfaction in their best-suited media by moderating the extent of both their psychic involvement and their disciplined method to produce a musical performance, picture, social exchange, or other creation that nurtures as it reflects the workings of the mind.[12]

Self-objectification in the employment of one's talents betrays not only the self but any art form that is exploited as an "art" for questionable ends. As Juliette Wells states, "that displaying . . . might eclipse playing" deeply concerned "conduct-book writers in Austen's era" ("Harpist" 108). In *Mansfield Park* and *Persuasion*, the harp lends itself to exhibitionist activities that violate the purity of intention that should characterize a cultivated mind. Mary Crawford's harp "added to her beauty, wit, and good humour; for she played . . . with an expression and taste which were peculiarly becoming, and there was something clever to be said at the close of every air. . . . A young woman, pretty, lively, with a harp as elegant as herself; and both placed near a window . . . was enough to catch any man's heart" (*MP* 64–65). Mary and her harp become interchangeable objects in this passage, "both placed near a window" looking out on a lush view, and the woman's mind—as manifest by her "wit" and "clever" remarks, which appear as afterthoughts to her "beauty"—is one incidental attraction among several in a relativistic inventory of details that relegate her to the role of artifact in an already framed picturesque.[13] Mary's choreographed allure and polish suggest she has performed her charmer persona numerous times before, perhaps even repeating some of the same one-liners between numbers, like a touring player. At the Great House in *Persuasion*, the more ingenuous Henrietta and Louisa Musgrove also lack a true artist's disinterestedness: "the present daughters of the house were gradually giving [the parlour] the proper air of confusion by a grand piano forte and a harp, [and] flower-stands and little tables placed in every direction" as if repeating history, playing the role of generic "daughters of the house" in a domestic theater filled with the obligatory accoutrements of feminine activity (*P* 40). Despite their sisterly geniality, the Musgrove girls' goal of "living to be fashionable, happy, and merry" reflects the redundancy of their shallow, "happy, and merry" minds (40).

In the context of Austen's collective references to flirty harpists, the narrator's pronouncement that Anne Elliot "played [the piano] a great deal better than either of the Miss Musgroves; but ha[d] no voice, no knowledge of the harp, and no fond parents to sit by and fancy themselves delighted" (*P* 46–47) is Austenian code for Anne's superiority of character as well as musical prowess. Her pursuit of piano rather than harp underscores her sincerity, and her disinterestedness aids her attainment of a true expertise unadorned by superficial staging or dependence on others' inflated approval. Mrs. Musgrove's preference for the harp over the piano, conversely, points toward her intellectual limitations. Like Anne, the genuine Elinor Dashwood is disassociated from the harp: she freely gazes where she chooses at a musical party, "unrestrained even by the presence of a harp" (*SS* 250), not merely because she is unmusical but because she shuns the trappings of romanticized female spectacle. Austen endorses the pursuit of excellence for its own sake and for personal fulfillment, but lampoons the exploitation of an ability for strategic self-display as Mary Crawford, Caroline Bingley, the Bertram sisters, Mary Bennet, and even the merry Musgrove girls do. Juliette Wells notes that Elizabeth plays when asked, whereas Caroline seizes opportunities to perform ("Fearsome"), though this may have as much to do with Elizabeth's awareness of her inferior skills as with her greater modesty. A woman's mind, like her body, is not to function as a tool of seduction or familial vanity; enlightenment and its offspring are their own rewards.

"Patroness of a Village": Female Intelligence as Community-Builder

Austen expects her heroines to share their intellectual wealth in ways that honor rather than objectify them, portraying their enhancement of others' and their own lives as mutual purposes. Communal women employ their mental resources to beautify other people's existence, whether they deserve it or not, and are ennobled by their beneficence. The innumerable methods of contributing to society's flourishing are demonstrated by both negative and positive exemplars. Characters' abuse of their brain power to others' detriment is easily identified. Marianne's self-obsessive piano playing, symptomatic of her "usual inattention to the forms of general civility" (*SS* 144), harms others as well as herself, as when she rudely rejects Lady Middleton's invitation to play cards in favor of isolation at the piano: "wrapt up in her own music and her own thoughts, [she] had . . . forgotten that any body was in the room besides herself" (145). Kathryn Libin even claims that "music unseats her reason, becoming a kind of narcotic" (140). The pre-reformed Emma debases her drawing skill when she exaggerates Harriet's attractiveness in the effort to manufacture a romance between her friend and Mr. Elton, and debases her wit when she insults Miss Bates.[14] Lucy Steele invests all her cleverness in parasitism. The only meretricious efforts are those that emanate from the sincere desire to benefit others rather than exclusively to gratify oneself. Austen's exemplary women draw on their visual, musical, and other abilities in ways that suggest a catalytic energy between selfless intent and the spark of their unique mode of genius. Elinor Dashwood, Eleanor Tilney, Emma Woodhouse (despite a few lapses), and Anne Elliot are liberal in their efforts to contribute to the common good.

These heroines function as natural leaders, household organizers, and social artists who endeavor to benefit others by sharing their vision. Three of the four are motherless, and Elinor is psychologically motherless (Mrs. Dashwood occupies a more filial than maternal role toward her), a factor that may explain these women's assumption of somewhat matriarchal roles. Their involvement with art or music reinforces their knowledge of math and logic as well, which enables them to help manage family resources, servants, schedules, and social life—all areas in which such elements as scale, proportion, pattern, and perspective are important. Elinor keeps the reduced Dashwood budget in line; Anne attempts to further the Elliots' retrenchment and compensates for their cold obtuseness and irresponsibility; and Emma and Eleanor oversee extensive households for demanding fathers. Inured to mostly indoor living and attuned to the visual or auditory effects in homes for which they feel responsible, these women possess a sensitized awareness of the spaces they occupy and their needs, flaws, and beauties, and a corresponding cognizance of these characteristics in their loved ones that invite their attentive assistance. In the process, they turn outward a circumstantially imposed domestic inwardness.

Austen identifies only a few characters as talented visual artists in her canon, implying that drawing is a specialized skill that perhaps relies more on inherent giftedness than does musicality. Judging from the cast-off projects they have dumped on Fanny for convenient storage, the Bertram sisters lack artistic ability. More ambiguous examples of visually oriented female characters include Mrs. Dashwood, who may demonstrate visual competence in her eager visions of a hypothetical redesign of Barton Cottage, but we never witness a successful renovation or tangible evidence of her spatial savvy and can only surmise that she possesses an educated gentlewoman's appreciation of art and music that she passes down in separate parcels to her daughters. By a reach, Lucy Steele may be somewhat artistic—she succeeds in assembling a basket for spoiled Annamaria Middleton, with artist Elinor's help. More promising is the example of *Persuasion*'s charitable Mrs. Smith, who, though poor herself, learns to craft decorative sewing items to sell to rich women as a fundraising project for the poorer.[15] The Bertram sisters' and Lucy's false generosity with their inartistic creations shows their throw-away attitude toward their minds and relationships. In addition, visual art displaces the gazer from the performer's body to her product in a way that may frustrate vainglorious desires. As with music, laziness or ulterior motives obstruct creativity and its power to unify.

Elinor Dashwood's attractive artwork decorates both her home and that of her half-brother and his particular wife, reflecting the communal spirit of her aesthetic. She chose to direct her artistic ability toward creating something beautiful for an ugly person when she "painted a very pretty pair of screens for her sister-in-law" (*SS* 234), a gesture characteristic of her effort to connect with the obnoxious Fanny Dashwood and of her modeling of unconditional giving to one's family circle, whether through material goods, social grace, or sound advice. Elinor evokes in her selfish sister-in-law a redemptive glimmer of ability to recognize and imitate beauty, when Fanny blushes at her mother's cold dismissal of the screens and markedly compliments their prettiness; in so doing, Fanny affirms Elinor's feelings as well as artistic merit and herself becomes appealing for one, brief moment in the novel (before immediately undermining this gesture).

Elinor's painting-giving also metaphorically reflects her pedagogy as an educator—she presents others with verbal sketches of what is and what could be, often in pairs, to exhort them to positive thought or action, while herself presenting a picture of social altruism. Elinor converses well with diverse personalities, serves as a buffer between people in tension, compensates for others' rudeness or offense and, of course, serves as the moral instructor of particularly Marianne, who affirms her influence in this role: "I compare [my conduct] with what it ought to have been; I compare it with yours" (345); "Your example was before me" (346). Thus, Elinor's artistry reflects the moral equilibrium for which she strives, within and without. In her own suffering and in that of others, she turns "to her drawing-table . . . [and]

busily employ[s] herself" (104) with conjuring images of realities and probabilities intended to encourage the good in and for others. As Jeffrey Nigro puts it, her "talent for capturing likeness on paper is matched by an acute perceptiveness in discerning the motives and personalities of others" ("Visualizing"). Only when she attempts to envision Edward to herself as Lucy's husband does her portraiture fail, from the force of her emotions and ambiguity of intention ("she knew not what she saw, nor what she wished to see;—happy or unhappy . . . she turned away her head from every sketch of him" [SS 357–358]). With this exception, emanating from the vulnerability to romantic emotionalism previously analyzed, Elinor as discerning artist conveys the same self-assurance in her figurative drawings as in her literal ones, showing people "what she saw" and "what she wished to see" to draw them closer to each other and to their better selves.[16]

For example, in serving as the comforter of both Marianne and Colonel Brandon, Elinor functions as the relational fulcrum between the two that maintains an ongoing connection between them throughout the novel. She paints verbal portraits of each to the other that shed positive light on their personalities, increasing their knowledge of each other and contributing to their ultimate alliance. Elinor first describes her sister to the Colonel as a romantic, then anticipates her "better acquaintance with the world . . . as her greatest possible advantage" (56); Colonel Brandon admires the familiar Eliza-like ebullience of the initial portrait, but learns to cherish Marianne in her deepened character of post-Willoughby experience as well, a state that enables her to appreciate his genteel sincerity in kind. Elinor likewise showcases the Colonel's good qualities to Marianne in an early sketch in response to her and Willoughby's caricature of him: " 'You decide on his imperfections so much in the mass,' replied Elinor, 'and so much on the strength of your own imagination, that the commendation *I* am able to give of him is comparatively cold and insipid. I can only pronounce him to be a sensible man, well-bred, well-informed, of gentle address, and I believe possessing an amiable heart'" (51). Elinor's tragic portrait of Colonel Brandon in retelling his woeful tale and Willoughby's role therein better impresses Marianne, as demonstrated by her "no longer avoiding Colonel Brandon . . . even voluntarily speaking [to him], with a kind of compassionate respect" (212); she reveals "an increase of good-will towards himself . . . [which] gave Elinor hopes of its being farther augmented hereafter" (216).[17] Elinor teaches both her sister and her chosen brother-in-law to seek hope and to value each other's experience, which deflects the Colonel from patronage of "a young mind" (56) and Marianne from bias against "age and infirmity" (37), clearing the way for their mutuality of friendship and marital fulfillment.

Elinor even seizes the chance to reform Willoughby when he appears at Cleveland in hopes of redeeming his image in her and Marianne's minds. Though Elinor easily cuts through "'what may comparatively be called, [his] justification'" and reminds him of her power to choose what portrait of his current self "'is necessary'" to depict to her sister (330), she acknowledges her improved opinion of him and "was even interested in his happiness—and added some gentle counsel as to the behaviour most likely to promote it" (332). She affirms in his self-portrait the reformative potential in his admission of wrongdoing, and shows him a sketch of his possible future self as a principled person. Like Fanny Dashwood, he rejects the opportunity to become the positive picture she has painted, but the beauty of Elinor's instructive art remains and benefits those who are receptive to it, such as not only Marianne and the Colonel but her mother and future husband.[18]

Northanger Abbey's Eleanor Tilney also exemplifies an intelligent artist who applies her ability to educating others. We learn little of her craft, except that she and her brother Henry share a practiced vision, "viewing the country with the eyes of persons accustomed to drawing, and decid[ing] on its capability of being formed into pictures, with all the eagerness of real taste" (*NA* 110). Eleanor assumes the role of sisterly mentor to Catherine Morland, teaching her "to love a hyacinth" (174) as well as a new understanding of the picturesque, and introducing her to a correspondingly enlarged vision of life. Eleanor encourages her protégée to love history, for example, delivering a lecture on the merits of the discipline in which she counters her pupil's assumption that fiction preponderates in it. She expresses her relative confidence in historians and appreciation of their narratives' creative dimension, asserting that she is

> 'very well contented to take the false with the true. In the principal facts they have sources of intelligence in former histories and records, which may be as much depended on, I conclude, as any thing that does not actually pass under one's own observation; and as for the little embellishments . . . I like them as such. If a speech be well drawn up, I read it with pleasure, by whomsoever it may be made—and probably with much greater, if the production of Mr. Hume or Mr. Robertson, than if the genuine words of Caractacus, Agricola, or Alfred the Great.' (109)

This commentary anticipates Catherine's primary lesson in the novel. Eleanor is able to enjoy historical accounts as artifacts whose "principal facts" she trusts and whose imaginative flourishes she appreciates "as such" from the perspective of a sophisticated reader who can discern the fundamentally false or true. Catherine's core intellectual weakness is her inability to make these distinctions with accuracy and consistency, as when she applies her Gothic novel reading to her reading of the General;

she superimposes farfetched plots over scanty details and goes beyond "embellishment" in viewing these interpretations as facts, whereas she naïvely accepts at face value the insincere General's embellished speeches.

Eleanor celebrates the inventive power of well-wrought language, like the hyacinth's ornate beauty; its design merits as much appreciation as strict questions of fact, but not within a vacuum of ignorance in which such questions are elided through misuse of the imagination. She encourages Catherine to embrace history as creative nonfiction, a more responsible genre than history as Gothic fictionalizing.[19] In so doing, Eleanor invites Catherine, not to lose her inventiveness, but, to direct it like a trained artist with an informed vision who embellishes only details that colorfully highlight rather than overstate the truth, as in the framing of a picturesque but essentially unadulterated landscape. Catherine's transgressive blurring of the line between fact and fiction is metaphorically foreshadowed in her childhood education, in which "[h]er greatest deficiency was in the pencil" (16) due to her inability to distinguish images, as shown in her "drawing houses and trees, hens and chickens, all very much like one another" (14). The adult heroine begins her bildungsroman with this lack of critical judgment, which Eleanor's lecture on perspective primes her to learn. Catherine's embarrassment at Henry's discovery of her morbid speculations at Northanger and his follow-up lecture on probabilities clinches the lesson, but her impulse to conceal her imaginings prior to their exposure reveals at least a partial awareness of overstepping the boundaries of plausibility as well as propriety.

In addition, Catherine's greater skepticism of history than Eleanor and her dialogues with both sister and brother about Gothic novels suggest her recognition of the genre's sensationalism. Catherine's character is more complex than it appears, and her Gothic reading of the General as murderer shows discernment of his misogynistic nature. However, she discovers that one cannot rewrite the fundamental facts of history; serious consequences to relationships occur when one's passion for creative flights goes beyond aesthetic elaborations to distortions of reality at others' expense. What Eleanor the artist teaches Catherine is the value of comprehending the view from which one draws. Through a mature friendship built on trust and esteem, she awakens her student to the appeal of fields of knowledge barely tapped by her—to literal and figurative alternate perspectives. Eleanor helps Catherine to reframe her perspective, as if providing "viewers" to aid her perceptual clarification and imaginative self-discipline.[20] That Eleanor and Elinor share the same names, though differently spelled, reinforces their similarity as artist-logicians who enlighten their pupils by striving to transform their vision.

Whereas Elinor Dashwood offers pictorial moral instruction through pairs of verbal portraits illustrating her students' current and prospective virtues, and Eleanor Tilney promotes a "big picture" framework for envisioning landscapes of reality, Emma Woodhouse strives to preserve her precarious familial community by idealizing people in her life and art, accentuating their best traits and minimizing their worst. She sometimes exploits this skill, as when she pictorially glamorizes Harriet for her own amusement; flirts with perceived beau Frank Churchill while anticipating rejecting him; and takes advantage of Miss Bates's good nature to vent her spleen on "an old friend" (*E* 371). However, Emma warrants some recognition for her continual selfless strivings to employ her cleverness to maintain unity among her divergently difficult loved ones. Elinor Dashwood offers no analysis of her artistry, suggesting that it functions as an organic outgrowth of her character that she refines through intuitive application. Emma, on the other hand, like Eleanor Tilney, is a self-conscious artist. Just as Emma has studied her craft with an interest in the relationships among her creative process, motives, subjects' behavior during sittings, and resulting portraits, she has carefully studied the characters of her familial "subjects" to determine how to emphasize their best features in social intercourse.

Despite Emma's preference for pleasing herself, she claims to have a convincing record as an accommodating artist. She has tried to gratify doting mother Isabella by drawing her multiple children, despite the challenges involved. She also produces what the narrator confirms to be "a pretty sketch" and what she considers her "last and . . . best" likeness—a deliberately complimentary image of John Knightley intended to please both her sister and her brother-in-law (45). She makes it "too handsome—too flattering—but that was a fault on the right side" (46), demonstrating her generous spirit toward a relative whose temperamental character and treatment of Isabella she disapproves.

Emma's versatility as a conversationalist mirrors her versatility as an artist. She blends contrasting palettes of personalities—those of her father and sister, and those of the two Knightley men—as the person best able to dip her brush into both: "their subjects totally distinct, or very rarely mixing—and Emma only occasionally joining in one or the other" (100). Emma's artistic enhancement of John Knightley translates into her efforts to preserve and improve his temper in family interactions, particularly in the midst of Mr. Woodhouse's perpetual medical officiousness. She not only distracts her father as much as possible from delivering monologues of unsolicited health advice, but also engages her brother-in-law in conversation topics to his taste, as when her father has just started in with the provoking claim that John is " 'very far from looking well' " (103):

> 'I did not thoroughly understand what you were telling your brother,' cried Emma, 'about your friend Mr. Graham's intending to have a bailiff from Scotland,

to look after his new estate. But will it answer? Will not the old prejudice be too strong?' And she talked in this way so long and successfully that, when forced to give her attention again to her father and sister, she had nothing worse to hear than Isabella's kind inquiry after Jane Fairfax;—and Jane Fairfax, though no great favourite with her in general, she was at that moment very happy to assist in praising. . . . This topic was discussed very happily, and others succeeded of similar moment, and passed away with similar harmony; but the evening did not close without a little return of agitation. (104)

Isabella then joins Mr. Woodhouse in a bowl of gruel, which encourages his relapse into implied criticism of her husband and unwelcome advice that he "unconsciously" credits to his physician, Mr. Perry (107). This entire scene showcases Emma's constant vigilance and solicitous maneuvering in the family circle and her greater discernment than her sister regarding the dynamic between John and their father and how to diffuse rather than exacerbate the problem.

Emma shows remarkable patience toward her nervous father, a taxing figure in both her portraiture and her daily life, striving to ease his anxieties and draw out his admirable qualities, such as his compassionate concern for the Bateses. She must be ever-ready to shift conversations to alleviate his many fears and brighten his outlook. She is prepared to postpone or forego marriage to devote herself to him throughout his lifetime. Emma is also gracious to the exasperating Mrs. Elton, though she despises the vulgar gadfly, a challenging task for even Mr. Knightley. Moreover, when atoning for her hurtful behavior, Emma knows exactly what to say, with sincerity, to please Miss Bates, Jane Fairfax, and Mr. Knightley. She knows where the standards of gentility and uprightness lie and ultimately strives to correct her deviations from them. In both her pre-reform complacence and her post-error humility, Emma manifests an artist's self-critical eye; repentance motivates her to come closer to her own picture of perfection. Her training in art sharpens her gift of social savvy. Emma's ability to critique herself and her portraiture and parallel efforts to redraw any rough edges in the social dynamics around her—whether fissures created by herself or by others—present a redemptive picture of this dynamic heroine's intellectual generosity. Although she "paints to exercise and display her own artistic talent and social power" (Losano 188), Emma also deserves credit for her big-heartedness, which predominates in the novel as a whole and wins out over her possessive preeminence or reactive pettiness, and for the "social dexterity" (Libin 141) she invests in others.

Artists Elinor and Eleanor encourage others to embody the moral ideals they advance through pictorializations, and artist and adequate pianist Emma deftly redirects conversations in a kind of auditory portraiture that somewhat succeeds in cohering her family circle and heartening her father. More talented pianist Anne Elliot fosters community by lending others her highly trained ear, not so much to redirect their social exchanges to draw out their better selves as to encourage their greater empathetic attunement to each other. Anne serves as the confidante and counselor of many; as the auditor of diverse voices, she strives to bring their atonal keys into heartfelt, lasting harmony. Despite occasionally drowning out her pain in her playing instead of submerging herself in its expressive pleasures, as previously noted, Anne nonetheless shows daring in unconditionally sharing her intellectual endowments. She "play[s] country dances . . . by the hour together" (*P* 47) for the Musgrove circle, though this furthers her rivals' opportunities to dance with the man she loves. When properly performed, the role of musical accompanist aptly illustrates Anne's social strengths. She carefully observes the intricate workings of the relationships around her from her place at the keyboard, and is thereby able to assess the whole piece and its component parts.

Anne hears multiple variations on a theme, including three characters' cause-effect theories of the Musgrove boys' behavior, two perspectives regarding Mary's right of precedence, and two opinions on who has the best servants between Upper Cross Cottage and the Great House:

> . . . being treated with too much confidence by all parties, and being too much in the secret of the complaints of each house. . . . How was Anne to set all these matters to rights? She could do little more than listen patiently, soften every grievance, and excuse each to the other; give them all hints of the forbearance necessary between such near neighbours, and make those hints broadest which were meant for her sister's benefit. (44, 46)

Anne subtly directs the social choir around her by identifying the false notes from the true and striving to soften disparate voices into a more melodious whole. She invests particular energy in lightening sour-note Mary, cheering her out of ill-humor, but she also cautions Elizabeth about Mrs. Clay, brings comfort to Mrs. Smith and Captain Benwick, gently enlightens Captain Wentworth and Lady Russell, and is a companionable presence to everyone because she knows how to play to their characters and contexts. She strives to open individuals' ears to each other's voices.

Moreover, Anne's skills as a seasoned musician enable her to strategize quickly in the crisis on the Cobb and help to save Louisa's life. Just as she can adjust her speed and volume and coordinate both hands and feet (keys and pedals) to play for spontaneous dances without depending on sheet music, she masterfully multitasks on the Cobb, delegating roles and "attending with all the strength and zeal, and thought, which instinct supplied" (111) to everyone involved, according to his or her need. She also proves herself "extremely useful" at the Great House, "both as an immediate companion, and as assisting in all those arrangements for the future" (121) that Louisa's parents are too traumatized to handle on their own. Until this incident, Anne's behind-the-scenes social efficacy receives little credit; afterward, Wentworth reveals his acute recognition of her intellectual superiority to the merely "amiable" Louisa-type (182) and his constancy as a man who " 'does not recover from such a devotion of the heart to such a woman!—He ought not—he does not' " (183). As suggested in chapter 2, Wentworth's reform is best signaled by his affirmation of Anne's stellar mind before he knows whether or not he will personally benefit from her superior nature as her spouse: " 'no one . . . so capable as Anne!' " (114).

"The Compliment of Attention": The Woman's Audience and the Woman as Audience

Austen conveys particular expectations regarding not only a woman's proper use of her intelligences, but also other people's responsibility to value her mind and its excellencies. Both male and female characters are frequently judged by their reactions to women's talents. Colonel Brandon's respectful attentiveness to Marianne's performing reflects well on his character, as contrasted with the false praise and distractedness of the others, comically captured by Lady Middleton's requesting "Marianne to sing a particular song which Marianne had just finished" (*SS* 35). Similarly, Edward's desirability as Elinor's life partner is early reflected in his implied enthusiasm for her artistic ability; as she coyly avers to her sister, "'He does not draw himself, indeed, but he has great pleasure in seeing the performances of other people, and I assure you he is by no means deficient in natural taste'" (19). Individuals' admiration or dismissal of the screens Elinor had painted for Fanny neatly delineates their degree of social sensitivity and moral worth. Thus, selfish John Dashwood pseudo-praises Elinor for manipulative ends as "in general reckoned to draw extremely well"; generous-hearted Colonel Brandon "warmly admired the screens, as he would have done any thing painted by Miss Dashwood"; and Mrs. Ferrars cruelly rejects them, disregarding Elinor's painting ability in favor of the asserted skill of acquaintance Miss Morton, who impossibly "'does every thing well'" (234–235).

In *Pride and Prejudice*, Charles Bingley's indiscriminate assumption of all women's being "so very accomplished" (39) manifests his respect for them, which may have been partially inspired by his observations of his smart sisters' zealous practice of their skills throughout their youth. Lady Catherine's arrogant rudeness shows in her loud talking over Elizabeth's playing and open criticism of her guest's performance, whereas Darcy, who "spoke with affectionate praise of his sister's proficiency" (173), displays his redeemability and dawning love for Elizabeth in the surprising compliment, "'No one admitted to the privilege of hearing you, can think any thing wanting'" (176). By this point, Elizabeth and Darcy have reached mutual agreement that the development of strong character supersedes "ornamental and snobbishly superficial accomplishments" (L. Brown 332). *Northanger Abbey*'s Henry Tilney clearly enjoys the company and conversation of his intelligent sister Eleanor, who seems to be his best friend. *Mansfield Park*'s Edmund likewise finds fulfillment in shared reading and philosophical discussion with Fanny. Emma and Mr. Knightley engage in multiple intense debates and, though she sometimes exploits it, he admires her shining intellect (*E* 64). In the aftermath of Emma's flirtation with Frank Churchill, Mr. Knightley goes off to visit John and Isabella "to learn to be indifferent" (432), but Isabella intensifies his love for her brighter sister: "Isabella was too much like Emma—differing only in those striking inferiorities, which always brought the other in brilliancy before him" (433). The smart, argumentative woman is resplendent, whereas the sweet, submissive one is merely "amiable"—Austen's code word for a respectable but commonplace person, an everywoman.[21]

Women's loyalty or disloyalty to other women in response to their achievements is particularly revelatory of their comparative integrity, a pattern Austen explores from personal experience of the crucial importance of the close female family members and friends who helped to sustain her literary endeavors (Kaplan, *Jane* 91).[22] Fanny Price's pleasure in Mary Crawford's harp playing, Emma's acknowledgment of Jane Fairfax's superior musicianship and Harriet's virtues, Elizabeth's declaration that Charlotte possesses "an excellent understanding" (*PP* 178), and Jane Bennet's protectiveness of Mary's study time all accentuate these heroines' largesse.[23] Marianne's eager defense of Elinor's artistic genius during the conversation about the painted screens shows that, despite her self-preoccupation, her heart is in the right place. Isabella's unjust criticism of Emma's extra-flattering portrait of her husband as "not do[ing] him justice" understandably offends Emma, who refuses to complete it, " 'to have it apologized over as an unfavourable likeness, to every morning visitor in Brunswick-square' " (*E* 46). In addition to showing Isabella's over-doting on her husband at the expense of her judgment, this example suggests that she feels threatened by her younger sister's greater cleverness. Considering the sociable nature of portrait-making as "a form of community entertainment" (Losano 187) in Austen's day, one can picture Isabella peering over Emma's shoulder, both fascinated by and tempted to find fault with her sister's skill. By contrast, Eleanor Tilney defends the less astute Catherine's intellectual capacity to her brother Henry when he teases them both for misinterpreting each other in conversation, insisting he assure Catherine that he " 'think[s] very highly of the understanding of women' " (*NA* 113). She then declares that despite his flippant sense of humor, " 'he must be entirely misunderstood, if he can ever appear to say an unjust thing of any woman at all, or an unkind one of me' " (114).[24] Eleanor emphasizes Catherine's right to a respectful audience, regardless of her degree of intelligence.

Women's generosity and aesthetic objectivity in celebrating each other's achievements is remarkable in a social system that sets them up for a Darwinian competition for mates. The aggressive self-promotion of such characters as Caroline Bingley, Lucy Steele, Isabella Thorpe, Mary Crawford, and Mary Bennet is more understandable in that context, though unjustified, and highlights the better women's honest appreciation of each other's gifts as the laudable outcome of committed investment in a stressful social environment.[25] Austen's culture's ambitious expectations for genteel female "accomplishments" à la Caroline Bingley and the intellectual acuity they require would seem to suggest its agreement with the author's egalitarian stance on the sexes' comparative intelligence. Yet, her society hypocritically claims to expect greatness from women while limiting the means through which they can achieve it. At the same time, the concept of female "accomplishments" was also becoming a subject of controversy in Austen's era, because some felt this form of training failed to prepare women for their domestic, social, and spiritual lives (Kelly 258), or incited them to rebel against their expected functions (Wells, "In music" 101, 99).[26]

"So Very Accomplished": Purity of Selfhood

Conversely, judging from her life and work, Austen accentuates the enormous possible benefit to self and others of women's intellect and its harvests. She critiques society's and individuals' mistaken motives, not female accomplishment in itself. What is Jane Austen's ultimate vision of the "accomplished woman"? On the one hand, her heroines of integrity reject marriage-market motives as the basis of self-cultivation, and she undercuts the assumption that women's worth depends on extrinsically measurable qualities. Elizabeth Bennet boldly defies nearly all the standards for female excellence cited by Caroline Bingley, and the radically ordinary Catherine Morland, "though she could not write sonnets . . . brought herself to read them; and though there seemed no chance of her throwing a whole party into raptures by a prelude on the pianoforte, of her own composition, she could listen to other people's performance with very little fatigue" (*NA* 16).[27] Austen satirizes stereotyped expectations of women, whether as virtuosas or idiots, as well as women's conformist garnering of "the usual stock of accomplishments . . . like thousands of other young ladies" (*P* 40). The author does not disdain the "very amiable, sweet-tempered" Louisas and Henriettas in the world, who are "not deficient in understanding" (182). Indeed, she critiques each character of both genders according to her or his role in building or fragmenting community, and offered her beloved niece Fanny Knight the epistolary advice that "Wisdom is better than Wit" in a husband (18–20 November 1814). Virtue and benevolence always seem to trump cleverness in Austen's hierarchy of values.

On the other hand, for Austen, well-employed cleverness *is* virtue. She and her readers expect "something more" (*P* 182) than feminine righteousness of her heroines to be able to admire and identify with them in that imaginative collusion that makes her fiction so compelling. The saucy wit of Elizabeth Bennet and Emma Woodhouse, even when based on delusions, defines their permanent appeal, and they both learn how best to utilize their sharp minds.[28] Austen's intellectually gifted women of all personality types provide the reader with endless cerebral stimulus; this chapter provides only an initial adumbration of some foundational patterns in her depiction of them. Namely, as we have seen, Austen illustrates the essential interconnectivity of multiple factors to intelligent women's realization of their potential: some innate aptitude as well as application; both emotional and rational investment in their skills; personal pleasure and communal beneficence in using them; and the reciprocal receipt of and payment to other women of "the compliment of attention" (*SS* 35). Without extolling the merit of one talent over another, Austen implies fascinating affinities among particular brain powers, as in her visual artists' pedagogical portraiture and her musicians' social orchestrations. Not surprisingly, the most likeable heroines generally possess the most intelligences, whereas the least likeable characters evince the fewest intelligences and suppress or misuse them. Thus, Lucy Steele's grotesquely ungrammatical speech parallels her grotesquely mediocre character. Austen affirms the value and fulfillment of the disciplined pursuit of excellence—whether in art, music, reading, physical activity, interpersonal communication, or a combination thereof—when free of toxic motivations. Beyond providing private pleasure, impeccable piano playing, painting, or clever conversation produces value only if and when it strengthens communal bonds. What Austen expects of intelligent women (and the not-so-smart ones, for that matter) is that they continuously assess, improve, and share their abilities, as part of their character development, for both self-actualization and the greater good.

Thus, the realization of peak selfhood—of the highest possible development of one's talents, in whatever form they consist and as expressed through available outlets—is a woman's preeminent accomplishment. Her mind can radiate such dramatic influence that when neglected or misguided, it can devastate individuals and divide families, but when well honed and directed, it can save lives and better an entire community. It is in society's interests to do its best to support women's intellectual advancement, thereby reinforcing their positive moral and pragmatic force. Whether society supports them or not, however, women must strive to become their truest and best selves. Every intelligent woman will function as "the patroness of a village" (*SS* 379).

CHAPTER 5

"Born to Be Connected"

*Female Monasticism and Vocation
in Austen's Novels*

Within the social "village" that intelligent patronesses fortify in the fiction of Jane Austen, the ascendancy of female relationships is everywhere apparent. As we have seen, sororal and matriarchal mentors enhance the lives of Austen's fictional women, who also serve as one another's companions, entertainers, audiences, emotional supports, and empathetic fellow strivers after selfhood in an often artificially constraining social sphere. This supportive sisterhood facilitates its members' self-knowledge and growth into their potential. In order to find and create coherence, each heroine must courageously discern and follow her vocation—the personal calling through which she can most ably serve God and humankind—aided by the sorority that helps her to pinpoint or refine her calling.

In depicting such a spiritual sisterhood, Austen draws on the traditions and ideals of medieval women's religious communities in striking ways, and anticipates monasticism's restoration in England with the Oxford Movement in the mid–nineteenth century. Education, hospitality, counsel, charity, and prayer have long been hallmarks of monastic service to society. Those who entered monasteries consecrated themselves to service to God through living out their religious faith in community, in accordance to Christian beliefs and traditions and the rules of their particular order. Striving for sacrificial lives of virtue in imitation of Christ, they commonly vowed adherence to the values of poverty, chastity, and obedience, and pursued some combination of the active and contemplative lives, or service work and prayer, respectively. Austen's heroines likewise embrace these ideals of poverty (through various forms of self-denial), chastity, and obedience to the duties of a reflective religious faith in action and need other women's assistance to realize them. Female characters' cultivation of the virtues, or Fruits of the Spirit, produces fruit in the lives of others within their sphere of influence in a manner closely associated with the female conventual tradition.

Roger E. Moore, author of *Jane Austen and the Reformation: Remembering the Sacred Landscape*, persuasively argues that Austen participated in "a tradition of nostalgia for the monasteries" (6) that were dissolved under Henry VIII's rule, a tradition "she encountered in eighteenth-century poetry and travelogues as well as contemporary reprints of seventeenth-century antiquarian writings" and that sheds light on "the many references to medieval abbeys, chapels, and hospitals that appear in her work" (9). Moore offers a fascinating explication of such works as the *History of England, Northanger Abbey, Mansfield Park*, and *Sanditon* within this canon of "literature of nostalgia" (23) and its contextual geography of historical monastic sites, figures, and cultural narratives that he identifies as shapers and reflectors of Austen's ideological stance. The young Austen overtly critiques Henry VIII's reign and the Dissolution in her satirical *History of England*. In addition, Moore emphasizes that Catherine Morland and Fanny Price experience an unmonastic inhospitality at Northanger Abbey and Mansfield Park, respectively, that is symptomatic of the post-Reformation suppression of the medieval monastic socio-spiritual infrastructure. Both heroines lament the loss of this religious, moral, and aesthetic foundation of English life.[1] Catherine intuitively disapproves of the way a convent that had "fed . . . many guests, as well as the community at large" as part of its dedication "to the well-being of the entire parish" (Moore 88) has become the habitation of a tyrannical patriarch and insatiable epicure who serves "only his delicate palate" (89). General Tilney forsakes the communal nurturing function of the monastic space he occupies, inculcating into his progeny only a principle of personal and familial aggrandizement.

Austen's worthy characters of both genders must oppose the negative example of parents, guardians, or peers and seek alternative role models in order to eschew corruption and seek noble ends. The author's *bildungsromane* feature courtship plots and imply familial rather than monastic futures for their heroines, but similar to nuns, these women face daily conflicts between temporal and transcendent moral values. As Laura Mooneyham White asserts, though "Austen was rarely explicit about her religious values" (*Jane* 4) because she considered fiction an inappropriate mode for extensive religious discourse, "[t]he world of her novels is a Christian one in which worldliness competes against traditional orthodoxy and moral precepts. Living in the real world, Austen shows, is the best test of one's Christian values, and the novels rest on this foundation of Christian purpose" (66). In addition, body is not excised from spirit or marriage from religiosity in Austen's sacramental Anglican worldview, and characters' marriages can also be read as religious allegories. For example, Michael Giffin suggests that the union of Fanny Price and Edmund Bertram embodies "the mystical marriage between Christ and [H]is church," with Fanny as the Christ figure and Edmund as the church (129)—a gender reversal of the biblical analogies.[2] However, the spiritual gifts of the women exist independently of men as if a spontaneous outgrowth of the essence of their identities. They must awaken to and embrace these gifts before marriage to continue their vocations throughout their lifetimes through authentic and mutually fulfilling alliances and, by extension, healthy family relationships. The circumstantial opportunities of daily living evoke Fanny Price's instructorship, Emma Woodhouse's hospitality, and Anne Elliot's healing powers, for example, qualities that flow naturally from them as if inspired by divine promptings.

By contrast, when Austen's heroines attempt forcibly to pursue roles for which they possess no vocation or to abuse their known powers—as in Emma's failed effort to play teacher to Harriet Smith or Elizabeth Bennet's assumption of the omniscient judge role—moral and social distortions occur. When heroines follow their purest and often simplest instincts, however, their actions produce reciprocal good for the biological or platonic "sisters" who most often call their vocations into action. Anne's sister Mary demands and Louisa Musgrove depends upon Anne's restorative influence. In a more compelling example, as will be shown, it is not Mr. Knightley but Miss Bates and Harriet who cause Emma to abandon her false path and ascertain her true one. Primarily through explication of the divergent examples of contemplative Fanny Price and active Emma Woodhouse, this chapter will illustrate how Austen's heroines discover their true vocations through the cultivation and honoring of a spiritual sisterhood. Fanny's abbess-like capacity is reflected through the monastic architecture of the spaces she occupies and activated by the inculcation she receives and gives, whereas Emma's already asserted social initiative requires the infusion of a wiser woman's spiritual acuity to be purified into the efficacy of an all-embracing monastic welcome.

The Abbess: Austen's Female Spiritual Directors

As considered in the previous chapter, women such as Elinor Dashwood and Eleanor Tilney invest their intelligence in teaching a sister and future sister-in-law, respectively. This educator function often involves a critical religious role—that of a kind of abbess (leader of a female monastic order) or spiritual director. The portrayal of female reliance upon spiritual mentors repeatedly emerges in Austen's novels. Sarah Emsley observes, "When an Austen heroine recognizes where she has erred, she . . . often confesses her error to another person" (9). That person is usually another woman. For example, Marianne makes a confession to Elinor in several scenes of self-flagellating regret and recommits her loyalty to her all-female nuclear family. Elinor, "though too honest to flatter," affirms her penitent spirit and resolutions of reform, extending her "that praise and support which her frankness and her contrition so well deserved" (*SS* 347). Even the glibly self-assured Elizabeth Bennet habitually seeks out the moral guidance of her older sister, Jane.

When Elizabeth recounts her hostile rejection of Mr. Darcy and mistaken view of his and Wickham's characters, she communicates regret but not contrition. Jane discerns this. She undercuts Elizabeth's flippant tone, pressing her to repent and admit wrongdoing, alluding to Elizabeth's early bias against Mr. Darcy and his likely suffering from her behavior: " 'It is really too distressing. I am sure you must feel it so. . . . Lizzy, when you first read that letter, I am sure you could not treat the matter as you do now. . . . How unfortunate that you should have used such very strong expressions in speaking of Wickham to Mr. Darcy, for now they *do* appear wholly undeserved' " (*PP* 225–226). Jane makes a surprisingly pointed critique of her sister's actions in this dialogue, reiterating that she did not share Elizabeth's negative first impression of Darcy and breaking through the prideful wit's self-protective jocularity, drawing her into empathetic identification with his pain. Rather than being offended, Elizabeth converts her casually delivered story into the confession it should be and experiences a resultant sense of disburdenment: "The tumult of

Elizabeth's mind was allayed by this conversation. She had got rid of two of the secrets which had weighed on her for a fortnight, and was certain of a willing listener in Jane, whenever she might wish to talk again of either" (227). Jane serves not only as a caring confidante, but also as a more spiritually mature and ever-available mentor who challenges Elizabeth with her greater disinterestedness and purity of mind. She insists on Elizabeth's serious admission of faults she prefers to package in jest, drawing her from emotional detachment into the state of penitence that enables her to progress.[3]

Just as Elizabeth Bennet humbles herself to the less witty but wiser Jane, Emma Woodhouse must admit her repeated misperceptions to the intellectually inferior Harriet Smith, who, although not a spiritual mentor in a full sense, assists her reform as the remarkably forgiving victim of her ill-judged romantic interference. Emma must profess her errors to Harriet (" 'you make me more ashamed of myself than I can bear' " [338], she briefly admits and later feels) and learn from Harriet's virtues, earlier recognition of Mr. Martin's and Mr. Knightley's good characters and husband potential, and forbearance toward Emma despite the pain she has caused. Emma must also relinquish her desire for control over another woman's method of fulfilling her vocation (of marriage, in Harriet's case) (408). The penitential scenes of Elizabeth Bennet and Emma Woodhouse reverse the power dynamic between women who pride themselves in their perceived superiority of discernment and the companions they have patronized as naïve. Intelligence and moral wisdom are distinct qualities, as Austen's witty women discover. They conjoin in her principal female spiritual mentors, however, whom men as well as women seek out for counsel (as in the examples of penitents Edmund Bertram, Edward Ferrars, and Captain Wentworth discussed in chapter 2). Sagacious guides Fanny Price, Elinor Dashwood, and Anne Elliot are generally at the periphery of their social circle's center stage, from which vantage point they observe and reflect upon the web of motives, actions, and reactions that unfold before them. They envision how things should be and provide direction to others intended to promote that vision.

Contemplative Spiritual Advisor: Fanny Price's Novitiate and Conventual Order

Mansfield Park and *Emma* are two of at least four novels in which Austen includes abbey references. *Mansfield Park* explores the topic of "Ordination" (29 January 1813), but depicts introspective heroine Fanny Price's vocational journey to "ordination" in much greater depth than that of her cousin, Edmund Bertram.[4] Austen's "best exempl[ar of] the contemplative life" (Emsley 25) leaves behind her nuclear family at Portsmouth and the bustling outside world to train for the future role of supervisory educator and spiritual counselor through her "novitiate" at Mansfield Park. There, she confronts physical, psychological, and ethical difficulties that encourage her practice of self-denial and reliance upon faith to persevere through myriad sufferings. Scholars tend to view the problematical Fanny Price as a reactive victim of an abusive childhood and frustrated young adulthood, an empowered naysayer who tenaciously resists coercion, a paragon of virtue, or a prudish irritant. While there is some truth in all of these characterizations, the successive metaphors of novice (a person training for monastic life who has not yet taken a vow) and abbess best describe her form of leadership. She most fully actualizes the abbess role when her sister Susan necessitates it. Fanny's combined education at Mansfield and during the extended return visit to Portsmouth gradually awakens her to a more active method of living out her deepening spiritual enlightenment.

As a novice at Mansfield, Fanny learns the Rule of poverty, chastity, and obedience through a critical series of character tests. Not only do Fanny's aunts Norris and Bertram represent opposite extremes of hyperactivity and sloth that encourage her pursuit of a median of healthy physical activity, as chapter 1 explains, they also function as parodies of the active and contemplative dimensions of religious life, in a serio-comic critique of a Georgian church in need of reform. Austen was thoroughly familiar with the Anglican church of her day and would have been aware of its "problems of absenteeism, pluralism, non-residence, worldliness, and nepotism" while optimistic "that the Church will reform itself, given time" (White, *Jane* 23, 24). Sir Thomas opposes such corruptions and anticipates his son's contrasting dedication as one who " 'knows that human nature needs more lessons than a weekly sermon can convey, and that if he does not live among his parishioners and prove himself by constant attention their well-wisher and friend, he does very little either for their good or his own' " (*MP* 248). Edmund also gives several earnest speeches in debates with Mary Crawford regarding a clergyman's responsibilities and critical spiritual and social influence. In the vocational dichotomy of Fanny's aunts, manically meddling caricature-abbess Aunt Norris seeks to lead only to feed her own purse and ego, her soulless worldliness rendering impotent her "charitable" activity, whereas Aunt Bertram's combined mental vacuity and physical stasis render her quietude an empty alternative to true contemplation.

No one questions Aunt Norris's authority over the other women at Mansfield, especially over Fanny, whom it is assumed on her widowhood she will relocate to her own home and supervise as a substitute mother figure or mother superior in a female order of sorts. Edmund defers to his aunt even when he disputes her treatment of Fanny, and encourages his horrified cousin to move into the White House as a matter of course:

"My aunt is acting like a sensible woman in wishing for you. She is choosing a friend and companion exactly where she ought, and I am glad her love of money does not interfere. You will be what you ought to be to her. I hope it does not distress you very much, Fanny. . . . And I am quite convinced that your being with Mrs. Norris, will be as good for your mind, as riding has been for your health—and as much for your ultimate happiness, too." (26–28)

Edmund wishfully envisions his aunt as improving Fanny's mind, and she her aunt's temperament, in a mutually fulfilling female community that is set apart from but integrated within the Mansfield family circle. Reality contradicts the noble motives and plans he imputes to his aunt: she deliberately moves into the smallest eligible house and creates bogus excuses to avoid supporting her niece in any way. Aunt Norris's calculated disloyalty sets up a contrast for Fanny's generous mentorship of her younger sister Susan in a clear counterexample of devotion to spiritual sisterhood.

Despite Aunt Norris's bad intentions, however, her instruction of her niece at Mansfield helps to prepare Fanny for eventual headship of her own "order." Her training includes the daily discipline of physical and emotional deprivation through obedience to demanding family members, in addition to a rigorous course of morally enlightening reading and Socratic dialogue with Edmund. Having come from the overpopulated, underfinanced Price household, Fanny has already faced scarcity, but then encounters it superfluously in a wealthy household. She is assigned to a cell-like "little white attic" (150) for a bedroom and embraces a lifestyle of privation under the watchful tutelage of "Abbess" Norris, who ensures her denial of a fire in the "East room" (151) she inherits as her study and book repository.[5] The east has significant Christian resonances, as the location in which the star announcing Christ's birth appeared and the region of the world in which He lived and died, as well as the direction of the daily sunrise connoting the resurrection; church altars traditionally face eastward. Fanny's living spaces at Mansfield are reminiscent of medieval nunneries, in which architectural research suggests that the dormitories were generally secluded and the communal gathering space, leader's chair, and lodging for visiting women and possibly novices tended to have an eastern orientation in the monastery.[6] Fanny resembles a lodger, a novice, and eventually the spiritual head of a household who hosts conferences in her eastern living space. In keeping with the monastic "renunciation of private property" (Gilchrist 19), Fanny recognizes possessions as community property at both Mansfield and Portsmouth. The East room displays her cousins' cast-offs mingled with the miscellaneous gifts she has received from them, like a mendicant's museum, and the items include a transparency of Tintern Abbey. The aptly named East room represents Fanny's intellectual and spiritual character and purpose in the Mansfield family, not her own space as such.[7] It is accessible to both the men and the women "lay people" of her circle, as medieval nunneries "were founded in order to interact closely with the local community" (Gilchrist 191).

As part of her asceticism, in addition to material self-denial, Fanny experiences regular mortification in the form of insults, scolding, and ordering about by Aunt Norris and exploitation and neglect by everyone. With quiet grace and self-restraint, she obeys her aunt's strictures and functions as a glorified servant to the family, even into adulthood. When her feckless cousin Tom declares, " 'we want your services,' " the narrator emphasizes that "Fanny was up in a moment, expecting some errand; for the habit of employing her in that way was not yet overcome, in spite of all that Edmund could do" (*MP* 145). Edmund misinterprets Fanny here. Tom and others, indeed, selfishly use her. However, Fanny is on a spiritual quest in which her dedicated service to others, including the undeserving, represents the essential apostolic dimension of her twofold active and contemplative monastic roles as well as her obedience to authority. She divides her time between labors for the community and observance of prayerful contemplation in the East room, performing only tasks that her conscience approves, as demonstrated by her refusal to perform in *Lovers' Vows*. She is not a slave to the Bertrams but a novice scrupulously pursuing her spiritual discipline. Although Fanny refuses to act in the morally questionable theatricals, she aids the participants by performing menial tasks, serving as resident counselor and coaching players like the hopeless Mr. Rushworth: she "was at great pains to teach him how to learn, giving him all the helps and directions in her power" (166).[8] She finds "great pleasure in feeling her usefulness" (390) in diverse contexts. In assisting others with sewing and theatrical practice (albeit of a worldly play), Fanny imitates medieval nuns, whose labors sometimes included handiwork such as sewing and weaving as well as the more cerebral copying and illumination of manuscripts, the composition and performance of religious dramas, reading and study, and the education of children (Rushworth counts as a child), in addition to regular prayer and charitable activities.

Fanny avoids experiencing too much gratification from her rare opportunities for personal enjoyment by enduring Aunt Norris's ruthless guilting cant, which parallels her own resistance of unalloyed pleasure in earthly diversions. More than an abusive hater to Fanny, Mrs. Norris sometimes becomes the mouthpiece of her heightened conscience, its monstrousness personifying her increasing guilt over her negative feelings, such as toward the Crawfords and Edmund's relationship with Mary. When Edmund initially surrenders his place to enable Fanny's expedition to the Rushworth estate, she appreciates but feels "pain" at his sacrifice and reflects that "her own satisfaction in seeing Sotherton would be nothing without him" (79). Yet he then pains her by going. On the carriage ride home after a day of touring and socializing overshadowed by Edmund and Mary's flirtation and others' bad behavior, it is as if Fanny's superego delivers a biting chastisement through Aunt Norris to counteract her bitter feelings: " 'Well, Fanny, this has been a fine day for you, upon my word! . . . Nothing but pleasure from beginning to end! I am sure you ought to be very much obliged to your aunt Bertram and me, for contriving to let you go. A pretty good day's amusement you have had!' " (105). Reminders of the primacy of selfless service over personal pleasure thus bookend Fanny's uncommon share in an outing. Aunt Norris often vocalizes her niece's perfectionist demands of herself as she struggles to achieve an altruistic spirit.

Fanny dislikes and is vigilant toward the hidden ugliness in herself that Aunt Norris both embodies and warns against. When "[s]he was full of jealousy and agitation" (159) at Edmund and Mary's intimacy during their flirty rehearsing, "reflection brought better feelings" (160) of humility, obedience to Sir Thomas's likely wishes, and empathy for the jilted Julia. Similarly, after reading Edmund's letter to her at Portsmouth, in which he reports Sir Thomas's postponement of her return to Mansfield and obsesses over Mary, Fanny is "within half a minute of starting the idea, that Sir Thomas was quite unkind" and "almost vexed into displeasure, and anger, against Edmund," narratorial qualifiers undercut by her inward diatribe against him for stupidly misreading Mary's corrupt character (and against Mary for her corruption) (424). Although Fanny's inward discourse showcases her anger, she soon drags herself back to righteousness: "Such sensations, however, were too near a kin to resentment to be long guiding Fanny's soliloquies" (424–425). Fanny *is* resentful but, after privately venting, strives not to be. The combination of continual self-repression with the obstruction of her desire by nearly everyone produces emotional and ethical quandaries that intensify the habitual self-scrutiny that fosters Fanny's insight into herself and others.

The mental and spiritual exercises Fanny practices at Mansfield develop her natural facility for the traditional monastic role of providing counsel to the community. During the actors' rehearsals, "being always a very courteous listener, and often the only listener at hand, [she] came in for the complaints and distresses of most of them" (164). Others take for granted Fanny's availability for empathy and support. Both Edmund and Mary seek her out, traveling to the East room as if on pilgrimage in quest of moral guidance from a wise nun or anchorite.[9] Fanny's pilgrims find her in a space apart from the worldly majority, where she performs "her works of charity and ingenuity" (151). She upgrades the former schoolroom of the family's girls, where Maria and Julia received no education in character, to a retreat wherein to host needy visitors who should benefit from her discerning guidance. Edmund first solicits her approval to capitulate to his and others' desire that he act opposite Mary in *Lovers' Vows*: " 'Give me your approbation. . . . I am not comfortable without it. . . . If you are against me, I ought to distrust myself—and yet—But . . .' " (155). Edmund views Fanny as his standard for moral conduct, almost as his conscience, though he rationalizes contradicting both.[10]

Edmund and Mary individually solicit Fanny's aid in rehearsing—subconsciously seeking justification (or, more redemptively, correction) for what they know to be an indecent script for a disrespectful scheme. When Mary visits, Fanny conveys a hospitable spirit, "endeavour[ing] to show herself mistress of the room by her civilities, and look[ing] at the bright bars of her empty grate with concern" (168). Mary bluntly calls Fanny's attention to multiple speeches in her part that she recognizes as objectionable, asking, " 'How am I ever to look him in the face and say such things? Could you do it?' " (168), confiding her concern as if she possesses moral standards and invites feedback on them from a trusted source. She quickly answers her own question, however, rationalizing Fanny's anticipated response and rushing onward to do as she pleases. In forestalling the input of a female mentor of superior character and perception, Mary subverts a critical opportunity for growth; she rejects her potential better self. Mary's later remark to Fanny encapsulates her longing for genuine female community, which she misdirects toward manipulative marital schemes: "'Who says we shall not be sisters? I know we shall. I feel that we are born to be connected'" (359). In another era, Mary, whose combined name and personality evoke the figure of Mary Magdalene, might have applied her energetic intelligence to the greater good as patroness or abbess of a nunnery.

Fanny begins her vocational training with a tough crowd—people who may recognize her wisdom and good example but resist gaining spiritual benefit from them—but then applies her gifts more fruitfully in the new "order" she establishes on being sent back to Portsmouth. Like the medieval women who entered convents in part as a socially sanctioned alternative to an unwelcome marriage, Fanny sometimes retreats to her conventual space to evade the unwelcome attentions of the man she dislikes, Henry Crawford.[11] He continues to pursue her at Portsmouth, but she maintains her vocational and sororal devotion. Fanny quickly bonds with her sister Susan, a kind of younger double, whom she prepares for a future of benevolent service by being a far more effectual mentor than Aunt Norris was for her. Portsmouth tests both sisters with its material, intellectual, and spiritual impoverishment. They confront the daily horrors of filth, noise, and chaos bred by ignorant, neglectful parents whose limited means exacerbate their character flaws. Fanny quickly discerns both the domestic conditions and Susan's temperamental strengths and weaknesses in endeavoring to address them. Circumstances "placed Susan before her sister as an object of mingled compassion and respect" (396), the phrasing, "placed . . . before her" suggesting a divine prompting, as if the movement of the Holy Spirit. Although Fanny recognizes the errors of her sister's ways,

> she began to hope they might be rectified. Susan, she found, looked up to her and wished for her good opinion; and new as any thing like an office of authority was to Fanny, new as it was to imagine herself capable of guiding or informing any one, she did resolve to give occasional hints to Susan, and endeavour to exercise for her advantage the juster notions of what was due to every body, and what would be wisest for herself, which her own more favoured education had fixed in her. (396)

As a wiser, more educated and experienced role model, Fanny assumes "an office of authority" that involves "guiding and informing" Susan regarding the combination of active and contemplative life, work with reflection, that best benefits Susan and her familial microvillage.

The gesture the narrator identifies as the catalyst for Fanny's authority with her pupil epitomizes this blend of reflection with action: "Her influence . . . originated in an act of kindness by Susan" (396) in which she purchases a silver knife for their younger sibling, Betsey, so that Betsey relinquishes Susan's similar memento of a deceased sister. The practical gesture "thoroughly answered" in winning Susan's confidence as well as restoring domestic peace (397). The silver knife is both useful and decorative, like Fanny herself, who exemplifies a mode of intervention that delicately cuts through to address concrete problems while preserving a decorous equanimity. Unlike any of the women Fanny serves at Mansfield, Susan both seeks and follows her guidance, beginning by confessionally "acknowledg[ing] her fears, blam[ing] herself for having contended so warmly" for her possession (397). Fanny and Susan Price share a painful history of being unloved by the women who have exploited their authority over them. By contrast, Fanny's humble, sensitive mode of spiritually intuited instructorship helps to preserve the mutuality of her and Susan's relationship: "The intimacy thus begun between them was a material advantage to each. By sitting together up stairs, they avoided a great deal of the disturbance of the house; Fanny had peace, and Susan learnt to think it no misfortune to be quietly employed" (398).

Thus, Fanny quickly establishes a new East room at Portsmouth, an alternative upstairs space for her female "order" that serves but is set apart from the rest of the community represented by the Price household, where Susan's tuition similarly begins "without a fire" (398). Having spent some of her funds purchasing the peace knife, Foundress Fanny then invests in a circulating library membership that enables her to school Susan in the balancing of an active life of service with the intellectually grounded contemplative life that should direct it. The upstairs represents contemplation and the downstairs, action, in this typology.[12] The sisters "came to spend the chief of the morning up stairs" in reading and discussion of the books Fanny chose for Susan's "improvement" (398) and in conversation about Mansfield's people and ways, as if the elder sister prepares the younger for the next stage of her vocational training in her postulancy there. The pleasures of cultivated thought and conversation open a world of culture to Susan that showcases the catalytic interplay and interdependency of knowledge, virtue, premeditated action, and social harmony, and the purity of the personal fulfillment that arises therefrom. She experiences the cultivation of self for others that monasticism has historically nurtured in society and that produces a level of self-actualization for women that the wasteland of either sheer domesticity or genteel female accomplishments—Mrs. Price's world or the Bertram and Crawford women's world, respectively—cannot engender. In a spirit of selfless egalitarianism, Fanny equips her sister with the intellectual and reflective tools for a moral life. The thanks she receives is a reciprocal supportive empathy from another woman, a true sisterhood that she has never previously experienced: "Susan was her only companion and listener on this, as on more common occasions. Susan was always ready to hear and to sympathize" (428).

An optimistic spirit regarding the future of female monasticism is suggested by Susan's transportation to Mansfield and even greater success than Fanny in fulfilling her role there. Fanny graduates to the role of implicit reigning spiritual head of both Thornton Lacey and Mansfield as the sought-after companion and advisor of the improved Sir Thomas's nearly daily existence. Meanwhile, Susan is promoted from Fanny's back-up and assistant to her yet more effective replacement as Lady Bertram's resident aid and the Mansfield household's immediate force for communal good:

> Susan became the stationary niece—delighted to be so!—and equally well adapted for it by a readiness of mind, and an inclination for usefulness, as Fanny had been by sweetness of temper, and strong feelings of gratitude. Susan could never be spared. First as a comfort to Fanny, then as an auxiliary, and last as her substitute, she was established at Mansfield, with every appearance of equal permanency. Her more fearless disposition and happier nerves made every thing easy to her there. . . . [S]he was soon welcome, and useful to all; and after Fanny's removal, succeeded so naturally to her influence over the hourly comfort of her aunt, as gradually to become, perhaps, the most beloved of the

two. In *her* usefulness, in Fanny's excellence . . . and in the general well-doing and success of the other members of the family, all assisting to advance each other, and doing credit to his countenance and aid, Sir Thomas saw repeated, and for ever repeated reason to rejoice in what he had done for them all, and acknowledge the advantages of early hardship and discipline, and the consciousness of being born to struggle and endure. (472–473)

This passage appears in the third-to-last and longest of the three concluding paragraphs of the novel. Another emphatic *her* appears earlier in the same paragraph that refers to the importance of Fanny, whereas the second *her* quoted above refers to the newly indispensable Susan. In fact, Sir Thomas lists Susan first in his mental summation of the redounding good of supporting the two adoptive Price women. Fanny infuses her moral excellence into Susan's bold energy to perpetuate an ongoing sisterhood of social beneficence in which strong female community magnifies into the social unity of "all assisting to advance each other" (473) like never before, not in material "success," but in righteous living.

Sir Thomas over-credits himself for the fruits of a lineage of female sacrificial influence that, ironically, began with the sacrifice (albeit tempered with selfishness) of Fanny's mother in releasing her daughters from her maternal hearth, not unlike a medieval mother relinquishing her child to monastic life. This pattern is further mirrored in Fanny's adoptive mother Lady Bertram's similar liberation of her in the adoption of Susan. The narrator conveys that "struggle and endur[ance]" (473) constitute components of the courageous young women's and, to a lesser extent, their mother figures' intervention to better other women's lives as part of a larger socio-symbolic monastic devotion whose feminocentric focus escapes Sir Thomas. The next "*her*" to supplant Susan will inevitably be Betsey, whose wayward feistiness, redirected through solicitous sisterly mentorship, will continue the pattern of "repeated, and for ever repeated" (473) female preservation of spiritual sisterhood and, consequentially, societal renewal.

Sir Thomas intuits, as symbolized by the Price sisters, the distinct virtues of "usefulness" (Susan) and "excellence" (Fanny)—the active and contemplative lives (473). Once Fanny discovers how to direct her sagacity into self-assertion, she is ready to assume matriarchal moral authority at Mansfield.[13] That Fanny earns a position of leadership at Mansfield through others' recognition of and dependence on her discernment also marks a shift from a hierarchical to a more meritocratic dynamic that opens new opportunities for all family members to contribute their talents to the community (Lenta 172, 181).

Active Banquet Host:
Emma Woodhouse's Growth in Hospitality

The pensive Fanny Price embodies a monastic contemplation that, when she learns to apply it in bolder action to enlighten her sister Susan and transform her family life, produces more concrete results in a genuine female solidarity that leads to individual and social gain. By contrast, the much more affluent and powerful Emma Woodhouse begins her vocational journey with a facility for practical action, but needs to develop the inwardness and scrupulosity to properly direct her energetic interventions.[14] Emma desires Fanny's vocation—to be a sage—but proves a disaster as a mentor to Harriet Smith. Instead, she must become a student and submit to another's instruction in order to learn how to be supplier of the feast. Pre-reform, Emma possesses tremendous potential for good, as manifest in her conversational skill described in chapter 4 and in her material generosity. However, she holds herself above the total self-giving of a true host. Austen celebrates the spiritual and social significance of female hospitality through her depiction of Emma's education in the role of benevolent banquet host.

The multiple medieval allusions in *Emma* highlight the heroine's desire for worldly homage and her amendment in eventually choosing a humbler service role.[15] At first, Emma enjoys the company of Frank Churchill because he seems to lionize her as her "gallant" admirer who claims to be " 'under [her] command' " (368). He proclaims, " 'You order me, whether you speak or not' " (369). However, Frank later crowns Jane Fairfax his queen instead, having his aunt's jewels reset in a headpiece for her. Several scholars suggest that the monarchial Emma chooses Harriet Smith as companion as part of her effort to retain her throne in Highbury society; she prefers an associate who "will defer to [her] and be grateful, paying court to her in her kingdom of Hartfield" (Flavin). Sandie Byrne identifies "a touch of the feudal act of fealty" in Emma's exchange of feasting and social elevation for Harriet Smith's "service [and] companionship," as signaled by the women's handshake and Harriet's humble kiss of Emma's hand (131). Of all of Austen's heroines, Emma is the one we can best picture sporting a crown, but she must relinquish it and accept her call to a more modest part.

Mr. Knightley wishes Emma would be more of a friend to Jane Fairfax, her more accomplished peer and somewhat the emblem of the feminine ideal she has failed to achieve. One of the novel's key convent allusions occurs with reference to Emma's almost-double. Before Jane's engagement becomes public and her marriage imminent, she prepares to pursue "her path of duty" as a governess "[w]ith the fortitude of a devoted noviciate" [*sic*], a career she melodramatically envisions as "retire[ment] from all the pleasures of life, of rational intercourse, equal society, peace and hope, to penance and mortification for ever" (*E* 165). Emma similarly views Jane's transitional visit with the Bateses (a familial sisterhood of sorts) as one "of privation and penance" (217). Although the narrator mocks Jane's extreme character-ization of both her pending job and the novitiate analogy she misappropriates to it, the description better applies to Emma's developmental paradigm and echoes the resigned tone of her inward resolutions later in the novel. The heroine has enjoyed an existence of comfortable self-complacence while falling short in her "path of duty" and example, and must undertake (though not "for ever") the "sacrifice . . . penance and mortification" (165) essential to her spiritual reform and vocational effective-ness. By novel's end, she has not realized her full potential, as hinted at by the fact that she and Mr. Knightley do not yet inhabit Donwell Abbey, the "earthly paradise . . . the entry to which must be earned" (Giffin 150). Considerations of Mr. Woodhouse's comfort aside, host Emma has not yet "done" as "well" as she could, nor shed her self-fixation in order to inhabit the metaphorical abbey, the goodly sisterhood, that she seeks but repulses. She makes progress, however, with the help of her spiritual advisor, Miss Bates.

Women have long fulfilled the ordinary yet significant role of serving food and drink, of nourishing others, inside and outside the monastic setting. Austen inherited a rich cultural trope of woman as both everyday and ritual feeder, sustainer, cupbearer. While Austen likely did not deliberately incorporate serious religious allusions into a genre she considered a legitimate but secular entertainment, the author was immersed in the incar-national theology of a liturgical religious and literary tradition that emerges in her work in evocative ways. Emma finds joy in feeding others, including disadvantaged women in her village, but simultaneously betrays glimpses of an emotional parsimony that begrudges others the full enjoyment of her provisions and company. She gradually develops into a more worthy leader who sublimates her social power into nurturing the community, a progression that is occasionally illustrated through images that convey subtle sacramental resonances.

Austen portrays hospitable women with affectionate approval in the likes of Mrs. Jennings, Mrs. Harville, Mrs. Musgrove and, of course, the Bates women. Mrs. Jennings is the archetypal nurturing matriarch; outraged by the cold injustice of Edward Ferrars's mother and family, she declares, " 'I am sure he should be very welcome to bed and board at my house. . . . It is not fit that he should be living about at his own charge now, at lodgings and taverns' " (*SS* 268). Mrs. Harville hosts and cares for people she has just met, including the injured Louisa Musgrove. Juliet McMaster describes the Harvilles' hospitality at their cramped home as nearly miraculous; the cottage's transformation into a literal hospital becomes "a kind of analogy, scaled down to the Austen world, to the gospel story of the loaves and the fishes that fed the multitude" ("Hospitality"). Even shy Georgiana Darcy recognizes and employs food's function as a social unifier; "the beautiful pyramids of grapes, nectarines, and peaches, soon collected" her guests "round the table" at Pemberley (*PP* 268). Austen's rules for hospitality make clear that it cannot be begrudging and cheap (Fanny and John Dashwood, Elizabeth Elliot) or self-serving (Lady Catherine, Charlotte Lucas, Mrs. Bennet, Mrs. Elton), nor should one deprive others of hospitality (Aunt Norris, General Tilney) or usurp it for oneself (Aunt Norris, the Steele sisters, Lydia Bennet). Emma romanticizes and pretends to the wisdom she lacks, while undervaluing her vocation as a host and feastmaker. Yet she seems to identify with a phenomenon that historians such as Caroline Walker Bynum observe, based on records of medieval saints, "that female spirituality was strongly linked to food practices" (ctd. in Gilchrist 89).

Emma is a feeder by nature, by contrast to a food-phobic father who endeavors to withhold or withdraw tasty dishes from others and to offer only diminished fare out of misplaced concern for their health—a " 'very small' " boiled egg, " 'a *very* little bit' " of apple tart, " '[a] *small* half glass' " of watered-down wine (*E* 24–25). Where Mr. Woodhouse rations or takes away with compassionate tyranny, his daughter gives "in a much more satisfactory style" (25), applying her astuteness to the practical and, sometimes, emotional support of others. The narrator boasts that toward the needy, she

> was very compassionate; and the distresses of the poor were as sure of relief from her personal attention and kindness, her counsel and her patience, as from her purse. She understood their ways . . . had no romantic expectations of extraordinary virtue from those, for whom education had done so little; entered into their troubles with ready sympathy, and always gave her assistance with as much intelligence as good-will. (86)

Emma's pragmatism and largesse toward the underprivileged reveal her gift for an intuitive hospitality through which she can capably meet people where she finds them and give them what they need. These qualities become distorted in the course of the novel by Emma's unfortunate insistence on playing a tutorial role toward Harriet, a narcissistic exercise that twists her reason and taints her generosity into a patronizing condescension toward other women. Yet, as we will see, the conflicted heroine ultimately approaches the realization of her spiritual gift when she wills with a purified heart the simultaneous feeding of others' spirits as well as bodies.

Emma's unexpected role model and catalyst for her spiritual renewal and development of her vocation is Miss Bates, the quintessential purveyor of goodwill. Throughout Emma's life, Miss Bates and her mother have demonstrated the true hospitality of complete self-giving, as epitomized in Miss Bates's simple gesture of offering Emma and Harriet cake:

> Mrs. and Miss Bates occupied the drawing-room floor; and there, in the very moderate sized apartment . . . the visitors were most cordially and even gratefully welcomed; the quiet neat old lady, who with her knitting was seated in the warmest corner, wanting even to give up her place to Miss Woodhouse, and her more active, talking daughter, almost ready to overpower them with care and kindness, thanks for their visit, solicitude for their shoes, anxious inquiries after Mr. Woodhouse's health, cheerful communications about her mother's, and sweet-cake from the beaufet—'Mrs. Cole had just been there . . . and had been so good as to sit an hour with them, and *she* had taken a piece of cake and been so kind as to say she liked it very much; and therefore she hoped Miss Woodhouse and Miss Smith would do them the favour to eat a piece too.' (155–156)

The Bates women's sacrificial gestures of welcome in this scene—their gifts of warmth, comfort, attentiveness, gratitude, sensitivity, nurturance, and generosity—are punctuated and emblematized by the "sweet-cake." This provision, suggesting a feminine Eucharistic offering, signifies and foreshadows Emma's eventual desire to participate in the communion of women, regardless of their class or personality type; though at different times, they all take and eat from the same proffered cake. While the narrator does not specify that Emma and Harriet accept the cake, the text intimates it; their refusal would have resulted in another speech on the subject by a concerned Miss Bates.

Yet Emma's sacrilege in this scene is that all of her polite forms—including her implied acceptance of the cake—are void. She makes the rare call on the Bateses to distract herself and Harriet from her guilt over the Harriet-Mr. Elton matchmaking debacle, and spends the visit hoping to avoid Miss Bates's greatest pleasure in it: the sharing of a letter from Jane Fairfax. At this point in the novel, Emma inwardly disdains Miss Bates, Harriet, Jane Fairfax, and Mrs. Cole as inferior. Miss Bates extends to Emma what she needs: more sweetness and, more importantly, the a priori forgiveness and unconditional love that imitate Christ's redemptive sacrifice. Emma's best but most disregarded spiritual mentor and an approximate Christ figure, Miss Bates offers her the cake, the bread sweetened by sacrifice, without the egotism of self-congratulatory fanfare. Hinting at the miraculous gesture of mysterious grace in which the small becomes great beyond measure, the true host offers the guest everything.

Emma seems to take Miss Bates's lessons to heart and to aspire to her mentor's munificence, telling Mr. Knightley, " 'I hope I am not often deficient in what is due to guests at Hartfield,' " to which her fussy father responds, " 'If any thing, you are too attentive. The muffin last night—if it had been handed round once, I think it would have been enough' " (*E* 170). Mr. Woodhouse's allusion to Emma's "hand[ing] round" of "[t]he muffin" (inclusive singular) obliquely suggests a comparison between her hospitality and the dissemination of the Host, further reinforcing the potential spiritual significance of her vocation as banquet host. Emma's preoccupation with preserving her image as one who provides "what is due to guests," however, reduces the gesture to the performance of a social duty. In a similarly mixed example, Mr. Woodhouse expresses the desire to help the Bateses, but hesitates to send them " 'a loin or a leg' " of pork that " 'is very small and delicate,' " in part from concern as to whether it will be prepared as he thinks proper (172). Emma responds, " 'My dear papa, I sent the whole hind-quarter. I knew you would wish it. There will be the leg to be salted, you know, which is so very nice, and the loin to be dressed directly in any manner they like'" (172). She acts on more generous instincts beneath the guise of serving as her father's proxy, and subtly reminds him of the recipients' liberty to prepare their food as they choose. And yet, as Susan E. Jones persuasively argues, Emma's chosen gift creates inconveniences for the Bateses, with their smaller home and cooking resources, and is ostentatiously lavish: "Mr. Woodhouse was thinking kindly of the economy of scale on which the Bates household operates; Emma, however, sends a more opulent present, one that is larger than the household can accommodate. Emma is thinking of the gift, not the recipients" ("Oysters").[16]

Likewise, when Mrs. Bates and Mrs. Goddard babysit Mr. Woodhouse the night of the Coles' dinner party, Emma's hospitality brings to light both her sincere bigheartedness and its contraction through embedded egoism.

> . . . her last pleasing duty, before she left the house, was to pay her respects to them as they sat together after dinner; and while her father was fondly noticing the beauty of her dress, to make the two ladies all the amends in her power, by helping them to large slices of cake and full glasses of wine, for whatever unwilling self-denial his care of their constitution might have obliged them to practise during the meal.—She had provided a plentiful dinner for them; she wished she could know that they had been allowed to eat it. (213)

Counteracting her father's rationing, Emma serves her guests "large" pieces of cake and "full glasses of wine," an action remi- niscent of Communion that suggests her desire for the completeness of the gift and its receipt. Mr. Woodhouse's fearful clinging to life through denying himself and others its richness serves as a foil for her more life-affirming sharing of bounty.

Nonetheless, in this pre-enlightenment scene, Emma willingly risks her utilitarian female visitors' inevitable disappointment for her own pleasure in being the guest of honor elsewhere. She is still in the house while aware that her father, an early diner, likely deprives their guests of the "plentiful dinner" she had ordered. At the very time that Emma is being attired in finery and having her hair styled to accentuate her social supremacy at the Coles' party, Mrs. Bates and Mrs. Goddard sit at her father's table being reminded of their insignificance through his probable usurpation of whatever portion of their meal he finds most terrifyingly substantial and tasty.[17] In light of Mr. Woodhouse's habitual deprivation of his guests, Emma's presentation of cake and wine at the dinner's end partially functions as a compensatory attempt to save face. She has an inborn affinity for hosting, but does not yet actualize the devotional essence of the activity because she lacks total commitment to her guests; she often suppresses or abandons her vocation. Emma's ego demands the recognizably elevated status of knowing instructor, and when not supposedly enlightening Harriet, she must occupy the starring role center stage by running off to be the guest of honor at the Coles' party, a position counter to her calling to serve. Having planned to repulse the unworthy Coles, Emma deigns to attend their gathering and then engages in a self-congratulatory fantasy of their grateful awe of her royal condescension: "She must have delighted the Coles—worthy people, who deserved to be made happy!—And left a name behind her that would not soon die away" (231). She eschews the servant role to indulge in "the splendour of popularity" (231), preferring to be first rather than last.[18]

The guileless Miss Bates unconsciously discerns and affirms Emma's potential as a bountiful hostess while hinting at her need for more involvement, telling Jane of her mother's inadequate dinner experience with Mr. Woodhouse during the Westons' ball at the Crown, in a voice loud enough for Emma to hear:

> 'I was telling you of your grandmamma, Jane,—There was a little disappointment.—The baked apples and biscuits, excellent in their way, you know; but there was a delicate fricassee of sweetbread and some asparagus brought in at first, and good Mr. Woodhouse, not thinking the asparagus quite boiled enough, sent it all out again. Now there is nothing grandmamma loves better than sweetbread and asparagus—so she was rather disappointed, but we agreed we would not speak of it to any body, for fear of its getting round to dear Miss Woodhouse, who would be so very much concerned!' (329-330)

As the lady of the house, Emma planned this meal, like the others designed for the delectation of her guests, but once again, was not there to supervise it. Miss Bates knows that Emma's direct oversight would have guaranteed her mother's enjoyment of the repast that Mr. Woodhouse snatches away.[19] Significantly, Miss Bates sets up and reinforces the above-quoted audible questioning of Emma's royal dedication by temporarily dethroning her in favor of Mrs. Elton. Shortly before describing Mr. Woodhouse's usurpation of her mother's favorite foods—her post-facto explanation for demoting Emma—Miss Bates designates Mrs. Elton the queen of the ball instead of the neglectful hostess: " 'Stop, stop, let us stand a little back, Mrs. Elton is going; dear Mrs. Elton, how elegant she looks!—Beautiful lace!—Now we all follow in her train. Quite the queen of the evening!' " (329). Mrs. Elton's superficial queenliness depends on her ostentatious dress and vulgar insistence on precedence over others; thus, in adulating Mrs. Elton, Miss Bates not only snubs Emma but comically presents her with a magnified image of her own ugly fault of self-glorification.

The absentee hostess-in-training knows that she can guarantee only guests' present pleasure in whatever she serves in person, as when she distributes muffins, ample dessert portions, and filled wine glasses. Miss Bates communicates to Emma the fact that others know she knows this, thereby disallowing her from hiding behind momentary liberality her miserliness in enabling the confiscation of the meal itself. What Emma gives, her father does not seize.[20] This reinforces the notion that the service is as important as the food to effective hosting. Just as Emma deprives guests of the material substance of the feast—the entrée—she omits its more significant sacramental dimension. Emma overemphasizes the trappings of the dinner, revealing a prideful, empty hospitality toward women she contemns but finds useful as intermittent babysitters. She must infuse a sacrificial spirit into her hosting in order to provide a real banquet that fills and fulfills others. Miss Bates's retelling of her mother's complaint reinforces that Emma is not fully present to other women, especially those beneath her in wealth or status, and takes away from their experience by eluding communion with them.

Emma's degeneration from her calling reaches its nadir, of course, at the picnic at Box Hill, where she plays queen-of-the-mountain while contributing only a partial share in the provision of sustenance but nearly all of the social conflict—the extreme opposite to a beneficent host (370). Danielle Spratt goes so far as to claim that Emma "exhibit[s a] nearly pathological [level] of incompetence for philanthropic acts" (193) in a critique of the Lady Bountiful role's hypocrisy and ineffectuality in an era fraught with "broad institutional inequalities" (205).

The heroine's hubris leads her to publicly insult Miss Bates. Instead of affirming the value of her mentor of hospitality, Emma punishes her role model for the virtuosity that Emma fails to achieve because she denies her vocation. After her cruel affront to Miss Bates, she feels an unformulated but acute regret at having participated in "the very questionable enjoyments of this day of pleasure" (374).[21] The narrator captures a psychologically nuanced and relatable sense of Emma's gnawing conscience—she feels an increasingly urgent desire to escape the scene of her misbehavior, and projects the blame for her discombobulation onto the social group: "Such another scheme, composed of so many ill-assorted people, she hoped never to be betrayed into again" (374). This flawed but maturing heroine feels guilty before Mr. Knightley's intervention; he only forces her to confront her conscience, on which Miss Bates has already been working. With an added push from Mr. Knightley, Emma acknowledges the ugliness behind her flaunted bounteousness:

> Miss Bates should never again—no, never! If attention, in future, could do away the past, she might hope to be forgiven. She had been often remiss, her conscience told her so; *remiss, perhaps, more in thought than fact; scornful, ungracious. But it should be so no more.* In the warmth of true contrition, she would call upon her the very next morning, and it should be the beginning, on her side, of a regular, *equal*, kindly intercourse. (377, emphases mine)

Emma finally comprehends that the spirit behind her actions is as fundamental as the gestures themselves. She internalizes and inhabits the role of hospitable host who views others as friends rather than tools or charity cases. She makes the transition from a preoccupation with the literal provision of food while seeking to exalt her social image, to the heartfelt provision of interest, support, and love from a place of humility and mutuality. The day after denigrating her spiritual mother and experiencing a consequential climax of self-dissatisfaction, Emma views visiting her as an honor. She enters the Bates home for the first time with the active "wish of giving pleasure" rather than assuming she is "conferring obligation" (378), seeking admittance into a worthier one's space like a humble communicant.

Emma acquires a sense of balance and joy when she embraces her genuine vocation as "the attentive lady of the house" (434). She finally discerns that her guests feed *her*, and shows her teachability in absorbing and applying Miss Bates's wisdom in wholehearted giving. After facing her suppressed awareness that she has never appreciated her female friends of longest standing, she gives them the food of friendship, gratitude, attention, affection—her full presence. Similar to the way she offers cake and wine whose ingredients have been transformed into something greater than their original form, Emma begins to transform herself from vainglorious socialite to servant, replacing her emphasis on the externals of the feast with an emphasis on its essence: the gift of herself.

Emma Woodhouse is called to be a gracious host, one who humbly serves the sisterhood that helped her to realize her vocation. Emma's hurtful mockery of Miss Bates ironically draws her attention back to where it should be; her remorse for this offense inspires her to follow in Miss Bates's footsteps and hone her natural gift for hospitality with a conscious effort and zeal that she has never before applied. Similarly, *Mansfield Park*'s Susan Price and her need for guidance propel the cloistered Fanny into overt action, and when Fanny compares herself to bolder agent Susan, she recognizes her comparative weakness: "Susan tried to be useful, where *she* could only have gone away and cried" amid the Portsmouth pandemonium (*MP* 395). Fanny partly learns from Susan the courage to answer her unexpected call to authority as the intellectual and moral teacher of this very sister and, by extension, an implied succession of women. Clever Emma initially longs for such a mentor role, but acquires the humility to defer to the superior wisdom of a woman she had relegated to an inferior place—Miss Bates—and to accept and honor her own calling to serve the feast.

Realist Jane Austen suggests a hint of tragedy or at least of severe frustration in the cramping of Fanny's and Emma's genius and its expression into the few available channels. Austen's heroines are all denied full autonomy in their culture, whether socially, economically, or expressively. Neither wealth nor virtue can purchase unequivocal freedom or diversified opportunities for them. However, like devout monastics, Austen's exemplary women view no form of oppression as justification for evasion of moral responsibility. They must make a committed study of the personal development essential to maximize their gifts, to the benefit of other women and society. Through striving to perfect their available vocations in a sacrificial spirit, they enact the sacramental significance of their roles. Neither Austen nor her orthodox heroines show interest in theological radicalism; like medieval nuns, they creatively exercise sanctioned forms of authority but depend on men for roles denied them. For example, only male clergy perform religious functions central to the women's practice as well, particularly the celebration of Holy Communion. This fact makes Fanny Price's grooming of Edmund Bertram for the priestly role in her female community particularly important, and her own greater spiritual sagacity a crucial determinant of his efficacy as a clergyman. It also makes more regrettable the moral stasis of such negative exemplars of the clergy as Mr. Elton, Dr. Grant, and Mr. Collins, who choose wives that enable their conceit and its destructive effects. Through all her novels, Austen brandishes and commends the sometimes unofficial but efficacious power of strong, spiritually discerning women to ameliorate flaws in themselves, others, and society. Fanny Price wields the influence of transcendent principle.[22] In the example of Emma Woodhouse, despite the critical error of prioritizing her relationship with "her paternalistic hero" over her friendship with "the spinster Miss Bates" (Looser, *Women* 91), the purified heroine extends hospitality to others with convivial expediency and fortifies her sororal circle. Personal and social progress are possible only when truth takes precedence over and directs desire in one's mode of leadership, and when women support each other in effecting that ideal.

Austen's women of diverse temperaments and talents can and do fulfill profoundly valuable vocations, largely through a sincere desire to learn from other women how best to combine the contemplative and active dimensions of their particular calling. Fanny emboldens herself to disseminate the insight she has gained from much meditation, and Emma enacts her social authority with more thoughtful intentionality. Both build stronger communities of women who augment each other in individual and societal good. Emma's reconciliation with Miss Bates facilitates her reconciliation with Jane Fairfax, who apologizes in kind, and her greater mutuality and intimacy with all the women in her circle. Fanny's daring offer of guidance gains her an expanded sisterhood in the proximity of Susan, the newly humbled Julia, and a likely futurity including Betsey Price and all the young women's eventual female descendants. Austen's best heroines bring others to the banquet—Elizabeth Darcy and Jane Bingley adopt Kitty Bennet and Georgiana Darcy, as Eleanor Tilney mentors Catherine Morland and Anne Elliot cheers Mary and befriends the Musgrove sisters; and Mrs. Jennings mothers the Dashwood sisters as Elinor mothers her own mother and sisters. Women's authentic use of their spiritual gifts results in a beautiful coherence that inspires other women's like recognition and cultivation of their gifts. In this way, truth to self is truth to other women, which explains why Austen's heroines cannot marry until they have first reconciled with their biological or social sisters.[23] In Austen's novels, as in medieval women's monastic life, such gifts as spiritual counsel, education, hospitality, charity, healing, and the modeling of virtue produce a ripple effect of benefits that contribute to social concord. In Austen's vision, to borrow Mary Crawford's phrasing, all human beings are "born to be connected" (*MP* 359).

Part 3

Women and Others

The Female Self in Environmental, Social, and Imaginative Space

CHAPTER 6

"Mamma says I am never within"

Heroines' Eco-affinities as Identityscapes

The sororal sacramentality of Christian women's spirituality in Austen's fiction inheres in her depiction of heroines' environmental associations as well. Through her oeuvre, the novelist endorses "the Augustinian aesthetic that everything is beautiful according to its nearness to God" (Capitani 197). The convalescent Marianne anticipates frequent perambulations to view the "new plantations at . . . the Abbeyland" and declares that she and her Dashwood sorority "will often go to the old ruins of the Priory, and try to trace its foundations as far as we are told they once reached. I know we shall be happy" (*SS* 343). She envisions finding healing joy through reconnection with the tradition of a shared faith. Similarly, the enthusiasm for abbeys and chapels of Catherine Morland, Emma Woodhouse, and Fanny Price reveals neither mere Romantic enthusiasm nor even solely religious conviction, but also loyalty to its communal expression and to the continuity it imbues in space and society. Just as Marianne values "old ruins" more than plantings, Emma admires Donwell Abbey for its blend of gradual change with a preservationist historicity that fosters longevity: "neither fashion nor extravagance had rooted up" its trees and the "rambling and irregular" but "comfortable" house "was just what it ought to be, and it looked what it was" (*E* 358). The aspiration to holism in the architecture of space, as of self, stems from belief in the inheritance of a divinely ordained natural order in which the human steward respectfully builds upon—rather than eradicates—the foundation of the past.[1] Heroines' fulfillment of their interwoven potentialities through vocation finds expression in their relationships to space. Distinctive topographies of characterization emerge in individual novels that help readers to understand each protagonist by tracing the symbolic spatial map of her progress.

A dichotomy pervades Austen's fictional landscape in which nature-lovers transcend the eco-callous in virtue and likeability. For example, the charismatic Elizabeth Bennet belongs in fields and groves and rarely "shut[s herself] into her own room" (*PP* 186) unless confronting a problem, whereas Bingley's artificial sisters nearly always appear indoors and Charlotte Lucas sells herself for a home she can enjoy only by giving her moronic husband monopoly of the garden.[2] Elizabeth's habit of outdoor tramps lends parody to Caroline Bingley's invitation to " 'take a turn about the room' " (56). Similarly, Anne Elliot "glorie[s] in the sea" (*P* 102) and its rejuvenating influence, while her shallow elder sister can only move "with exultation from one drawing-room to the other" (138). The green Catherine Morland claims to need no superadded incentive for outdoor activity, declaring to Henry that " '[t]he pleasure of walking and breathing fresh air is enough for me, and in fine weather I am out more than half my time.—Mamma says, I am never within' " (*NA* 174); by contrast, her false friend Isabella Thorpe man-chases her way through ballrooms, city streets, and country drives without heeding her surroundings. More famously, Fanny Price admires the Mansfield parsonage's shrubberies and evergreens and feels protective toward the avenue of trees Mr. Rushworth threatens with leveling by an "improver," whereas foil Mary Crawford infamously admits to " 'see[ing] no wonder in this shrubbery equal to seeing [her]self in it' " (*MP* 209–210).[3] Felicia Bonaparte observes that "Fanny . . . is the very idea of rootedness" (59). Indeed, she and trees are almost interchangeable and Edmund seems to court both when he finally falls in love with the conservationist rather than the consumer. Whereas Mary uses Sotherton's woods as mere backdrop for her flirtatious self-flaunting at Edmund, Fanny can admire and commune with a beauty outside herself; by "wandering about and sitting under trees with Fanny all the summer evenings" (462), Edmund allies himself with both her and nature and becomes re-rooted.[4]

Austen's female characters implicitly identify with nature and its vulnerability to men's oppression or nurturance in ways that manifest the novelist's participation in this fundamental paradigm of ecofeminist literature. Barbara Seeber delineates patterns in Austen's portrayal of the correlative oppression of women, animals, and nature in general (*Jane* 71) and cites as examples "tree-cutting," the consumption of animal flesh, and Fanny Price's empathy with her overtaxed mare that also suffers from "the treatment of those constructed as subordinate" ("Nature" 269, 272).[5] Heroines must not only challenge their men into husband-readiness, but also intuit that a man's harmonious integration of the feral with the domesticated through a minimal modulation of wildness bodes well for his supportiveness of nature's as well as his wife's authentic vitality. Elizabeth Bennet values the beauty that results from the collaboration of man and nature at Pemberley—she marries "the proverbial biblical 'good steward' " (Sulloway 207).[6] Emma Woodhouse chooses a spouse who liberates the environment to follow to an even greater degree its own way from its original rooting. Donwell Abbey's grounds flourish in their independent, acknowledged life, apart from considerations of the occupants' views—"the Abbey, with all the old neglect of prospect, had scarcely a sight" of its "ample gardens stretching down to meadows washed by a stream," just as its many trees remain "in rows and avenues, which neither fashion nor extravagance had rooted up" (*E* 358). Like several other Austen heroines, Emma equates "true gentility" (358) with a preservationism in which "fashion" is satirized as destructive but the allowance of a continuity that produces gradual growth is praised. Mr. Knightley accepts the sufficiency of an ancestral order and cultivation evidenced by old "rows and avenues" and gives the longstanding trees freeplay, just as he refrains from renovating the abbey into unnecessary uniformity or ostentation and thus safeguards its significance, and as he learns to cherish the sovereignty of Emma's peculiar form of "brilliancy" (433).[7]

Jane Austen imparts that love of nature constitutes a desirable ideal for both genders as evidence of the capacity to look beyond themselves, thus reaping the reward of self-preservation—what we would call sustainability. The novelist's environmental commentary is commonly viewed as influenced by the "long tradition of anti-improvement literature" that criticizes the destructive artifice of landscape designers such as Lancelot "Capability" Brown and Humphry Repton (Duckworth xviii–xix), and by "eighteenth-century moralists" who upheld country over city for productive moral atmosphere (Butler 97). Alison G. Sulloway asseverates that the author herself "had seen and suffered enough casual exploitation so that she took the pastoral world under her tender but unobtrusive fictional protection, just as she felt protective toward human figures under threat of abuse or neglect" (187).[8] Humankind's humble collaboration with the environment produces an expressively beautiful setting that furthers the survival of the earth and its inhabitants. In this sense, the narrator affirms the over-exuberant Marianne for the very " 'passion for dead leaves' " (*SS* 88) about which Elinor teases her. Elinor remarks that their former home's " 'woods and walks' " are probably " 'thickly covered with dead leaves' " (87) as usual for the season, but Marianne fears that with her brother and sister-in-law in residence at Norland, " 'Now there is no one to regard them. They are seen only as a nuisance, swept hastily off, and driven as much as possible from the sight' " (88). Though it might be a stretch to suggest that Austen advocates composting in this scene, Marianne's rather melodramatic observation reflects her awareness of John and Fanny Dashwood's exploitative attitude toward their newly acquired resources; they are more likely to sweep away organic matter than to nurture it. Forcing nature into cosmetic sterility for mere appearances shows short-term thinking as well as poor taste.

Austen portrays a feminine conservationist zeal in her heroines' landscape aesthetics that presages their propagation of scrupulous estate stewardship in succeeding generations. She emphasizes the inextricable link between women and nature through depiction of parallels between female characters and particular locations or elements such as earth, leaf, shrub, or sea. A woman's "place"—her occupation of space and how she acts upon and is reflected in it—sheds light on her personality and mode of relating to the world and supports her growth in and through it. Like an organism or rising waters, she absorbs critical insights into herself and her context, seeking both individuation and connection by finding her place. To achieve this goal, with nature's help, she must expand her perspective. Laura Mooneyham White claims that "each of Austen's heroines" seeks "to find a home in her self, for only then may she be rewarded with the idealized physical space that represents this inner integration" ("Traveling" 201).[9] Ongoing interaction with place also facilitates the heroine's attainment of this literal and metaphorical home. As Eleanor Tilney taught Catherine Morland to step back and admire the picturesque appeal of rugged wilderness, the hyacinth, and a vibrantly tinted human history, Austen's heroines all need to look farther outside of themselves to see more deeply into themselves and others. They enact on a living stage-set a striving toward and attainment of a healthy marriage of self-nurture with social integration.

Daughter of the Soil: Elizabeth Bennet

Elizabeth Bennet is Austen's most earthy heroine. She expresses her sassy self-assurance in her free occupation of space, but chooses a self-isolating path. On her way to Netherfield to visit the recuperating Jane, Elizabeth walks Kitty and Lydia to Meryton, where they go "to the lodgings of one of the officers' wives" while she strides on "alone, crossing field after field at a quick pace" (*PP* 32), muddy fields that connote her fecundity of mind and body. The generic sisters and wives Elizabeth leaves behind are "lodged" together in man-made buildings defined by the men they follow, whereas Elizabeth shows contrasting independence through her mobility. She overleaps all obstacles and emphatically connects with the land, "jumping over stiles and springing over puddles with impatient activity . . . and find[s] herself at last within view of the house, with weary ancles [*sic*], dirty stockings, and a face glowing with the warmth of exercise" (32). Elizabeth awakens to the house's proximity as if from a thorough communion with the earth, which she carries with her into the artificial domestic space through the dirt on her clothes. Unlike Jane, she rejects the mediating transport of even horseback, finding "transport" in nature itself and receiving its mark of kinship on her petticoat (which Louisa Hurst observes is " 'six inches deep in mud' " [36]). It is as if Elizabeth plants and replants her feet in the soil with each leap.[10] Louisa and Caroline are shocked that she walks so far alone (32); their reaction accentuates the prevalence of women's claustrophobic enclosure that likely intensifies the heroine's near-bursting zeal for outdoor treks. Bingley's sisters attempt to denigrate Elizabeth with animal associations in characterizing her as " 'look[ing] almost wild' " (35) and her trip to Netherfield as " 'scampering about the country' " (36). Their primitivization of her is rooted in jealousy of her bold liberty and the more deeply established values and traditions of the landed gentry from which she descends. Insecure, reactive Caroline is apt in her profile of Elizabeth as possessing " 'an abominable sort of conceited independence, a most country town indifference to decorum' " (36), in that Elizabeth's bond with the agrarian landscape reinforces her rejection of strict conformism in favor of agentic expediency. She disregards the expectation that an unaccompanied woman will "keep inside the house, or at least its grounds" and limit herself to "a walk in the shrubbery or through the park" (Selwyn 89), for the higher goal of expediting her visit to a sick sister while protecting family farm resources, and because she wants to get out.

Elizabeth feels an affinity for cultivated wildness, for the harmonious coexistence of nature and its stewards in which the latter group plays a conscientious role. On her visit to Charlotte Collins, "she ha[s] often great enjoyment out of doors" and takes possession of some park land as a "favourite walk, and where she frequently went while the others were calling on Lady Catherine . . . along the open grove which edged that side of the park, where there was a nice sheltered path, which no one seemed to value but herself" (*PP* 169). Elizabeth's attraction to the fringe of a planted park suggests her subconscious awareness of her need to moderate her staunch individualism to allow for more connectedness to community. According to Barbara Wenner, this position enables her to "remain in touch simultaneously with society and nature—a good place to hide and a good place from which to seek" (59). Wenner denotes the scene one of the "[e]dge-of-the-wood experiences" that function as an "important way for Austen's heroines to understand and control where they are in the landscapes" and in "their lives" (9). That Elizabeth occupies a space that "edge[s]" Lady Catherine's park while escaping her surveillance and company proves fitting in that she ultimately edges Darcy's aunt out of her schemes for him and his property by usurping both (*PP* 169). Elizabeth's home "grove" with Darcy will be both "open" and "sheltered," as if her taste in nature forecasts her ideal for marriage and social life: rooted, yet selectively thinned out and thus "open" to sunlight and nutrients, to new growth (169).

Elizabeth's assumed equality with men and even lordship over them is manifest in her competitiveness toward them in the demarcation of space. She takes offense at Darcy's perceived encroachment into "her" realm at Rosings Park:

> More than once did Elizabeth in her ramble within the Park, unexpectedly meet Mr. Darcy.—She felt all the perverseness of the mischance that should bring him where no one else was brought; and to prevent its ever happening again, took care to inform him at first, that it was a favourite haunt of hers.—How it could occur a second time therefore was very odd!—Yet it did, and even a third. It seemed like wilful [*sic*] ill-nature, or a voluntary penance, for on these occasions it was not merely a few formal enquiries and an awkward pause and then away, but he actually thought it necessary to turn back and walk with her. (182)

The ironic humor of this scene resides in Elizabeth's brazen attitude of entitlement toward someone else's land (to which Darcy has more a right than she), and her obliviousness to his attempt at courtship. She misreads as "ill-nature" his investigation into her tastes, in which his query about "her love of solitary walks" (182) and escort suggest at least his desire to comprehend and honor her boundaries while sharing in her life (as a landowner who treats the environment with this delicate circumspection). However, the descriptor "ill-nature" somewhat applies to Darcy at this stage, because he does not yet respect Elizabeth as fully as he should; her territorialism reveals her suspicion of this—she refuses male patronage and shows skepticism of the possibility of a reciprocal romantic relationship. She even demands an explanation from the genial Colonel Fitzwilliam when he appears in her self-designated walk as if in Darcy's stead one day: "forcing a smile, she said, 'I did not know before that you ever walked this way'" (182). After rejecting Darcy's heavy-handed first proposal, Elizabeth alters her walking route at first, but unable to resist the propitious "verdure of the early trees," she wanders back to "the sort of grove which edged the park," where her woodland escort approaches her from inside it (195). They meet at the gate to the grove, where Darcy hands over his explanatory letter about his treatment of the perfidious Wickham and division of Bingley and Jane. Although the gate demarcates Elizabeth and Darcy's emotional division, her act of accepting his letter from the other side foreshadows their later reconciliation at the verdant Pemberley estate.

Elizabeth's conquest of space parallels her surmounting of gender and class barriers to claim entitlement to air her views with surety, telling both men and women, like a Darcy or a Lady Catherine, "'exactly what to think'" (86). Instead of taking a survey first, she races from impression to conviction, traversing social and perceptual space with an immediacy that is refreshingly frank. Nonetheless, this heroine is near-sighted; bounding as briskly along the surface of issues as she does land, she sometimes willfully ignores alternative perspectives and steps on others' feelings in the process. The novel visually foreshadows this fault by portraying not only her overleaping of "stiles" but her endeavor to obscure the mud on her petticoat by " 'let[ting] down' " her dress " 'to hide it' " (36). This complicates Elizabeth's appearance of earthy openness—she often disregards both the rich soil of positive potential in others and the negative qualities or otiose "dirt" in her own character. She fails to perceive proximal realities that should be self-evident or to look far afield enough to interpret events accurately in context. Yet Darcy's verbal and epistolary revelations in response to her stinging rejection force Elizabeth to acknowledge to herself that she can be wrong and unjust. Holding herself apart has distorted her character; she discovers "the limitations of a private view" (Duckworth 41).[11]

Elizabeth's essential expansion of insight into herself and Darcy appears in her diversified views of his home setting in the Pemberley landscape. When she visits Darbyshire with her appropriately named Aunt and Uncle Gardiner, she watches for the first appearance of Pemberley Woods with some perturbation:

> . . . when at length they turned in at the lodge, her spirits were in a high flutter. The park was very large, and contained a great variety of ground. They entered it in one of its lowest points, and drove for some time through a beautiful wood, stretching over a wide extent. Elizabeth's mind was too full for conversation. . . . She had never seen a place for which nature had done more, or where natural beauty had been so little counteracted by an awkward taste. (*PP* 245)

She marvels over the park's vastness and resplendent "great variety of ground" as she and the Gardiners travel from "one of its lowest points" to the hilltop lookout, from which they view Pemberley House, and then down again, over the river and partway upward to reach the house, "standing well on rising ground" (245). Their trip through the park depicts in codified form Elizabeth's widened sympathies—she has learned to entertain others' perspectives, whether from below or above her usual line of sight, ultimately embracing the midway point represented by the position of the house, which perches between wooded hills and a lush river valley. From the grounds, she "saw and admired every remarkable spot and point of view" (245), and likewise from inside the house, "she looked on the whole scene, the river, the trees scattered on its banks, and the winding of the valley . . . with delight" (246). Elizabeth speaks no more than the truth when she quips to Jane that her love for Darcy dawned "from [her] first seeing his beautiful grounds at Pemberley" (373)—from the point in her development when she could see beyond her own field of view to that of another and, thus, be capable of perceiving his inward admirability.

Elizabeth's climactic revelation "that to be mistress of Pemberley might be something!" occurs on the hilltop overlooking the "wide extent" (245) of Pemberley's myriad naturescapes.[12] This does not signify her exultation in an imagined social-materialist power in which she has succumbed to Darcy's temptation, "All this Power will I give thee, and the glory of them; for that is delivered unto me, & to whomsoever I will, I give it. If thou therefore wilt worship me, all shalbe thine" (Luke 4: 6–7).[13] Though that was Darcy's attitude toward Elizabeth in the first proposal, both characters have already been humbled into reform by this point. Rather, this scene allegorizes the speechless Elizabeth's almost mystical apprehension of the paradoxical splendor of well-cultivated authenticity, whether in the self or the soil. Whereas the perusal of Darcy's blunt letter had awakened her to "kn[o]w [her]self" in her defects (*PP* 208), this scenic-view moment constitutes her recollection, in a humbled but more optimistic spirit, of her positive potential as well as his.

Elizabeth seeks to redirect her energies toward preservation of the physical and social landscape in partnership with one whose vision the landscape itself verifies. She encounters Darcy in person after her perspectival shift as traced in her tour of the multileveled grounds and house. Darrel Mansell describes her journey as mapped in relation to him: "she entered the park, then the house. Moving closer and closer to the true man, she confronted his miniature, then his large portrait. Finally, . . . she confronts the true, three-dimensional Darcy himself" (93). This reunion occurs after Elizabeth and company exit the house and enter the garden, an intermediary space between interior and exterior that makes an apt setting for Elizabeth's exercise of her amplified vision—she immediately recognizes Darcy's self-improvement. This once overly individualistic heroine no longer stomps over or hovers at the edge of an ecosystem, but judiciously chooses one, gets to know it from all vantage points and, with her marriage, will plant herself in its epicenter as a pledge of communal self-investment.[14] No longer holding herself above her flawed humanity, she comes down from her righteous pride and meets Darcy in the middle, where both characters display the humility necessary for relational sustainability. They will co-steward a flourishing—because mutual—family life.

A Leaf in Search of a Tree: Marianne Dashwood

Marianne Dashwood must also broaden her point of view in order for her distinctive identity to enhance rather than to fragment her familial and environmental bonds. She often expresses her ardor for nature, as when she bids the personified trees of Norland an emotive farewell: " 'And you, ye well-known trees!—but you will continue the same.—No leaf will decay because we are removed, nor any branch become motionless although we can observe you no longer!—No; you will continue . . . unconscious of the pleasure or the regret you occasion, and insensible of any change in those who walk under your shade!—But who will remain to enjoy you?' " (*SS* 27).[15] Marianne describes her immature self in this monologue: her absorption in an existential sensationism that renders her oblivious to others whom she "shades" with her inflated sufferings, and her subconscious curiosity over who will persevere with her. Yet she emulates the "dead leaves" she loves more than the trees onto which she projects herself, in being " 'driven . . . about . . . by the wind' " (88) of extreme impulses and avoidable consequences that could have landed her in the pile with the respectively physically or socially dead Elizas.

Substantial critical emphasis has rightly been placed on Marianne's fall downhill as a manifestation of her moral and psychological downslide. She hurls herself precipitately into life, a leaf whirling downward in faster pursuit of more socially suspect inclinations than more grounded field- and grove-hiker Elizabeth Bennet pursues. Marianne's cultish Romanticism is encapsulated in her superlative-filled commentary on the outdoors and, of course, the famous plummet "with all possible speed down the steep side of the hill" that causes her accident (41). Elizabeth's zeal for Darcy's expansive grounds and budding interest in Darcy himself emanate from deepened self-knowledge, and sharing Pemberley's environmental and domestic beauties with a select circle of family members will strengthen the heroine's bonds with them. Marianne's loss of self is evidenced in her inability to experience nature apart from its associations with Willoughby, whereas her recovery shows through in her desire to co-inhabit myriad spaces with her family and Colonel Brandon. In her dysfunctional state, she correlates Willoughby with the phallic protrusions of "fine bold hills" (69) visible from his estate and "ridge of hills" (303) visible from Cleveland (the Palmers' estate where she sickens herself in the wettest grounds), and also with all the scenery at Barton: "every field and every tree brought some peculiar, some painful recollection" (342).

However, even before she has completely extricated herself from Willoughby, Marianne puts into motion her self-restoration by choosing Colonel Brandon. She is still a vulnerable leaf after the discovery of Willoughby's infamy—when Mrs. Jennings remarks, "'tis a true saying about an ill wind, for it will be all the better for Colonel Brandon. He will have her at last'" (196)—but she does not remain so. Perhaps the wind of circumstance blows her closer to the Colonel, but she is not passive in her choice of partner. She feels increasingly drawn to his romantic tale of personal loss and to his loyal friendship. During her convalescence, Marianne consciously determines to include him in her community: "at her own particular request, for she was impatient to pour forth her thanks to him for fetching her mother, Colonel Brandon was invited to visit her" in the feminine personal space of "Mrs. Palmer's dressing-room" (340). Furthermore, she suggests to Elinor that Barton Park's library will be insufficient for her reading needs and, conveniently, require supplementation with books "'of more modern production which I know I can borrow of Colonel Brandon'" (343)), a scheme that creates an excuse for frequent interaction with him. The book-borrowing idea flows out of Marianne's delineation of her plans for post-recovery outings earlier in this same paragraph, as if she already unconsciously includes the Colonel with her female family group: "'[W]e will take long walks together every day. We will walk to the farm at the edge of the down, and see how the children go on; we will walk to Sir John's new plantations at Barton-Cross, and the Abbeyland; and we will often go to the old ruins of the Priory, and try to trace its foundations as far as we are told they once reached. I know we shall be happy'" (343). Marianne's maturation process is manifest in her change in preference from lonely country roams, to sociable strolls with her "dear family party" (343) to places replete with communal associations—farm, children, plantations, abbey, priory. She has learned to long for the agrarian proximity and fertility that Colonel Brandon's Edenic gardenscape at Delaford will ultimately provide. Along the way, by reattaching to her vital family tree, she regains enough strength to reclaim herself and the landscape from Willoughby.

Marianne exorcises Willoughby from her life by ceremonially returning with Elinor and dismissing him to "the important hill" (344) where she fell under his influence: " 'There, exactly there'— pointing with one hand, 'on that projecting mound,—there I fell; and there I first saw Willoughby' " (344). In particularizing the exact site of Willoughby's first entrance into her life, she reduces and expels his presence, as if burying his memory in the "projecting mound." The modifier "projecting" in this phrase can be grammatically interpreted as describing the mound's purpose for the heroine, who projects her unworthy beau into it, as well as the erectile quality of his narcissistic sensualism, which she rejects and buries along with her illusory image of him. According to Kelly M. McDonald, "Place name analysis suggests Willoughby's Combe Magna to be a 'giant enclosed hollow,' while Brandon's Delaford is a 'point of crossing or passage' " (24). Willoughby had lured Marianne on a tour of playacted housekeeping that revealed itself to be hollow, like her inflated fantasy of him and their future together and like the hill in which she inters his empty shell.

By contrast, Colonel Brandon's home will support its new mistress's "passage" (McDonald 24) into adulthood, in the transitional space of the garden harbor—a yonic utopia that matriarch Mrs. Jennings depicts as " 'quite shut in with great garden walls' " that are not confining, but supportive of a prolific harvest, " 'covered with the best fruit-trees in the country: and such a mulberry tree in one corner! Lord! how Charlotte and I did stuff the only time we were there!' " (*SS* 196–197). Marianne will further transform a tree associated with the ancient Babylonian tragedy of Pyramis and Thisbe—whose forbidden love leads them to suicide, their blood reddening the tree's fruit (Lehner 71)—into an image of female prosperity in not only berry consumption, but romantic love and life as a whole. Delaford also features " 'an old yew arbour behind the house' " from whose branches " 'you may see all the carriages that pass along' " (*SS* 197). Marianne looks within the garden of her self to sow its fruits, and looks into the wider world without for the understanding that nurtures this effort, from the firmly rooted yew tree associated with longevity, death, and immortal life—a fitting perch for a heroine who has gone from near-death to rebirth.

Elizabeth Bennet and Marianne Dashwood share in common a sincere zeal for nature that stems from living in their bodies and asserting the liberty of their minds in space. Yet land—whether field, park, hill, or valley—becomes a living canvas for the registration of their independent thoughts and feelings with an insistence that can produce repetition and predictability.[16] Both of these lively, contrary women become more real when they enlarge their visions of themselves and of nature. Rather than exploiting the landscape as the backdrop for projection of the role of self-reliant " 'impertinence' " (*PP* 380) or Romantic heroism, they become more present to its and their own complexity, opening a broader field for the play of their minds and a more balanced, realistic outlook. Elizabeth achieves this by both ascending and descending Marianne's preferred hills to extend the scope and variety of her formerly cropped view, while Marianne comes down from the hills to connect more closely to the Elizabeth-identified soil. Marianne's downward plunge, though foolhardy, on some level represents what she subconsciously knew she needed: to become more down-to-earth in her views and behaviors.

Rather than being subsumed in a man's identity and patriarchal authority as may appear to be the case, Marianne, like Elizabeth, selects as partner one who supports her continuing journey into her fullest nature in a well-nurtured naturescape. After her haphazard fall, the fragile but more focused Marianne invites the devoted Colonel Brandon to enter the inner room of her heart, as she moves outward into the garden of his, revitalized by grafting herself to a firmly established tree—not in the windy hills, but in a buttressed enclave of well-protected soil. In addition, "she will have plenty of wild places on the Delaford estate to which to repair. Colonel Brandon will not be the husband to try to stop her" (Sulloway 204) and will likely join in her rambles in their garden or judiciously bordered wilderness, whenever invited. Along with Elinor and Edward Ferrars, the Brandons will jointly serve as "preservers of lands and of domestic serenity alike" (205).

"Hurrying into the Shrubbery": Emma Woodhouse

The turbulent Marianne eventually embraces voluntary domesticity for its solidity as a foundation for further growth. Emma Woodhouse, on the other hand, allows her father to imprison her in a physical stasis that breeds cerebral atrophy and misappropriation. She lacks a developed relationship to nature because of her lifelong deference to her agoraphobic father. Evidence for this quandary proliferates in the text. The narrator early establishes that Mr. Woodhouse "never went beyond the shrubbery" (*E* 26) and even fears for the inanimate Harriet Smith of Emma's portraiture because " 'it is never safe to sit out of doors' " (48). Emma's social plans revolve around assuaging her father's anxieties, and Mr. Knightley collaborates with her in this, aware in planning his Donwell party "that to have any of [the guests] sitting down out of doors to eat would inevitably make him ill" (356). The "too much confined" heroine lacks female "walking companion[s]" (26) before her adoption of Harriet and, after, must dread the sabotage of her increased mobility if her father becomes "scarcely . . . satisfied without their promising never to go beyond the shrubbery again" (336). Thus, Hartfield's shrubbery initially signifies a paternal impediment to Emma's self-actualization, the unnatural trimming back and hedging in of her vitality.

Shrubberies in Austen's fiction and era can connote both liberation and constraint as ambiguous yonic symbols. Although conventionally female-designated outdoor features of prosperous country homes that provided women a safe, pretty place where they could "escape . . . for privacy" (Sulloway 187), shrubberies, like all "provinces" of a property, tended to be overseen by the patriarch in possession (187–188).[17] After their conflict, Sir Thomas Bertram tells Fanny Price to " 'go out for an hour on the gravel' " where she " 'will have the shrubbery to [her]self, and will be the better for air and exercise' " (*MP* 322), and Lady Bertram advises Mr. Rushworth to create one in his makeover of Sotherton (55). Mr. Woodhouse enshrouds himself in Hartfield's shrubbery as the border of his walks in all seasons, and strives to enclose his vibrant daughter in it as well, using her as a hedge-like buffer against the vigorous outside world.

As outlined in the previous chapter, Emma must align her motives and exertions with a humble service role to fulfill, as heiress of a sororal spiritual tradition, her calling to feed others. Examination of how this reformation process occurs in space reveals both Emma's hunger for the wide green world and how it subtly aids and illustrates her budding comprehension. She must descend her high hill and take possession of the shrubbery as emblem of the introspection she wants. She must confront the cramped enclosure of her mind and heart and open it to the light of grace and reason.

Emma rebels against interment in the shrubbery by escaping up Box Hill for a picnic free of her father, where she unleashes pent-up frustration by asserting her social prerogative and attacking Miss Bates, an act a number of scholars agree in attributing to continual self-suppression and ennui. For Emma, "Box Hill" combines a yonic and a phallic symbol in a juxtaposition that underscores her greater virility in mind and body than the father whose impotence boxes her in. She must navigate a way to thrive within that irony as delineated in her alteration of the shrubbery into her eco-conscious space for self-redefinition. Marianne Dashwood reclaims her landscape on a new footing by shifting her attention from preoccupation with isolating masculine hills to communal enjoyment of fields and gardens. Emma faces circumstantial isolation from women of compatible intellect and personality and exacerbates this estrangement through her hilltop hostility to Miss Bates; like Marianne, she must return to even ground and learn to see, both near and far, what is there. The shrubbery will become hers, as a symbol of the courageous interiorization that enables her self-knowledge and attendant embracement of the previously explicated role of hospitable host.

When Emma possesses the opportunity to enjoy the lovely scenery right before her on Box Hill, she ignores it, deflecting both her own and others' attention from natural glories to her false flirtation with Frank Churchill and aggressive wit. Throughout this important chapter of the novel, the narrator forecloses readers' view from Box Hill to induce our participation in Emma's willful insentience and our experience of everyone's disconnect from the setting and each other. We receive no concrete description of the landscape whatever. Though "every body had a burst of admiration on first arriving" (of an unspecified sight), we are told that the social fragmentation that directly sets in proves "too strong for any fine prospects" to alleviate (*E* 367), and find only a few more, vague allusions to the site. In this scene, the heroine "limits her contact with nature—a corollary to limiting self-examination" (Curry 111). We are blinded from seeing the external beauty that Emma refuses to see, while forced to watch her turn a blind eye to herself. After her mockery of Miss Bates and the social unraveling it aggravates, Emma soon "wished herself rather walking quietly about with any of the others" than those who condoned or fomented her egotism, "or sitting almost alone, and quite unattended to, in tranquil observation of the beautiful views beneath her" (*E* 374). Having subconsciously repented her role in "the very questionable enjoyments of this day of pleasure" (374), the heroine awakens to regret at missing "the beautiful views beneath her" and begins descending closer to them as if sensing the profounder self-awareness awaiting her within them. The deepest sorrowing penitence overtakes Emma when the carriage transporting her and Harriet is "half way down the hill," at which point "[s]he was vexed beyond what could have been expressed—almost beyond what she could conceal. Never had she felt so agitated, mortified, grieved, at any circumstance in her life" (376). Throughout this chapter and especially as Emma lowers herself down her hill, we view the landscape, not of nature as such, but of the heroine's emotions and moral amplification that displace it to the background.

Once grounded, the penitent Emma freely and sacrificially reenters confining indoor and outdoor spaces or "boxes," not in obedience to a father figure but to her own dictates of conscience as a woman. In four successive scenes, the long-caged Emma ingresses into a kind of moral-psychological birth canal in search of maturation. She enacts her empathetic identification with other women's feelings through humbly entering their residential interiors or dignifying them in hers, in a spirit of tenderness toward those she has injured. For example, "In the warmth of true contrition" (377), for the first time Emma "entered the passage" and "walked up the stairs" (378) to the Bateses' "very moderate sized apartment" (155) with humility, reconciling with Miss Bates (though not yet with the still-inaccessible Jane Fairfax, who hides further inside the constricting apartment in the bedroom (378)). Emma faces a more daunting test by hosting Harriet Smith in her room at Hartfield, ostensibly for the unpleasant task of confessing yet another error in encouraging her protégée's attachment to Frank Churchill. Instead, after "[h]er heart beat[s] quick on hearing Harriet's footstep and voice" and her guest sweeps "eagerly into the room" (404), Emma discovers Harriet's and simultaneously her own love for Mr. Knightley. Incited by her romantic double's ready occupation of her intimate living space, Emma looks more deeply into her own motives and feels intensified impetus to take redemptive action, encouraging Harriet's narration of her perceived romantic relationship with Mr. Knightley (409). In each of these scenes, Emma gains clarity about "her own heart" (408) and compassion for other women as her shrinking ego gains her entry into their hearts.

In this way, Emma relinquishes her hilly height and takes ownership of her fuller self-knowledge—metaphorically speaking, her shrubbery. Although "[a] mind like her's . . . ma[kes] rapid progress" (407) and she wills herself off her hill from the first revelation of serious error, Emma experiences the reform process in stages, like terracing. With each discovery she makes about her treatment of Miss Bates and Harriet and about her own suppressed sentiments, she comes further down from vainglory and climbs further up into others' spaces and points of view. Emma's arrival at consistency of self-perception is signaled by her uniform recognition of "the blindness of her own head and heart" while successively occupying her boxlike interior and exterior spaces: "she sat still, she walked about, she tried her own room, she tried the shrubbery—in every place, every posture, she perceived that she had acted most weakly; that she had been imposed on by others in a most mortifying degree; that she had been imposing on herself in a degree yet more mortifying" (411–412). Note that in committing to self-scrutiny and reform, Emma neither views her sins in isolation nor abandons her self-esteem. She has rendered herself vulnerable to others' imposition ("others" plural—more people than Frank Churchill projected agendas onto her) and reinforcement of her greater self-deception; having repented and begun her program of redress, she also identifies the communal toxicity that produces reciprocal weakness. Emma takes responsibility for her fall while identifying the enervated social soil that contributed to it and from which she uproots herself in order to regrow on the soil of her own decontaminated and more fecund principles.[18]

At a point when she foresees only a future of "wretchedness" alone with herself, Emma resolves to "thoroughly understand her own heart" (412) and live a better life, regardless of personal happiness. In her quest for sustained wholeness, she longs for the shrubbery that now symbolizes her reshaped selfhood: morally autonomous but accessible and revitalizing to others and, therefore, to herself. In achieving this powerful shift, Emma opens for herself a wider and wilder landscape of experience and influence, metaphorically as well as literally

> resolv[ing] to be out of doors as soon as possible. Never had the exquisite sight, smell, sensation of nature, tranquil, warm, and brilliant after a storm, been more attractive to her. She longed for the serenity they might gradually introduce; and on Mr. Perry's coming in soon after dinner, with a disengaged hour to give her father, she lost no time in hurrying into the shrubbery.—There, with spirits freshened, and thoughts a little relieved, she had taken a few turns, when she saw Mr. Knightley passing through the garden door, and coming towards her. (424)

Without any hope of her own love being reciprocated, Emma looks outside of herself, and for the first time attentively appreciates and communes with nature's splendors. At the same time, she communes with her replanted, reshaped, more truthful and entire (though suffering) self. Only at this point in her development can a now-deserving man enter her heart.

This scene is the eco-climax of *Emma*, and recalls similar scenes in other Austen novels. Mr. Darcy re-proposes in Elizabeth's landscape after she has abandoned her territorialism of space and judgment, enabling the two to "wander together over and beyond the boundaries of Longbourn plantation" (Sulloway 210).[19] Colonel Brandon waits for Marianne's invitation into her personal space and affections before assisting in the rerouting and stabilization of her landscape by giving her his walled gardens, trees, and company on perambulations. Likewise, Mr. Knightley enters the shrubbery of Emma's heart only after it is self-redefined, deferring to her liberty of movement over whether she leaves the shrubbery alone, they leave together, or they " 'take another turn' " (*E* 429). Having repossessed the shrubbery as a feminine space and her own character through the developmental process it allegorizes, Emma rebirths herself into a larger spatial and experiential environment. She selects a spouse who "is familiar with the solid earth, and takes it at its word" (Mansell 176)—the man who willingly lives in her domestic sphere of "Hartfield" while collaborating with her in stewardship of the earth, or at least of two estates' worth of it.

The engaged Emma then completes her reconciliation with the women she has alienated by successfully reattempting her visit to Jane Fairfax. Jane functions as the protagonist's double in multiple ways, including in the quest for liberty in the landscape—the claustrophobic Jane desires " 'to be out of doors as much as [she] can' " (*E* 296). Emma begins to "walk up" the stairs into Jane's transitional interior world at the Bateses', but "a moment afterwards she was met on the stairs by Jane herself, coming eagerly forward, as if no other reception of her were felt sufficient.—Emma had never seen her look so well, so lovely, so engaging. There was consciousness, animation, and warmth" (452–453). Emma experiences the same "warm" (424) sense of renewal here as in her rejuvenated shrubbery, as if further reuniting with her better self. Like the now open Jane, she no longer needs to back herself unnaturally through the canal into the sterile uterine house of a foreclosed psyche. Rather, in identifying with and affirming Jane, Emma rejoins herself, carrying her own and others' hearts together into the expanding outer world as she completes her rebirth in this third reconciliation with a woman she has harmed.[20]

Emma achieves wholeness through reunification with herself, other women, and the linked organic worlds of nature and self-knowledge that her shrubbery has come to signify. She is now ready to participate in a female-friendly, collaborative marital relationship. Emma and Mr. Knightley will honeymoon at a fitting destination—the sea—a feminine nature image that connotes a vast horizon of possibilities, and then our precocious heroine will assume her broadened vocation of hospitable stewardship of an increased topographical and social terrain.

"The Worth of Lyme": Oceanic Anne Elliot

Elizabeth Bennet, Marianne Dashwood, and Emma Woodhouse all need to trim down their egos and diversify their angles of vision to better comprehend themselves and others. *Persuasion*'s introspective Anne Elliot, on the other hand, already empathizes with everyone almost too much, her panopticon vision of their various emotions and motivations paralleled by her all-encompassing generosity in sharing the environments she loves from the position of marginal ally. It is others who must come down off their hills and learn to compassionate their family and friends as they do themselves: Henrietta Musgrove goes "down the hill" (*P* 86) to Winthrop in a "relenting" (89) spirit and reconciles with her beloved Charles Hayter; Louisa Musgrove hurls herself off the "steep flight" at the Cobb and precipitates her transition to a calmer, more thoughtful path (109); and Wentworth gradually lowers himself from vengeful vanity toward humble understanding, like the entry down "the long hill into Lyme, and . . . the still steeper street of the town itself" (95) where, in "the scenes on the Cobb, and at Captain Harville's," he discerns Anne's "superiority" (242). Her social sensitivity is a strength founded in the self-knowledge and reflectiveness she also possesses from her bildungsroman's beginning. Her feminist values and the mixed blessing of her selflessness will be interpreted in more detail in the remaining chapters. The point here is to note how, while still fulfilling her social duty, Anne begins to redirect her primary efforts from self-obscuring service to pursuit of her own goals. She ruminates less and acts more, while using space to take small steps toward center stage of her social theater. From saturating herself in others' and her own disappointments in a macro-landscape whose cheery qualities she cannot always see, Anne works inward to enlarge her perspective, practicing the agency in social intercourse that will enhance her appreciation for the great outdoors as well.

There is an oceanic quality to Anne's personality and to the narrative point of view that often assumes her perspective. Places associated with water are fundamental to her plotline: the heroine's rejuvenation has its nascence at the seaside town of Lyme, and her sifting of society for reconfirmation of her desired spouse and friends occurs at Lyme and especially at Bath, where the hot springs attract visitors for their believed healing benefits. We previously examined how, as a skilled pianist, Anne manifests a talent for bringing people of dissonant tones into closer social harmonization; this skill also evokes the way water carries disparate elements into a more fluid coexistence and shared direction-ality.[21] She unifies the divergent people the social tides bring and imaginatively permeates their characters. "[S]he was only Anne" (5) to her nuclear family, but for her readers and social circle alike, she is the essential element. The motherless, emotionally homeless heroine occupies an ambiguous psychological space in her own and others' lives and they in hers that the narrator reproduces in readers' experience of *Persuasion*—we float along Anne's consciousness and view characters and events through her filter.[22] She conveys a depth of substance and insight that ebbs and flows among her more superficial associates with the consistency of ocean tides. Her strength emerges at key moments and carries the aimless on her own current, like a captain whose crew "look[s] to her for directions" (111), whether for childcare, recommended reading, or responding to an accident.

Anne's relationship with the outdoors commonly evokes her sympathetic identification with others and showcases her listener-supporter role. During the group outing in the countryside around Uppercross and Winthrop, Anne keeps Mary company until she wanders off and then sits "under the hedge-row" (87), overhearing Wentworth's conversation with Louisa containing his impassioned hazelnut speech: "she could imagine what Louisa was feeling" while "a bush of low rambling holly protected her" from being seen (88). Although the jilted lover in this situation, Anne vicariously identifies with Louisa. "[E]ntering into the feel-ings of" (103) Henrietta with equal sympathy as the two walk along the shore together and "glor[y] in the sea" (102), Anne agrees with her that Dr. Shirley deserves to retire to Lyme and leave a "respectable young man, as a resident curate, and was even courteous enough to hint at the advantage of such resident curate's being married" (103). The heroine displays a generous spirit in being so able to sympathize with two young women's apparent success in love, one with her former fiancé, while she has been unhappily single for eight years. The narrative description of the Lyme region emphasizes its variety of elements: bays, cliffs, high and low ground, rock, sands, woods, "and, above all, Pinny, with its green chasms between romantic rocks, where the scattered forest trees and orchards of luxuriant growth declare that many a generation must have passed away since the first partial falling of the cliff prepared the ground for such a state, where a scene so wonderful and so lovely is exhibited" (95–96). Having had a partial fall, a major personal loss that created a "green chasm between romantic rocks" in her own experience, perhaps Anne's sufferings have nurtured the soil of her abundantly caring attitude toward others, which she demonstrates again shortly after exploring these sights by commiserating with and bracing the grieving Captain Benwick and aiding the entire party during Louisa's accident. The continual oscillations between higher and lower ground, climbing upward and downward, falling and recovering, occur multiple times in the novel. It is as if Anne watches, through other people's changing altitudes—such as Mary's continual emotional dips and rises from the couch of malaise, and little Charles's and Louisa's falls and restorations—the vacillations in her own moods and hopes. By aiding others in recovering from their lowest points, Anne feels her value and somewhat helps herself. Only by the ocean that resembles, in a more joyful spirit, her own encompassing empathy does she seem to find a place that draws her out of dejection and into an exuberant immediacy. However, Anne lives too vicarious an existence. There is a self-suppression—an inner room in her heart like the "shut up" (95), "deserted and melancholy looking rooms" (96) of Lyme's buildings during post-season—that calls for expressive release.

In addition, the narrator betrays in Anne an occasional Marianne-like manipulation of the environment to wallow in despondency. She regrets moving away from Kellynch so soon because she must "forego all the influence so sweet and so sad of the autumnal months in the country" (33); reads this same sorrow in the "last smiles of the year upon the tawny leaves and withered hedges" at Uppercross (84); and even finds inspiration for fatalism after touring the beautiful variety and vitality of Lyme's natural wonders, reflecting on hearing about Captain Benwick that " 'he has not, perhaps, a more sorrowing heart than I have. I cannot believe his prospects so blighted for ever' " (97). Anne projects her dreary mood onto several different ecologies, viewing them all through the monolithic visual aesthetic of her grief and predisposed to read her "poetical despondence" (85) in any setting. Displaying a tinge of the co-dependency Austen discourages in women, the heroine needs to resist this unhealthy temptation. Despite her original reluctance to leave "her own dear country" (33) and distaste for Bath, she transitions from companionate wanderings in outdoor landscape and seascape to increasing attention to indoor spaces, which seems to facilitate redirection of her gaze from the past to the future. She has repeatedly proven her ability, anywhere, to act on behalf of others, and learns to carry that energy inward to help herself.

The heroine studies homes as models of different types of domesticity and begins to envision her own ideal household and social circle. From her family's frosty elegance at Kellynch, she moves to observation of the attractive but cluttered Uppercross Cottage and Great House of the Musgrove clan, which reflect the affectionate but conflicted relationships within and between the families. When Anne accompanies the Musgroves and Wentworth to visit Lyme and meet his naval friends, her scrutiny of the Harvilles' miniscule rental cottage at Lyme validates her taste for big hearts over big houses. After the Harvilles insist on hosting everyone for dinner but are finally convinced the preordered inn meal prevents it, the visitors enter their home and "f[ind] rooms so small as none but those who invite from the heart could think capable of accommodating so many. Anne had a moment's astonishment on the subject" but admires "all the ingenious contrivances and nice arrangements of Captain Harville" to maximize the space and "the picture of repose and domestic happiness it presented" (98). She recognizes in the tiny home a microcosm of a healthy, cohesive family that extends its love outward to others in a way that stretches space, and wishes she could count the Harvilles as friends.

By contrast, Anne rejoins her father and sister in Bath at a larger but sterile rented habitation in which, as at Kellynch, she is unloved. The arrogant Elizabeth knows she should host a dinner for the Musgroves while they visit Bath, "but she could not bear to have the difference of style, the reduction of servants, which a dinner must betray, witnessed by those who had always been so inferior to the Elliots of Kellynch" (219), so she hosts an evening party instead, minimizing her investment in others as much as possible. The least sympathetic characters—Elizabeth, Sir Walter, Mr. Elliot, Mrs. Clay, and somewhat Lady Russell—are drawn to artificial indoor spaces that reflect their preoccupation with appearances.[23] Anne's instinctive resistance of Mr. Elliot's suit foreshadows her choice against this focus on status and materialism in favor of a fluid future with Wentworth and his naval circle, whose warmhearted hominess is portable and shared.[24]

Having studied sample households to clarify her marital goals, Anne emboldens herself to strive toward attaining them by performing social theatricals of her own scripting in building interiors—of shop, assembly rooms, and hotel—transformed into momentary stages. We are moved by Anne's serial performances because they consist of spontaneous outpourings of her true feelings in decorously coded form, thus excusing the calculation employed. Her maneuverings also humorously recall the flirtatious behavior of Louisa, who had "put . . . forward for [Wentworth's] notice" (84). While out shopping at Molland's with Elizabeth and Mrs. Clay, Anne spots Wentworth through the store window and stages her first, brief show: "She now felt a great inclination to go to the outer door; she wanted to see if it rained. Why was she to suspect herself of another motive? Captain Wentworth must be out of sight. She left her seat, she would go, one half of her should not be always so much wiser than the other half, or always suspecting the other of being worse than it was. She would see if it rained" (175). Anne mocks her self-rationalizing while daring herself covertly to initiate an encounter; as intended, she runs into Wentworth coming into the shop, triggering their first conversation since the Louisa-Benwick engagement. Her part in this tableau ends with Wentworth offering her his umbrella, her politely refusing it, and Mr. Elliot arriving and escorting her away as she delivers "a gentle and embarrassed glance" with her farewell (177); then Wentworth's anonymous acquaintances chime in with chorus-like commentary on Mr. Elliot's attachment and Anne's beauty.[25] The narrator backs Anne's performance by accentuating the stagey quality of the scene, while goading Wentworth into jealousy.

Anne's role-playing initiatives continue when Wentworth enters the octagon room where she and her family are gathered before the concert: "He was preparing only to bow and pass on, but her gentle 'How do you do?' brought him out of the straight line to stand near her, and make enquiries in return, in spite of the formidable father and sister in the back ground" (181). She ignores her family and engages Wentworth in a genial conversation that reveals his reawakened interest. Anne becomes "more anxious to be encouraging" by trying to stop him from leaving the concert (" 'Is not this song worth staying for?' " [190]) and then twice communicating her disinterest in Mr. Elliot at the Musgroves' hotel. With Wentworth as primary audience, she downplays her knowledge of Mr. Elliot's travel schedule when Mary spots him still in town: " 'He has changed his hour of going,

I suppose, that is all—or I may be mistaken; I might not attend;' and [she] walked back to her chair, recomposed, and with the comfortable hope of having acquitted herself well" (223). Anne also voices emphatic preference for attending the theater with the Musgroves over the evening party featuring Mr. Elliot, while aware of Wentworth's rapt attention to her own theatrical, concluding, " 'I have no pleasure in the sort of meeting, and should be too happy to change it for a play, and with you. But, it had better not be attempted, perhaps.' She had spoken it; but she trembled when it was done, conscious that her words were listened to, and daring not even to try to observe their effect" (225). This inspires Wentworth to maneuver in kind, near enough to reminisce with Anne about her previous distaste for cards; her daring response—" 'I am not yet so much changed' " (225)—foreshadows her final performance: the famous dialogue with Captain Harville containing her pronouncement of women " 'loving longest, when existence or when hope is gone' " (235), which she tells herself Wentworth strains but is unable to hear (234).[26]

These seven performances, from running into Wentworth at a shop door to proclaiming her faithful love for him via generalities about women to Captain Harville, demonstrate the everbolder nature of Anne's coded but clear messages to her former lover. In each case, the actress preserves her feminine propriety and Wentworth's role as pursuing suitor, never crossing the line into direct declaration and displaying particularly scrupulous consideration to everyone on stage in her boldest scenes. She generates and delivers a script, choreographs her movements and predicts those of fellow players, and craves and receives audience feedback that she has achieved the intended effects—Wentworth proposes and she accepts. All of this conveys the effectiveness for Anne of being backed into a corner in both space and plot. Under the incentive of real urgency, she finds in interior spaces the courage to express herself more expansively through creative performativity, to become more like the sea she loves. Using the feminine tools of verbal abstraction, indirection, qualification, and substitution, she finds room within female decorum for strategic, even playful self-assertion. With greater confidence in her voice and the confirmed joy of the renewed engagement that finally occurs on the streets of Bath—a transitional space between indoor rooms and countryside and seaside in scale—Anne is ready to board ship and landaulette alike and recognize the range of verdant possibilities in both naturescapes.[27] It is no surprise that she selects as exploring companion the man who can overleap a "hedge in a moment" (91) and appreciates the "very fine" (183) scenery at Lyme instead of the one who yammers on about staying at the same inn and compares travel routes, as if oblivious to the natural world (143). Anne retains her caring personality, but places protective borders around her happiness, breaking away from hurtful relatives and, like Elizabeth Bennet, redrawing her family circle. Having practiced in smaller indoor settings the assertion of her needs and desires, she is ready to head back out to the seashore. Limiting her inward gaze on her own as well as others' feelings, she is better able to see renewal in the outer world, to say yes to an ocean of possibilities for herself and Wentworth.

Yet Anne's is, after eight years, a near-miss happiness. The narrator has tormented us along with the heroine and Wentworth by prolonging the suspense, repeatedly introducing disruptions to all seven of the above mini-dramas to postpone romantic closure, though each of the six interactions after the first was moving toward a proposal. After Anne's seventh strong hint is interrupted, Wentworth resorts to proposing by letter, and then the two meet up on the street and reach an understanding only by accident. In this sense, the heroine never really makes things happen; she helps them along and then limits her level of assertion, pulling back a bit into her hedge of passive observer again even as she moves eagerly forward toward the sea of love. The real world produces uncertainty as well: Julia Prewitt Brown states that "[w]hen Austen wrote" the novel "she knew she was leaving the hero and heroine about six months before Waterloo; the main action of *Persuasion* is set during the false peace" (57). Anne has discovered her ability to make tactical moves both indoors and out for her benefit as well as for others. She now sees beyond autumnal empathy to room for herself in an ocean of bliss. However, she still trusts too much in unpredictable conditions, ultimately "leav[ing] things to take their course" (*P* 221) in her love life, as if "watch[ing] the flowing of the tide" (102). Perhaps this letting go may itself reflect the heroine's acceptance of the real world's instability. As Mrs. Croft matter-of-factly states, " 'We none of us expect to be in smooth water all our days' " (70).

Conclusion: Sustaining the Self

Austen brilliantly illustrates a complex interdependent relationship between women and nature in which the landscape or seascape of their identity functions as simultaneously a medium, projection, and symbol for their clarification of self.[28] The interplay between heroines and distinct nature elements in Austen's novels offers readers a revelatory way to trace and co-experience their organic inner lives. Whether earth, leaf, shrub, or ocean, these women's eco-affinities speak to and about them and their ways of growing as individual and social beings. Elizabeth Bennet, Marianne Dashwood, Emma Woodhouse, and Anne Elliot come to understand that they must diversify their vision of the world in order to strike a sustainable relationship between their individual selves and their society and environment alike.[29] This involves looking both within and beyond the self, as aided by alternating occupation of larger and smaller, higher and lower spaces. As Susan Morgan aptly states, "Growing up is learning that the self does not encompass the entire world. It is a sort of shrinking into definable shape" (*Meantime* 38). Austen depicts parallels between women and the environment that promote a conservationist cultivation, a carefully cultured wildness, a combined tradition and diversification that enables sustainability amid and because of flux and change. Both the individual and nature need room for and guidance in optimal ongoing growth. After Anne's static isolation in an alienating home and family, the flux of a naval life will likely energize her, whereas after Marianne Dashwood's wild fluctuations of emotion on hill and down dale, she will enjoy the serenity and relative insularity of a self-reliant estate that has "every thing . . . that one could wish for" (*SS* 197). Yet both heroines, along with the rest, may need or be required to face another dramatic change in space and self-discovery down the road in order to keep growing.

Nature becomes a sacramental vehicle for redemptive self-transformation through the heroine's expanded experience in, of, and through it, in an ever-widening landscape or seascape of the self that highlights the reciprocity of the human–nature relationship in Austen's fiction. One can certainly imagine that if Jane Austen and her heroines lived among us today, they would oppose such aberrations as industrial-chemical toxification and GMOs, and would buy local organic produce, fill their yards with climate-suitable trees and plants, and promote cleaner air and waters.[30] While Austen might leave the tree-hugging to Marianne Dashwood and Fanny Price, she unequivocally conveys that preservation of the environment is critical to female self-knowledge and that society's future depends on the literal and figurative fruits of women's self-cultivation in diversified naturescapes.

CHAPTER 7

"What is the foolish girl about?"

Austen's Feminist Fools Speak Out

Just as Austen's women articulate and reshape themselves through physical space as a topography of their interior lives, so, too, does their occupation of the dialogic space of society represent in distinctive ways the author's own expression of her gendered ideological landscape. One of her most compelling methods is the use of dismissible characters as the mouthpiece for social protest. Austen's obnoxious or undiscerning female characters, like Shakespeare's fools, voice truths that can be easily heard by those who are open to receiving them or ignored by those who wish to reject or suppress those truths. Austen relies on a combination of direct and indirect rhetorical modes to interrogate specific social norms. She puts explicit feminist commentary into the speech of typecast female fools and of heroines at their most immature stage of development, thus permitting their fellow characters as well as readers to discount it as lacking credibility.[1] This illusion of superiority and control may render such fools less threatening and draw listeners into inadvertent attention to their claims, which are often reiterated in the more respectably feminine packaging of proper heroines' more restrained and coded language. Thereby, the author connects with a culture in which the promulgated feminine ideal was much closer to a Jane Fairfax than an Elizabeth Bennet: a virtuosa of elegant self-abdication, almost a still life.[2] Parallel assertions of gender injustice that differ in degree, timing, or manner produce a kind of syncopated lyrical score in which seemingly divergent individual tones are homophonic. This ingenious literary technique is easy to miss, but Austen's most blatant fools and her sweetest ingénues speak on critical issues with one voice.[3]

All of Austen's novels contain fools of different kinds, genders, ages, and functions, including such laughable characters as Mr. Collins, Mrs. Bennet, Robert Ferrars, Mrs. Palmer, John Thorpe, Mr. Rushworth, Lady Bertram, Miss Bates, Mr. Woodhouse, and Sir Walter Elliot.[4] John Lauber provides a useful catalogue of Austenian types, such as the "snob," the "rattle" and the "puppy" (borrowing Austen's terms), the "insipid fool," the "bore," the "learned fool," the "noisy fool," the "malignant" and "languid" fools, and even the "holy fool" ("Fools" 512–524). The effective portrayal of such multifarious foolish figures depends upon the author's artful isolation and magnification of a universal human foible; this defamiliarization of an unmistakable human weakness preserves the ironic distance essential to readers' enjoyment of comedy.[5]

The group of characters I denote "feminist fools" manifest an understated intelligence and keen cognizance of gender bias but are undercut by their absurd comportment, lifestyle choice, or blind spot—the "tick" that lends humor, irony, or even a touch of tragedy to their characters as it appears to separate them from the nobler heroine.[6] Pedantic Mary Bennet, materialist Charlotte Lucas, meddling Mrs. Elton, whiny Mary Musgrove, and even naïve Catherine Morland are all physically plain as well; the narratorial derogation of women's appearances accentuates their defining defect of character in the comic tradition while further enabling auditors who are uncomfortable with their proclamations to disregard them in favor of a more admirable character's apparently more palatable but equivalent convictions. We have seen how old, fat, garrulous Mrs. Jennings and her silly daughter know and live out the only emotionally healthy lifestyle available to women of their time, while Elinor Dashwood lectures Marianne about her similar views but fails wholly to live them out (chapter 3), and how Mrs. Jennings invites her guests to "laugh at [her] odd ways" (*SS* 154) while she freely broadcasts her opinions with little or no filter. The exaggeration of a foolish character's flaw or eccentricity by the narrator or the woman herself invites others to relegate her to a one-dimensional caricature that they can tolerate from the safe distance of mockery, as if sensing a peripheral noise they need not heed. In addition, the fool's pronouncement of her truth claim in social discourse is often inappropriate, whether in its timing or application, producing a disjointure that conveniently frames and excuses her offense against patriarchal gender conventions as it offsets the seeming propriety of the "better" woman—the heroine who, in fact, shares her stance.[7]

Thus, for example, self-described " 'noisy evil' " (*MP* 289) Mary Crawford serves as the flippant "feminist fool" to Fanny Price's decorously downplayed subversion in *Mansfield Park*.[8] Mary announces on her delinquent return of Fanny's horse that " 'Nothing ever fatigues me, but doing what I do not like' " and boasts that " 'Selfishness must always be forgiven . . . because there is no hope of a cure,' " yet Fanny shares the same conviction of her right to do as she chooses and likewise experiences "fatigue" whenever doing what she "do[es] not like" (68). She particularly dislikes sharing Edmund with Mary. Whereas Mary declares her belief in a life philosophy of selfishness, Fanny's rare verbalization of her similar belief in her free will seems more narrowly focused on a woman's liberty to refuse unwelcome marriage proposals (and, by extension, to marry the man of her choice), a more acceptable view during Austen's time:

> 'I *should* have thought,' said Fanny [to Edmund],
> after a pause of recollection and exertion, 'that every
> woman must have felt the possibility of a man's not
> being approved, not being loved by some one of her
> sex, at least, let him be ever so generally agreeable.
> Let him have all the perfections in the world, I think
> it ought not to be set down as certain, that a man
> must be acceptable to every woman he may happen
> to like himself.' (353)

The narrator may insist that the demure Fanny must "exert" herself to make this pointed observation to Edmund, but she has been harangued by three men in collusion against her will, including him, and he has just mentioned Mary Crawford and Mrs. Grant's displeasure at her refusing Henry. Fanny perceives that Edmund uses the absent Mary as coercive leverage to advance his own agenda for both women. Her joint betrayal by Edmund and Mary incites her response; she seethes with anger and sarcasm and directs her retort to the man, not the woman.[9] Although Mary openly insists on her way according to the pleasure principle while Fanny more abstractly channels her desire through the argument for a woman's right of individual feeling and prefer-ence, Fanny is as surely speaking of herself, and both women argue for the same thing—self-determination. " '[V]itiated' " (456) Mary and virtuous Fanny react against an embattled system that conspires against their fulfillment, whether that fulfillment arises from despicable or admirable desires and whether it pits them against one another or not. Fanny's declaration of independence quoted above comes later than Mary's and is less direct, but communicates a more resentful tone and almost as obvious an application. Her transparent speech is lost on Edmund, however, who reinterprets it to mean what he chooses in a decontextual-ized assertion of presumptuous, though ultimately impotent, male volition. Both women set up their "I" as implicitly at odds with the pervasive "he" that Edmund represents and whose polarizing effect on their relationship he enacts.

The commonality of Mary and Fanny's frustrated position, despite differences of income and character, surfaces not only in their shared experience of expressing their will and being contradicted or held in suspension, but also in Mary's hilarious satire on female accomplishment. While Edmund extends his visit to a friend who has three marriageable sisters, both Mary and Fanny pretend not to care, the former by asking questions and imagining scenarios and the latter by denying any interest in their new competition for Edmund. Mary asks about the Miss Owens' musical background, and Fanny states with negative emphasis, " 'I do not at all know. I never heard' " (288), as if to erase the trio. Mary's responding hypothesis is revealing:

> 'That is the first question, you know,' said Miss Craw-
> ford, trying to appear gay and unconcerned, 'which
> every woman who plays herself is sure to ask about
> another. But it is very foolish to ask questions about
> any young ladies—about any three sisters just grown
> up; for one knows, without being told, exactly what
> they are—all very accomplished and pleasing, and *one*
> very pretty. There is a beauty in every family.—It is a
> regular thing. Two play on the piano-forte, and one
> on the harp—and all sing—or would sing if they were
> taught—or sing all the better for not being taught—or
> something like it.' (288)

Again, Fanny answers with negation: " 'I know nothing of the Miss Owens.' " In her glib critique of the conventions of female accomplishment, "foolish" questioner Mary parodies the empty discourse that negates the acknowledgment of genuine excellence in women by leveling any diversity among them as further evidence of their homogeneity. She exposes the condescension behind the masquerade of good-natured flattery toward women who are always already typecast into predictable variations of a monolithic, illusory perfection—" 'one knows . . . exactly what they are—all very accomplished and pleasing' " (288). The pause indicated by the dash after "what they are" sets up the generic characterization. Mary expresses her individuality by citing criteria as normative that she does not consistently meet. Although she exemplifies the "*one* very pretty" sister and the "one" who plays "on the harp," she represents one of only two half-sisters and knows full well that she is not always "very pleasing" (288). Fanny resists social expectations by refusing to play at all, early rejecting music and drawing lessons for the book-learning that contributes to her vocation. Any time it would require compromising her principles or wished-for alliance, Fanny, as tenaciously as Mary, forfeits being "pleasing."

As *Mansfield Park*'s improper Mary Crawford proclaims her prerogative actively to achieve her wishes while proper Fanny Price implies her negative right as "some one of her sex" (353) to refuse what she does not wish, other pairings of fools and heroines in Austen's novels also present seemingly contrasting but kin models of female truth-telling amid a society defined by gender double-standards. In *Pride and Prejudice*, several fools speak to the gender concerns that protagonist Elizabeth Bennet likewise confronts within a conspiratorial system of male entitlement. Lady Catherine de Bourgh's brassy self-consequence emanates from her status as a wealthy widow for whom, as for heiress Emma Woodhouse, money has purchased a rare level of female authority. She critiques male inheritance laws during a conversation about the entailment of Longbourn: " 'For your sake,' turning to Charlotte, 'I am glad of it; but otherwise I see no occasion for entailing estates from the female line' " (*PP* 164).

Lady Catherine claims to be "glad" about the Bennet entail only because it benefits Charlotte, not Mr. Collins, and rejects the practice of deflecting wealth from women in favor of men. She also proves prophetic in questioning the wisdom of the younger Bennets being prematurely " 'out before the elder are married' " (165), a reaction that anticipates Lydia's " 'infamous elopement' " (357) with Wickham and its threat to Elizabeth's and Jane's marriageability. Lady Catherine's realism about a limited and biased marriage market is further reinforced by her criticisms of the inadequacy of the Bennet girls' education and their resulting dearth of accomplishments: " '[I]f I had known your mother, I should have advised her most strenuously to engage [a governess]. I always say that nothing is to be done in education without steady and regular instruction, and nobody but a governess can give it' " (165). She urges Elizabeth to become a better pianist: " 'I have told Miss Bennet several times, that she will never play really well, unless she practises more' " (173).

Lady Catherine's indecorum in delivering blunt, unsolicited advice on multiple subjects to a new acquaintance seems to justify Elizabeth in her equally frank pronouncements. Implying agreement with her host regarding women's restrictive choices but not in the best response to them, she defends her sisters' " 'right to the pleasures of youth' " considering that " 'the elder may not have the means or inclination to marry early' " and provokes Lady Catherine's surprised reaction: " '[Y]ou give your opinion very decidedly for so young a person' " (165–166). Darcy's pompous aunt believes in and even seeks to further equality for women, when pursuit of their ends does not conflict with her will, similar to her obstinate nephew. Elizabeth speaks to both in the same style, telling Darcy regarding his first proposal that " 'I have never desired your good opinion, and you have certainly bestowed it most unwillingly' " (190) and later informing Lady Catherine regarding the potential marriage that " 'I am only resolved to act in that manner, which will, in my own opinion, constitute my happiness, without reference to *you*, or to any person so wholly unconnected with me' " (358). More blatantly than does Fanny Price, Elizabeth Bennet claims her right to subjectivity and to fulfillment for her own sake. She and Lady Catherine are kindred spirits in their sometimes overemphatic self-assertion, as if they overcompensate for a culture that privileges male self-interest. Both women test others through this feminist trumpeting—Lady Catherine measures their malleability to her power, and Elizabeth tests Darcy's marriageability. Elizabeth's declamations seem softened by their greater justification and her greater likeability, but she demands liberty of word and deed with as much boldness and goes through a superiority complex nearly as pompous as that of her more absurd oratorical double.[10] What redeems Elizabeth is what the lady who caricatures her central vice cannot or will not achieve—the acknowledgment of her pride in an opinionatedness divorced from justice.

In addition to increasing the heroine's awareness of the social demands and dangers of a male-centric society, Lady Catherine also benefits the socioeconomic interests of another woman (who could have been Elizabeth if she had acquiesced) by urging Mr. Collins to marry—sad fool Charlotte Lucas. Charlotte shares with her patroness a cynical pragmatism in promoting women's strategizing as best they can within an unfair system. She also resembles Lady Catherine in her prophetic role in Elizabeth's life, having rightly predicted of Jane Bennet that " 'a woman had better shew *more* affection than she feels' " (22) to avoid " 'los[ing] the opportunity of fixing' " (21) her man. Jane's subtlety does leave Bingley open to Darcy's claims of her "indifference" (199) and result in a separation that easily could have been permanent. Elizabeth indirectly admits the veracity of both women's prognostications, conceding to Lady Catherine that the Bennet sisters' lack of formal lessons meant that " '[t]hose who chose to be idle, certainly might' " (165) and later recognizing in Darcy's misinterpretation of Jane's "composure" (21) some validation of Charlotte's viewpoint (208). When the disappointed Jane remarks that " 'Women fancy admiration means more than it does,' " Elizabeth retorts, " 'And men take care that they should' " (136), reinforcing her agreement with Charlotte and Lady Catherine regarding women's vulnerability in the courtship game. Charlotte believes women should play the game, too, checkmating men's dishonesty with self-protective playacting of their own. Righteous ingénue Elizabeth disassociates herself from her friend's argument for women's counter-deception to "secure" a man, stating, " 'You know it is not sound, and that you would never act in this way yourself' " (23). She reveals her naïveté regarding her less marriageable friend's position and the depth of conflicts and temptations a gender-biased marriage market produces, while acknowledging that bias and its aberrant conventionalization of men's deception of women. Still a "fool" in her immaturity and smug knowingness early in the novel, Elizabeth does not grasp the implications of the truths she voices in common with her apparent foils. Sad fool Charlotte Lucas takes her more extreme philosophy too far by insisting on marrying a fool herself, thereby undercutting her intelligence and coloring Elizabeth's feminist outrage with comparative virtue and moderation. Charlotte's deliberate distortion of a knowledge she, Elizabeth, and Lady Catherine share produces its own punishment in the limits of a self-abnegation that denies her emotional nurture in favor of "an establishment" (122).

The point is not that Austen's dismissible women are always correct in the way they frame or apply truths, but that they more flagrantly expose the gender discrimination with which the heroine also grapples. After Lydia's elopement, Elizabeth employs coded linguistic gaps and vague clichés to voice her concern to a newly considerate Darcy: " 'She has no money, no connections, nothing that can tempt him to—she is lost for ever. . . . I have not the smallest hope. It is every way horrible!' " (277). Significantly, Mary Bennet expresses this dire view in similarly unoriginal language, though her parroting of conduct-book aphorisms sounds more heartlessly condemnatory: " 'Unhappy as the event must be for Lydia, we may draw from it this useful lesson; that loss of virtue in a female is irretrievable—that one false step involves her in endless ruin—that her reputation is no less brittle than it is beautiful,—and that she cannot be too much guarded in her behaviour towards the undeserving of the other sex' " (289). The sisters make the same point. Mary both corroborates Elizabeth's justification for anxiety and sets off her more sincere and compassionate tone. While "one false step" does not quite lead to "endless ruin" for Lydia, she barely gains an indifferent rake for a husband who collaborates with her only in living by selfish impulse in a relationship whose unlikelihood of long-term success Elizabeth "could easily conjecture" (312).

The combined advice of Lady Catherine, Charlotte Lucas, and Mary Bennet heightens Elizabeth's and readers' awareness of women's precarious place in a society in which the diligent pursuit of feminine accomplishments such as piano and drawing and even of virtues such as being modestly "too much guarded" like Jane Bennet can prove as likely to produce disappointment as outright scandalous behavior, though of a different order. Although Elizabeth opposes her more foolish foils' pragmatic amorality, she agrees with them regarding the economic, educational, and romantic disadvantages women face. However, the fools mostly respond to women's precariousness by encouraging strategic cooperation with the biased status quo, reciting their words as if delivered almost disembodied from their consciousness: "practise more," "shew more affection," shun "the undeserving of the other sex," and be, as Mary Crawford describes society's generic feminine ideal, "very accomplished and pleasing." Though flawed, Elizabeth speaks from a more authentic connection to her words as a holistic female subject. Fools naming truths are often impotent by themselves; they gain ideological and literary impact by their similitude to the more sympathetic heroine, whose forceful remarks sound more moderate in the context of others' tactless speeches. Whereas the fools often transgress the bounds of courtesy, volunteering judgments critical of others, the righteous heroine responds to provocation. The collective repetition of both female types' common feminist ideology through their divergent voices—one apparently discredited and the other sanctioned—increases its likelihood of permeating unsuspecting listeners' consciousness.

Mrs. Elton functions as a "feminist fool" for Emma in much the same way that Lady Catherine does for Elizabeth Bennet. Both Mrs. Elton and Lady Catherine parade and parody a female power defined by unwelcome imposition, which makes both characters dismissible as performers in the carnival of Austen's fictional society.[11] Their assumption of an omnipotence that encompasses such minute and inappropriately personal concerns as instructing Charlotte on the care of her cows and chickens or offering to select as well as invite the guests for Mr. Knightley's strawberry-picking party neutralizes the horror of their strident authoritarianism in laughter at their insatiable intrusiveness.

In keeping with Austen's method, overbearing narcissist Mrs. Elton functions as the novelist's most outspoken proponent of female solidarity. She declares to Mr. Weston, " 'I always take the part of my own sex. I do indeed. I give you notice—You will find me a formidable antagonist on that point. I always stand up for women' " (*E* 306). Kindhearted Mr. Weston is not one of the several men in Highbury society most in need of chastening into greater respect for women. The provocation for Mrs. Elton's warning—his questioning the changeable nature of Mrs. Churchill's health and reference to " 'delicate ladies hav[ing] very extraordinary constitutions'" (306)—is incidentally sexist, but understandable as an attempt to blame someone other than his son for neglect. Mrs. Elton makes her insincere declaration of loyalty to her sex as applied to a stranger and contradicts it in her behavior toward women she knows: Harriet, Emma, and Jane Fairfax. And yet, Mrs. Churchill does turn out to be terminally ill rather than a "delicate lady" with a fictional "extraordinary constitution." In addition, although Mrs. Elton assists Jane Fairfax from the desire to control others and aggrandize herself, she finds Jane a job and thereby motivates Frank to reveal their engagement and expedite their marriage in the aftermath of Mrs. Churchill's death. This effect resembles (though in a less cruel and more effective way) the manner in which Mrs. Norris's aggressive interest in Fanny Price elicits Edmund's return of attention to her. More significantly, Mrs. Elton's assertion of opposed convictions mimics in bipolar fashion Austen's pairing of fools and heroines to convey feminist messages alongside more traditional feminine values.[12] Her pretense of submission to the husband she dominates demonstrates this pattern. Mrs. Elton vocalizes the importance of a supportive female community in a sexist culture, but compromises her credibility as a comic sham. As demonstrated in chapter 5, it is equally bold (though usually more decorous) Emma who learns to live out this principle, developing a spirit of genuine solidarity with other women and transforming from manipulating Harriet and neglecting the Bates women and Jane to supporting all of them in the free pursuit of their own paths. She chooses as model the "fool of God" Miss Bates with her "saintly simplicity" (Lauber, "Fools" 521) rather than self-promoting gadabout Mrs. Elton.

Before this amendment, Emma experiences a fool phase as well, in which she does not promote conflicting creeds like Mrs. Elton, but both speaks truths and reveals blind spots that overshadow her asserted convictions (most notably by manipulating Harriet and insulting Miss Bates).[13] When Mr. Knightley comments on Harriet's foolishness in her initial refusal of Mr. Martin, exclaiming, " 'What is the foolish girl about?' " (*E* 60), his outburst also applies to the immature, interfering Emma. He fails to grasp the import of her role as a "foolish girl" and must learn its feminist implications, as demonstrated in her successful test of him via Harriet discussed in chapter 2. Emma later looks back on her former self and tells Mr. Knightley that " 'at that time I was a fool' " (474), as if to discredit her past declarations in light of her subsequent growth. In fact, the opposite is true. Although Emma has become more perceptive and disinterested, endorsing the Harriet–Robert Martin alliance and supporting others' aspirations, she never negates her previous, biting gender generalizations, whether regarding men's objectification of women or women's right to marital self-determination. She lives out these very convictions by challenging and then choosing the humbled Mr. Knightley. He must first learn from Emma the " '[n]onsensical girl!' " (214), a phrase he employs affectionately, and then asks Emma the " 'woman' " to marry him (430), volunteering to move into her house, a sacrificial gesture of more than equality or acceptance but of affirming and meeting her where she is.

It is paradigmatic of Austen's methodology that Emma's designation of her more outspoken former self as "a fool" signals the legitimacy of her pronouncements in that role. Though wrong in particulars, such as regarding desirable romantic pairings, Emma-as-fool proves correct throughout the novel in her theory of the misogynistic system of courtship and marriage in her culture. She lives in a world that preserves conditions known to produce torturous social anxiety for single women who lack either status, money, or sex appeal, such as Harriet, Jane Fairfax, and the Bates women (who lack all three advantages).[14] Even prosperous but unattractive vulgarian Mrs. Elton displays a forced self-complacence in her purchased marriage—another form of selling out—that resembles the emotional self-deadening of Charlotte Lucas. That Emma succeeds in circumventing her society's entrenched pitfalls for women with her selfhood intact accentuates at once Emma's exceptionality and the treachery of the social order all women inhabit.

The most important "feminist fool" in all of Austen's fiction appears in her final completed novel. Mary Musgrove of *Persuasion* dares to utter the most explicit, detailed commentary on domestic inequality and the stereotyped assumptions underlying it. In this respect, Mary is the novel's covert heroine and the author's foremost conduit for persuading the reader of her egalitarian ideology. The author's female commentators on sexism in the earlier novels publicize their concerns over gender bias in courtship, definitions of accomplishment, inheritance laws, personal agency, and self-expression; they all also happen to be single, married with no children, or widowed with grown children.

The spokeswoman of Austen's last finished novel, on the other hand, gets into the grit of daily life and exposes the hypocritical double-standards in the expected conduct and sentiments of mothers as directly contrasted with fathers. Although as a self-absorbed hypochondriac, Mary Musgrove somewhat resembles Mrs. Bennet, she employs more precision and logic in her complaints, cutting through her surface vexation to the core problem of male entitlement.[15] The fact that Mary Musgrove, unlike Mrs. Bennet, has never possessed any physical beauty (disturbing her father with her "coarse" complexion [*P* 6, 142]) also indicates a more emphatic narrative discrediting of her on a surface level to offset her higher intelligence and more controversial contentions. Charles Musgrove, like Mr. Bennet, sadistically exercises his power to make his wife unhappy, "tak[ing] delight in vexing" her (*PP* 5). Mary chafes against the mandate of a female domesticity in which she feels perpetually left behind. She resents and is ever alert to the prospect of being denied a full life—to deprivation of pleasures and experiences that seem a birthright of manhood. She confronts a kind of experiential entail that generations of patriarchs have inscribed in heirs and their less fortunate sisters.

Meanwhile, Mary's "almost too good" (23–25 March 1817)[16] sister Anne Elliot appears through her surface speech and some actions to accept categorical female roles as natural and ordained, thereby establishing within the text a safe mooring of condescending approval for Austen's chauvinistic male readers and of identification for her anxiously compliant female readers. The "too excellent creature" (*P* 237) gently lectures her younger sister on a woman's duty and offers "hints" intended "for her . . . benefit" (46), while readers who reject Mary's feminism imaginatively join righteous Anne in gazing down on her knowingly, tsk-tsking with tender deprecation.

The most significant example of Mary's—and arguably the author's—feminist truth-speaking occurs in chapter 7 of *Persuasion*, which brings into sharp relief the gender double-standard in parenting and the assumption of male privilege that bolsters it. Mary and Anne are beginning their trek to the Great House for a visit, when they are immediately pulled back to the Cottage, "stopped by the eldest boy's being at that moment brought home in consequence of a bad fall" which "put the visit entirely aside" (53). The narrator sets up the gender conflict at the heart of this chapter by showing the mother being prevented from leaving the house by the child, whereas the independent father, already out in the world of action, must be "pursued and informed" (53). At first, little Charles's dislocated collar bone and potentially serious back injury cause both parents to be unified in their desire to stay home and care for their child rather than attending a dinner party at the Great House the next day to meet the much-discussed Captain Wentworth: " 'Oh, no! as to leaving the little boy!'—both father and mother were in much too strong and recent alarm to bear the thought; and Anne, in the joy of the escape, could not help adding her warm protestations to theirs" (55).

However, by the very next sentence, which begins a new paragraph, the father is changing his mind in favor of pleasure for himself and laying the groundwork with Mary for his already intended desertion: "Charles Musgrove, indeed, afterwards shewed more of inclination; 'the child was going on so well—and he wished so much to be introduced to Captain Wentworth, that, perhaps, he might join them in the evening; he would not dine from home, but he might walk in for half an hour.' But in this he was eagerly opposed by his wife" (55). Here, Charles minimizes his pending escape from his son's sickbed by framing it as a possible thirty-minute drop-in at his parents' place after dining at home; the presentation of his speech in free indirect discourse accentuates his artifice and emotional detachment from his family. In the third paragraph of the Mary-Charles conflict, the boy has continued to improve into the next day, and the narrator enters the father's mind to register his inward reaction: although "it must be a work of time" to determine the state of the boy's spine, the apothecary "found nothing to increase alarm, and Charles Musgrove began consequently to feel no necessity for longer confinement. The child was to be kept in bed, and amused as quietly as possible; but what was there for a father to do? This was quite a female case, and it would be highly absurd in him, who could be of no use at home, to shut himself up" (55); Charles also tells himself that his father wants him to attend the dinner. This interior monologue is both his self-justification and a rehearsal of his next, more provoking speech to Mary. The fact that he invests effort in composing a script to delude himself into feeling warranted in neglecting his son manifests not only his anticipation of further wifely opposition, but his awareness of the parental duty he dodges. Only readers are privy to Charles's thoughts, as if conspiring with him and the narrator behind Mary's back, but this information serves to confirm the accuracy of her interpretation of his selfish maneuvering. In reality, the narrator and Mary are conspiring against Charles and resistive readers to expose his—and through him these readers'—male chauvinism.

Charles delivers the "bold public declaration" (55) in the next paragraph that he will go to his parents' dinner, contradicting his previous proposition of a brief post-meal visit. He recites to Mary several of the arguments he had rehearsed in his head, pointing out their son's progress and his father's approval of his plan, as if buttressing his position with patriarchal approval, and concluding with the kicker, " 'Your sister being with you, my love, I have no scruple at all. You would not like to leave him yourself, but you see I can be of no use. Anne will send for me if any thing is the matter' " (55). Charles imputes to Mary feelings that suit his convenience and exploits her female supporter, Anne, as his implicit replacement to justify entrapping both women in the tedium he evades, while betraying his assumption that parenting should be a two-person job. By dipping into his private consciousness as well as sharing his spoken words through quoting of direct and indirect discourse, the narrator reveals and satirizes Charles's carefully constructed rationalization for doing what he wishes, which is to seek swift liberty from the self-acknowledged "confinement" of being "shut up" with an injured child at home in favor of a lively gathering elsewhere.

Then follows Mary's protest speech to Anne, which appears halfway through the account of the boy's accident and the couple's conflict surrounding it, as if to endow the speech with pivotal importance to the subplot and its purpose:

> 'So! You and I are to be left to shift by ourselves, with this poor sick child—and not a creature coming near us all the evening! I knew how it would be. This is always my luck! If there is any thing disagreeable going

on, men are always sure to get out of it, and Charles
is as bad as any of them. Very unfeeling! I must say it
is very unfeeling of him, to be running away from his
poor little boy. . . . So, here he is to go away and enjoy
himself, and because I am the poor mother, I am not
allowed to stir;—and yet. . . . My being the mother is
the very reason why my feelings should not be tried.
I am not at all equal to it. You saw how hysterical I
was yesterday.' (56)

Mary begins her invective by including Anne as sharing with her
in women's marginalization, then shifts to total self-absorption
from the next sentence, bemoaning the systemic injustice to herself of Charles's male prerogative. She refers to her son as "this
poor sick child" and to herself as "the poor mother" in a generic
manner that underlines their representative function in a society
that imposes restrictive typecasting on mothers (while she insinu-
ates the possessive pronoun into the phrase "his poor little boy"
to highlight Charles's abjuration of his paternal responsibilities).
However, Mary also employs that very stereotype of maternal
sensibility to reverse Charles's logic, claiming in rehearsing her
counter-argument to Anne that the dedicated-as-"hysterical"
mother is more justified in being spared the sickroom than the
father. Anne responds by first reassuring Mary that all will be
well, then briefly introducing the gender party line: " '. . . I cannot
wonder at your husband. Nursing does not belong to a man, it
is not his province. A sick child is always the mother's property,
her own feelings generally make it so' " (56). Mary noncommit-
tally " 'hope[s]' " she feels as much affection for her son " 'as any
mother' " and adds that " 'I do not know that I am of any more
use in the sick-room than Charles' " (56), reminding Anne that
little Charles habitually disobeys her. Likewise, throughout the
rest of her dialogue with Anne and then her husband on this

subject, Mary redirects the focus from an abstract debate over gender roles that she intuits she cannot win, to a trenchant comparison between herself and her husband.

This pattern becomes more clear when one studies the remaining dialogue of the subplot with the interspersed narrative and some of Mary's commentary removed and surveys her repetition of a forcibly paralleled female "I" with a male "he" and "you." Alison G. Sulloway names Austen as among those female novelists who borrowed " 'the HE . . . she' substructure that shaped feminist discourse" of her time, which interrogated "what 'HE' could do, and why throughout history 'HE' had been permitted to do it, and what 'she' could not do, and all the myths and all the masculine assumptions about feminine utility that had perpetuated women's predicament" (78). Note that in Mary's concluding statement to Anne and climactic follow-up declaration to Charles, she incorporates borrowed pieces of Charles's own language, as if to reinforce the similarity in their positions.[17] Most significantly, Mary even mysteriously manages to include two phrases from his unspoken thoughts (the words she recycled from his speech are underlined, with her variations or additions in brackets, and the words she impossibly usurped from his thoughts are also in bold):

> ANNE: "But, could you be comfortable yourself, to be spending the whole evening away from the poor boy?"

> MARY: "Yes; you see his papa can, and why should not I? . . . I am not more alarmed about little Charles now than he is. I was dreadfully alarmed yesterday, but the case is very different to-day."

> ANNE: "Well—if you do not think it too late to give notice for yourself, suppose you were to go, as well

as your husband. Leave little Charles to my care. Mr. and Mrs. Musgrove cannot think it wrong, while I remain with him."

MARY: ". . . To be sure I may just as well go as not, for I [am] of no use **at home**—am I? . . . You, who have not a mother's feelings, are a great deal the properest person. . . . I will certainly go; I am sure I ought if I can, quite as much as Charles. . . . You can send for [us, you know, at a moment's notice,] if any thing is the matter. . . . I should not go, you may be sure, if I did not feel quite at ease about my dear child."

[. . .]

MARY: "I mean to go with you, Charles, for [I am] of no [more] use **at home** than you are. If I were to **shut [my]self up** for ever with the child, I should not be able to persuade him to do any thing he did not like. Anne will stay; Anne undertakes to stay at home and take care of him. It is Anne's own proposal, and so I shall go with you, which will be a great deal better, for I have not dined at the other house since Tuesday."

CHARLES: "This is very kind of Anne . . . and I should be very glad to have you go; but it seems rather hard that she should be left at home by herself, to nurse our sick child." (56–58)

Including the previously quoted asseverations and the exchanges immediately above, Mary makes a total of at least five statements comparing herself to Charles in the "little Charles" subplot—four to Anne and one to Charles. This subplot explores the adult Charles's "littleness" of character as a central theme, albeit as exposed by Mary's reactive littleness. Mary rehearses her stance prior to broaching it to the spouse, as he has done, but she practices longer and before the live audience of the sister who releases her from the "confinement" of her maternal role. For example, both parents claim to be of "no use," but Charles delivers the point once in his head and then pronounces it once to Mary, as if he feels more entitled to parental ineptitude at the sickbed as a badge of masculinity, whereas Mary twice tries on the descriptor in discussions with Anne before proclaiming it to Charles. Mary's parting speech to Anne as she goes to perform the practiced script on her husband also imitates his parting words to her after announcing his decision—she not only describes herself as "of no use" but also repeats his remark that Anne can "send for" them "if any thing is the matter" (55, 57). She usurps the script he had used to incarcerate her and employs it to liberate herself, while further reminding Anne and the reader of the couple's likeness and shared right to equality. The silliness and inconsistency of Charles's case for his entitlement reflect "Austen's expos[ure of] the egotism behind arguments for male supremacy by portraying men who make such claims as fools and buffoons" (Bilger 141). In this respect, Charles Musgrove is as much a "fool" as Mary is.

Yet more noteworthy is Mary's vocalization of two phrases from Charles's inner monologue—to be useless "at home" and to "shut [one]self up"—as if she penetrates the male conspiracy in his heart (55, 57). Together and in context, these two thoughts that Mary lifted from Charles's private consciousness emphasize the loneliness and claustrophobia of the mother's solitary burden, of which the narrator and the mother jointly expose the father's cognizance. Perhaps Mary is able to invoke her husband's lexis because it is already well known to her from his previous abdications, but Austen implies that he merely takes advantage of a script provided him by a patriarchal society that has assigned him the preferential role in an absurdist gender theatrical.

In addition, these critical dialogues regarding gender-defined parental roles manifest a subtle over-arching perspectival parallel between two seemingly opposite sisters. Both Mary and Anne make conformist feminine speeches that seem half-hearted and obligatory in light of the women's behavior. After Mary gains release to go out through Anne, her concluding punchline of their discussion is to aver that " 'I should not go, you may be sure, if I did not feel quite at ease about' " the son whom she happily reclaims as " 'my dear child' " (57), now that she can join his father in "running away from" him (56). She assures Anne of her motherly devotion and Charles that it was Anne's idea that she go out, repeating her sister's name three times to emphasize her substitutionary caregiver role. Anne has become the willing scapegoat for both father and mother, the only responsible parent. However, the narrator also undercuts Anne's image of devotion to her traumatized nephew, indicating that she mechanically inhabits the sick-nurse role while totally preoccupied with thoughts of her former lover. The chapter begins by describing Captain Wentworth's expected visit to Uppercross and Anne's consequent disquiet, and even the second paragraph that introduces the child's accident concludes that "she could not hear of her escape [from seeing Wentworth] with indifference, even in the midst of the serious anxiety which they afterwards felt on [little Charles's] account" (53). After some exposition about the child, the narrator returns to the subject of Wentworth and describes other family members' enthusiastic admiration for him, as if heard through Anne's consciousness. Then Mary's previously quoted dialogues with Anne and Charles occur, and after Anne urges the couple on their way, she only briefly remembers her charge before ruminating on Wentworth again, whom she encounters within the next two pages and who becomes the focus of the chapter's remainder. The narrator quips,

"She knew herself to be of the first utility to the child; and what was it to her, if Frederick Wentworth were only half a mile distant, making himself agreeable to others!" (58). Clearly, it "was . . . to her" a great deal more than the quickly glossed circumstance of babysitting "the child"; she goes through the motions of a maternal "utility" (58) that functions as her cover while she busily contemplates the man she still loves with the "agitation which . . . eight years" (60) of separation could not obviate.

Despite Anne's seeming adherence to the backhanded idealization of women as sacrificial motherers and her unswerving commitment to serving others, her substantiated passion is for the fulfillment of her personal desire, like the most radical of Austenian fools. She chooses as a husband not the self-indulgent landowner who habitually abandons his wife to single-parenthood in "any thing disagreeable" (56), but rather the more progressive sea captain who instinctively liberates her from demanding childcare. During a memorable babysitting scene, the Musgroves' younger son Walter attaches himself to Anne twice in succession while she cares for his older brother. Walter's second, more tenacious adhesion occurs after she has briefly managed "to push him away" but found that "the boy had the greater pleasure in getting upon her back again directly" (80). Captain Wentworth initiates removing the toddler when "she could not shake him off" as if disburdening her of the albatross of an immobilizing, solitary maternity: "she found herself in the state of being released from him; some one was taking him from her, though he had bent down her head so much, that his little sturdy hands were unfastened from around her neck, and he was resolutely borne away, before she knew that Captain Wentworth had done it" (80). Anne acutely feels "[h]is kindness in stepping forward to her relief" (80), in contrast to Charles Hayter's reactive embarrassment at neglecting to intervene himself, as the other male witness to the boy's misbehavior and as his uncle (80–81).

Both men recognize participation in childcare as at least somewhat part of the male chivalric code, contradicting Charles Musgrove's selfish presumption of the manliness of child-evasion. Wentworth acts on this awareness by "taking [Walter] from" Anne and engaging the boy in noisy play "to avoid hearing her thanks," whereas Charles Hayter impotently playacts the patriarchal disciplinarian from his disengaged position on the couch: " 'You ought to have minded *me*, Walter; I told you not to teaze your aunt' " (80–81). Charles Hayter's lazy, inadequate address of the unaffected, boisterous Walter mimics the unwilling pseudo-parenting of his future brother-in-law, another Charles, which lends greater credence to Mary's feminist protest. The Charleses jointly signify egocentric everymen, who eschew real involvement with children in favor of a symbolic headship through which they can feed their independent pleasures while minimizing any discomfort or inconvenience to themselves. By contrast, the narrator's combined depictions of Anne's repeated efforts to detach a burdensome child from her and Frederick Wentworth's successful removal of him can be read as foreshadowing either their team parenting or their future of childless freedom for adventure in the style of the Crofts. Anne's words may fleetingly romanticize maternal care, but her thoughts and actions do not.

Moreover, Anne never disagrees with Mary's emphatic assertions about either Charles (a man she has already rejected as inferior) or men as a group and, in fact, affirms Mary's key convictions. Anne's only stated case for maternal devotion to the sickbed is the ambiguous remark noted earlier, delivered as if an afterthought, " '. . . and indeed, Mary, I cannot wonder at your husband. Nursing does not belong to a man, it is not his province. A sick child is always the mother's property, her own feelings generally make it so' " (56). Anne speaks the literal truth in declaring that she "cannot wonder at" the behavior of the everyman—Charles acts in predictable accordance to his privileged position. On the literary stage, she here half-heartedly gestures toward her role as a proper heroine who "cannot wonder" at Charles's behavior in the mode of open ideological interrogation, which would be counter to Austen's elusive technique of double-voiced feminist harmony between fool and apparent foil. Three of Anne's four explanatory phrases in the lukewarm mother's-province speech merely emphasize the fact of the systematized inevitability of ill children being a woman's "property," an inheritance concerning which she has no more choice than an estate under primogeniture.[18] Anne's qualifier regarding the mother's presumed preference for sickbed duty also stands out—she "generally" embraces the role, but not always, and when "her own feelings" do not urge her to the bedside, she is nevertheless compelled there. After Mary points out that she does not fit the profile of hypothetical nurturing mothers and is as ineffectual a parent as her husband, Anne encourages her to go out, using the same language of comparison that Mary has repeatedly employed: "'. . . suppose you were to go, as well as your husband. Leave little Charles to my care. Mr. and Mrs. Musgrove cannot think it wrong, while I remain with him'" (57). Anne abets Mary's escape while helping her to preserve appearances, though she privately wonders at the "oddly constructed . . . happiness" (58) that her shallow sister and brother-in-law share in common.

Both sisters give lip service to feminine nurturance as if by rote, but undercut it through their thoughts, speech, and actions. Mary does not even endeavor to sound convincing in her parting pronouncements of motherly concern as she rushes to overtake her husband in fleeing parental cares in pursuit of pleasure. Her short-term liberty seems to foreshadow Anne's long-term liberty from the hearthside type of wife and mother role to which Lady Russell considers "her to be peculiarly fitted by her warm affections and domestic habits" (29) but for which Anne never expressly aspires. When Mary catches up to Charles, he claims to be pleased for his wife's company out, but suddenly cares about burdening Anne with what he now admits is a " 'rather hard' " and alienating task of " 'be[ing] left at home by herself, to nurse our sick child' " (58). He had considered the tedium of this job perfectly acceptable for two women to share—Anne as well as his wife—but finds it harder to justify abandoning his son for revelry when his wife does the same.

Anne possesses a generous heart, but she has no more zeal for maternal domesticity than her sister Mary. Her indirect declaration of love for Wentworth, delivered via her conversation with Captain Harville, is simultaneously a cry for release from the physical, social, and emotional imprisonment that characterizes women's existence. Claiming women love longer than men, she explains, " 'We cannot help ourselves. We live at home, quiet, confined, and our feelings prey upon us. You are forced on exertion. You have always a profession, pursuits, business of some sort or other, to take you back into the world immediately, and continual occupation and change soon weaken impressions' " (232). Note that Anne's use of the word "confined" echoes Charles Musgrove's earlier internal application of the word "confinement" to staying home with his injured boy.

Anne's remark to Captain Harville applies to the gender divisions of everyday life—whether single or married, fathers or childless, men are engaged with the world and stimulated by action and variety, whereas women more passively await opportunities to escape the home fires they are forced to tend, opportunities that may never come or may involve a mere transfer from one hearth to another. The attentively listening Wentworth knows that Anne seeks a life and love that thrive in the open air rather than becoming self-consumed by entrapment in compulsory domesticity; his epistolary proposal emphasizes her place at the center of his eager preparations for a shared adventure: " 'You alone have brought me to Bath. For you alone I think and plan' " (237). Anne, like her sister Mary, refuses to accept as her own familial role that of being, in Charles Musgrove's words, "left at home" (58).

Austen appears to absolve both sexes of culpability for the gender double-standard, but underscores the existence of this double-standard. "Coarse" whiner Mary Musgrove relentlessly rails against sexism, while elegant heroine Anne Elliot, with her understated manner and timing, communicates the same concerns. In *Persuasion*, as in Austen's other novels, the fool who broadcasts her feminist ideology joins forces with the heroine who shares her core views while embodying feminine correctness. The narrator colludes with both the strident Mary and the sweet-tempered Anne to "persuade" the reader of their united perspective. A number of details suggest this, from the deliberate language of rationalization used to report Charles's self-serving logic, to Mary's whiny but accurate portrayal of the inequity in her marriage, to Anne's feminine platitudes designed to soothe the sting of Mary's acerbic exposure of her husband's sexism. The overall structure of the "little Charles" plot follows the couple's interaction from unity, to immediate disunity (triggered by Charles's exercise of his arbitrary privilege as the "father" who is supposedly helpless in the sick room), to Mary's malcontentedness, to Anne's intervention as the surrogate mother who liberates Mary to do as she pleases, to the couple's precarious reunification to attend the dinner party. As they prepare to depart, Charles acknowledges the injustice of someone else caring for their child while they go out, but never acknowledges his role in creating that circumstance; all implied responsibility rests with his wife. Once no longer a matter of life or death, the oversight of a recuperating child automatically becomes the mother's menial task while the father resumes his independent existence. Time stops for the woman to witness every stage of their child's recovery; time advances for the man, who will go about his business, perhaps observing their son's full recovery with pleasure whenever he remembers to notice it. Anne functions as the fulcrum between two equally selfish characters. Austen does not approve the puerile Musgroves' projection of responsibility for their child onto someone else, but she clearly promulgates the view that the two of them should possess the equal "right" to be selfish, without relying on gender stereotypes as a convenient cover for that selfishness.

Austen democratically holds her female and male characters to the same moral and ethical standards, but stresses that this is not so in a sexist society. Thus, Charles rationalizes that he can do whatever he likes because a father supposedly does not tend to a sick child, while Mary counter-argues that she should avoid the sick room precisely because of her supposed maternal devotion: " 'My being the mother is the very reason why my feelings should not be tried' " (56), she reasons. Both characters are negotiating a dysfunctional gender paradigm, when the simple truth is that they should both be more devoted to each other and to their children. Austen constructs with neoclassical symmetry, mathematical precision, and moral logic the disordered gender roles and values of a couple whose perceptions of themselves and each other are out of balance. The "Fall" of the Musgroves' heir underscores their loss of a collaborative Eden as manifest in the sexism of the parents' familial roles and reactive failures. Charles gets his just punishment for wishing confinement on Mary—he will never escape her perpetual song of sexism, featuring relentless accusations of conspiracies to marginalize or exploit her, some of which will continue to be proven true. At the end of *Persuasion*, Anne is happily married but no children are mentioned. In choosing Wentworth, she sails away from the mandate of daily self-abandonment to lonely domesticity. Whether or not she and her husband ever have offspring, live at sea or on land, or face intermittent separation, Anne disowns the spider-monkey child that had clung to her and refused to let go, and the claustrophobic, all-consuming maternity he symbolizes. While some readers may join Charles in endeavoring to elude Mary's shrill protests, they likely do not realize that the soothing voice they welcome—that of her serene sister, Anne—sings the same song.

Like the village idiot, Austen's female fool disarms suspicion. Others can "laugh at [her] odd ways behind [her] back" (*SS* 154) because she speaks unwelcome truths from a fringe position. The novelist allows auditors the illusion of bypassing these messages through laughter at the messenger and her delivery, as the female-identified narrator does in her own disarmingly self-ironic feminist commentary. Yet Austen's "feminist fools" and their attestations are impossible to ignore. They convey the courage of ruthless speech—speech that is often loud, declarative, contrarian, and mercilessly repetitive.[19] Mary Musgrove hounds readers as she does her family, ever reminding everyone of her importance, insisting on being at the center of activity as men like Charles, pre-reformed Wentworth, and even household collaborator Captain Harville assume they are. Although she sometimes imagines slights, Mary Musgrove rightly perceives and relentlessly names the reality of women's relegation to Otherness: their perpetual risk of being defined only by home, husband, children, circumstance; of being left behind. And to some extent, this incessant railing works—Mary gains mobility, achieving her goals of going to dinner at the Great House, to Lyme, to Bath. Austen as novelist resembles and relies upon her fools in the constancy of their voices; neither she nor they allow us to forget their grievances. Like the inexorable Aunt Norris haunts Sir Thomas (until she miraculously releases him), the galling fools become "a part of [ourselves], that must be borne for ever" (*MP* 465–466).

The apparent extremity of the fool's perspective, accentuated by the unfeminine trappings of physical homeliness, the immaturity of youth or age, or brazen self-assurance, neutralizes her sister heroine's parallel feminism into seeming conventionality. The feminine rectitude of servant-like Fanny Price and sweetheart Anne Elliot palliates their criticisms, despite Fanny's bitter rage toward both her future husband and her adopted patriarch and Anne's palpable distaste for conscription to the sacrificial maternity she apes. Even the more overt, spitfire protests of rebellious Emma Woodhouse and Elizabeth Bennet that are misplaced in degree or motivation can be attributed to pre-enlightenment reactivity. Thus, though clearly evidenced when the reader conducts a methodical comparison, the identical nature of fools' and proper jeunes filles' gender ideology in Austen's novels fades into imperceptibility.

Austen's respectively least and most mature heroines, Catherine Morland and Anne Elliot, both point out that men construct history as they choose to see it. Austen creates an alternative female history in her novels—in which her narrators, fools, and ingénues work in concert and tell the same tale of women's lives—and does so to hilariously ironic effect. The social and behavioral absolutes for women that female as well as male characters parrot sound so trite and unilateral as to be farcical, regardless of who mouths them, and are undercut by the shared gender critiques communicated in their diverging styles by admirable and foolish women alike. Both types are essential to this literary-ideological collaboration. Nonetheless, Austen punishes the fools whose accommodation of their desires to unjust impediments perverts their characters, thereby also undermining women's and society's emancipatory growth. Some of Austen's women succumb to gender injustice—Charlotte Lucas's "realistic" philosophy of material self-preservation proves morally and emotionally self-assassinating. In addition, those who argue theory without compassion, such as Lady Catherine and Mary Bennet, limit their potential for positive influence and for the genuine relationships it garners. The grotesque self-reductive narcissism of Mary Crawford, Mrs. Elton, and Mary Musgrove similarly alienates them from the very sororal community they endorse through brash feminist declamation.

Thus, although Austen's truth-speaking feminist fools play an essential role in validating their worthier sisters' quest for fulfillment, they perpetuate their own marginalization through a self-typecasting that reflects their abandonment of both themselves and society. While we may empathize with the cynicism that drew these fools down such a path, we must abjure it. Only the imperfect but deserving heroine who refuses to compromise her principles to the daunting pressures and encumbrances of gender oppression is rewarded with the prizes of love fulfilled, joy, economic stability, social consequence, and adventure. Austen's legacy to us is the ultimate fictional gratification of her protagonists' wishes in the very social landscape that seeks to disempower them, a landscape they have proven themselves determined—with no expectation of worldly reward—to rescue and renew. This is the heartbeat of the powerful female heroism the author holds up to us, one that eschews demoralization and the suspect oratory of the ideologue in favor of fearless magnanimity. As the concluding chapter explains, the insistent nurture of society at the anticipated cost of a merely personal desire reveals heroic hope. Through the consummate giving of self, a true heroine gains rewards of sublime value that only she knows how to treasure.

CHAPTER 8

"Unpropitious for Heroism"

Female Greatness in the Austenian Imagination

Austen's best women inspire readers with dreams of what we could be. They respond to circumstantial extremes in ways that, for the reader, assume heroic proportions. Each novel dramatizes a woman's didactic growth parable counterbalanced by a realism that both mocks and embellishes her rising greatness within a quest in which she plays not only maiden, but knight of her own deliverance. She requires deliverance from her own faults as well as from the injustices perpetuated by others' and social structures' iniquities or inequities, and only she can provide it. Austen does not present her protagonists as heroic. She assumes their share in the duty of all to God, society, and self to live a moral life, assuming universal knowledge of what that signifies. Her heroines demonstrate varying degrees of zeal for and success in accomplishing this obligatory goal.[1] Despite Austen's reinforcement of the gender-neutrality of virtue and the onus to cultivate it, her fiction also invokes the timeless tradition of female philanthropy in which the author herself participated. A peculiar social genius emerges in the exercise of not only material benevolence but an everyday charity that requires individual sacrifice and reflects the tremendous force of character needed to heal and preserve community. Based on our examination of their identities as reflected and refined through their physical, cerebral, spiritual, ecological, and social selves, to what extent do Austen's women merit our admiration?

Although the author presents lived virtue as an inherent human responsibility, she recognizes its difficulty and champions her heroines' courage when they choose to grow from unwelcome trials. She employs the courtship plot primarily toward this end, testing her women with the conviction of the permanent unattainability of their beloveds. Along the way, Catherine Morland, Elizabeth Bennet, and Emma Woodhouse face instructive interventions by their would-be lovers that intensify rather than instigating their self-improvement, while the comparatively blameless Elinor Dashwood, Fanny Price, and Anne Elliot despair of the romantic obstacles their heroes' weaknesses have produced. Austen hits her heroines where they hurt, creating barriers of circumstance or female competition that push them past belief in the possibility of realizing their loves. In so doing, she exposes their level of commitment to a fulfillment whose source exists outside of their own desire, beyond the self and its coveted earthly gratifications. Climactic moments of enlightenment and resolutions of reform or triumph over despair count for nothing unless they further motivate sacrificial efforts to benefit the greater good. What demonstrated nobility Austen credits in her women shines through in their pristine decorum amid the darkening clouds of severe disappointment. In the effort to achieve this feat, each heroine must alone confront and define her self, without the crutch of a man to determine either her plotline or her metaphysical purpose. This is no mean mission in a context in which even gilded singlehood has been stripped of its vocational dignity and marriage constitutes middle-class women's expected and only socially viable occupation. Austen shows "how one may transform commonplace reality into an epic of the individual conscience" (Ehrenpreis 43) under the most onerous conditions. Undergirding this effort, of course, is the Anglican Christian worldview in which "her heroines seek to imitate Jesus" through "taking up their cross, and making their journey to the place of their metaphorical crucifixion" (Giffin 27) in a world where "[r]eligious issues were still held to be of public importance" (23).

In a survey of the relative merit of Austen's leading ladies, we could argue that tomboy-turned-"almost pretty" (*NA* 15) Catherine Morland and *Sense and Sensibility*'s lesser heroine, Marianne Dashwood, prove least heroic because they never see their lives' higher purpose extrinsic to their chosen love object (or, by implication, beyond themselves). Even after a self-inflicted near-death experience, Marianne can only " 'wish for no change' " (*SS* 350) and envision an existence of uncharacteristic studiousness until she embraces her consolation-prize lover with equal co-dependency; the joke is that despite his age and flannel waistcoat, Colonel Brandon represents the hero of sensibility for which she has yearned all along. Catherine Morland imaginatively role-plays the Gothic hero on a quest to rescue an imprisoned lady, but the only one she aids is her crush's sister, the unwilling agent of a dictatorial father's orders. Catherine assuages Eleanor's terror and humiliation at her guest's expulsion from Northanger, declaring that " 'the journey is nothing' " (*NA* 230), and sends the begged-for confirmation of her safety post-eviction-insult. However, once at home, she continues to pout until Henry arrives to propose.

Elizabeth Bennet, with her prideful prejudices, evinces more serious character flaws than Catherine but also greater forbearance in the face of severer letdowns. She forgives Lydia and Wickham not only for their near-destruction of the entire family, but for their assumed destruction of her own potential happiness with Darcy. Elizabeth collaborates with Jane in arranging for the couple's awkward visit to Longbourn, even though, "had she consulted only her own inclination, any meeting with him would have been the last object of her wishes" (*PP* 314). She never reproves either of her betrayers, only obliquely alluding to Wickham's deceptiveness during a gesture of reconciliation: " 'Come, Mr. Wickham, we are brother and sister, you know. Do not let us quarrel about the past. In future, I hope we shall be always of one mind' " (329). For one with Elizabeth's strong opinions, habituated to "run[ning] on in the wild manner that [she is] suffered to do at home" (42), this leniency reveals concerted effort.

We could also argue that just as Elizabeth exceeds Catherine in the degree of both her errors and her compensatory gestures, Emma Woodhouse exceeds Elizabeth Bennet in both. Whereas the latter bears no responsibility for Lydia and Wickham's fall or its consequences and indirectly tries to prevent it, Emma creates the conditions that most threaten her happiness. Upon discovering that she and Harriet "love" the same man, she recognizes in hindsight "[h]ow inconsiderate, how indelicate, how irrational, how unfeeling had been her conduct!" (*E* 408) and that "it had been all her own work" (423). She offers herself as the romantic confidante of both Harriet and Mr. Knightley, even as she mediates between her presumptuous and penitential selves. Emma invites Harriet to share the story of her affection for Mr. Knightley and evidence of its reciprocation and, after a momentary evasion, invites Mr. Knightley to divulge his feelings as well (for Harriet, she assumes). She braces herself to provide whatever support he most needs, even to encourage the relationship with Harriet, "cost her what it would," as a truly disinterested "friend" ready to "give just praise to" her rival (429). Mr. Knightley can claim no credit for Emma's willingness to endure alone "every future winter of her life" (423) for his happiness.

However, this altruism is brief, unrealized, and based on illusory circumstances attributable to Emma's own machinations.

The minute she realizes that Mr. Knightley loves her, "that Harriet was nothing; that she was every thing herself" (430), she snaps him up, for she lacks the "heroism of sentiment" to refuse him for Harriet or to beg him to marry her friend instead. Though the narrator characterizes such hypothetical reactions as "generosity run mad" (431), a hint of satire manifests itself in the immediacy and gusto with which a supposedly reformed Emma seizes her own fulfillment. In addition, although her devotion to her father and commitment to suspending her personal life indefinitely to serve him shows selflessness, there is a tinge of Marianne-like melodrama to it as well: "While her dear father lived, any change of condition must be impossible for her. She could never quit him" (448). After a short-lived readiness for martyrdom in reparation for her errors, Emma continues to get what she wants and even reverts somewhat in "submitt[ing] . . . to a little more praise than she deserve[s]" (475). Perhaps the motherless hero-ine's repeated relinquishments of female connections that did or could help to assuage her maternal loss—Mrs. Weston, Harriet, and even Jane Fairfax, with whom she briefly bonds before their paths diverge again—represents a more substantiated example of Emma's capacity for emotional courage and sacrifice. She surrenders Miss Taylor to marital happiness, though "the very sight of Mrs. Weston, her smile, her touch, her voice was grateful to" one who houses an inner child that desperately desires to continue clinging to her mother-substitute (117).[2] Yet, in these instances of letting go of other women who possess the right to their own lives, does Emma have a choice?

We can easily identify Fanny Price, Anne Elliot, and Elinor Dashwood as Austen's most irreproachable yet most tortured heroines, whose reactions to their undeserved sufferings seem most akin to heroism. Fanny Price merits credit for demonstrat-ing the heroic potential of resistance, of the power of negation (as in her resolve against marrying Henry Crawford despite Sir

Thomas's ruthless bullying), yet the defense of her own interests and feelings largely motivates that tenacity. Her transformative impact on the character and life of her younger sister Susan, as described in chapter 5, is more meritorious. In addition, Fanny's less dramatic but more exigent challenge throughout her maturation may be her uniform consideration toward forced "friend" and romantic competition Mary Crawford, who puts her propriety to the severest test. Mary sees through Fanny's attempt to behave with simultaneous honesty and decorum as in her cagey remark in response to Mary's "fishing" for a compliment: "Fanny felt obliged to speak. 'You cannot doubt your being missed by many,' said she. 'You will be very much missed'" (*MP* 289). Mary's jocular response indicates her recognition of Fanny's real feeling as implied in her statements' calculated grammatical passivity, that *she* will *not* miss Mary, and showcases the latter's good-natured tolerance. Such moments suggest the irony of a perfectionism that risks forfeiture of the very authenticity and sensitivity to others that it strains to preserve.

A similar moral complexity emerges in Austen's depiction of "too excellent" (*P* 237) protagonist Anne Elliot. This soft-spoken healer saves as many as eight lives. Through her continual, clever exertions, she heals sister Mary's psychosomatic illnesses and restores her emotional equilibrium, thereby salvaging Charles Musgrove's sanity as well. She arguably saves the young Musgrove boy's life by nursing him back to health on behalf of his bungling parents. She counsels the depressive, possibly suicidal Captain Benwick, and proves the social salvation of ostracized Mrs. Smith. Of course, she saves Louisa's life through quick, sensible action during the critical aftermath of the accident at Lyme. Finally, modest, self-effacing Anne decides to save her own life by acknowledging her worthiness of happiness and accepting her second chance at it with Wentworth (and in so doing, she also safeguards Wentworth's reformed self from another thwarting in love and potential moral backslide). Therein lies the heroine's central weakness as well as strength—she originally reneges on her engagement from superfluous self-denial, then very nearly misses her love's second spring through submission to wintry despair. While we can admire Anne's thoroughly giving spirit and understand her fear to hazard hope after loss of mother, lover, and home, we cannot excuse her surrender to a self-paralyzing despondency that, to borrow her own words regarding pragmatic marital deferrals, "seems to insult exertion and distrust Providence!" (30). Perhaps Anne has learned this lesson by her renewed engagement, but she has been too willing for too long to sacrifice herself to inward agonies that benefit no one and deny the Redemption in which this almost-Christ figure believes. Her joy must practically be handed off to her, or at least placed on a table nearby like Wentworth's proposal note.

Anne Elliot ends her engagement unnecessarily and then endures over-punishment for this well-intentioned mistake in years of depression and in her former fiancé's gratuitous flirtations. Elinor Dashwood unwittingly falls for an already engaged man, and endures the even more gratuitous taunts of his fiancée. Both heroines, like Fanny Price and the chastened Emma Woodhouse, show consideration toward everyone during their private agonies, and remain loyal to the very women they believe will live the lives they wanted with the men they love. Whereas protagonists Anne and Emma resign themselves to the likelihood of this painful outcome, however, Elinor actively furthers it. She honors her promise of confidentiality to Lucy, supports Edward in fulfilling his promise to Lucy, and communicates Colonel Brandon's offer of the living intended to accelerate the very marriage that would complete Edward's and her misery and her rival's triumph. She feels more for his unhappiness than for her own, but takes comfort in her ability to "*esteem* Edward as much as ever, however they might be divided in future" (*SS* 179).

Although Elinor is the purest in pursuit of pure principle, Austen tests her most of all her characters, as if Elinor represents the Job to Lucy's Satan, the latter of whom the omnipotent author empowers to inflict successive trials on the heroine. Elinor remains faithful to her divine and literary authors. She even serves as "the comforter of others in her own distresses, no less than in theirs" (261), as when Marianne cries upon discovering her sister's longstanding knowledge of Edward's engagement. Yet Elinor is no angel, either, but a passionate person who has played mind games with Lucy to preserve her pride and invested two pages' worth of commentary in detailing her sufferings to Marianne.[3] She must also be disabused of a secretly harbored fantasy, "in spite of herself, . . . that something would occur to prevent [Edward's] marrying Lucy" (357), and stripped of all hope for her yearned-for future.

This foundation of human weakness and presumed loss is essential to the reader's sense of the excruciating difficulty and almost superhuman valiance of Elinor's greatest moment in the novel. When Edward visits the Dashwoods at Barton after his supposed marriage, she compels herself to the painful politeness of asking after the new "Mrs. Ferrars":

> Elinor, resolving to exert herself, though fearing the sound of her own voice, now said, "Is Mrs. Ferrars at Longstaple?"
>
> "At Longstaple!" [Edward] replied, with an air of surprise—"No, my mother is in town."
>
> "I meant," said Elinor, taking up some work from the table, "to inquire after Mrs. *Edward* Ferrars." (359)

This scene captures with beautiful simplicity the extent of Elinor's agonized effort to maintain her decorum toward the man she has lost and his undeserving wife; her self-distracting and self-concealing gesture of attempted sewing emphasizes her heroism with special poignancy.[4] She follows through on the sacrifice she has already made, accepting its distressing consequences while trying to avoid multiplying them for others. Edward's stammered revelation of Lucy's alliance to Robert presents Elinor with an unanticipated reward for her total subdual of self to honor. Upon realizing her miraculous accession to her heart's desire, Elinor finally releases her overwrought emotions: "She almost ran out of the room, and as soon as the door was closed, burst into tears of joy, which at first she thought would never cease" (360).

Austen puts her readers and heroines through a tragicomic catharsis that shocks us out of complacence and into a hope that has its remittance in pain. There is a touch of sadism in Austen's minute depiction of Fanny Price's and Anne Elliot's observations of their lovers' shallow fawnings over other women; Fanny must hear Edmund's fatuous praise of Mary's kindness to her and Anne must watch Wentworth look about for a wife in anyone but her and hear that he thinks her appearance decayed past recognition. Elinor chokes out civilities to a supposedly married Edward, about his snaky wife, through a built-up anguish she can but just forcibly contain. We sit beside Austen in her narrative theater, vicariously experiencing her heroines' thwartings, purgations, aspiring resignations to emotional widowhood, and tardy raptures, hoping she is fooled by our pretended identification with her dispassionate authorial sagacity.

Austen's heroines are or become warriors for politesse. The novelist "stresses . . . the 'exertion' that it takes to achieve civility towards fools and enemies, the heroism that can be involved in the expression of 'good Cheer,' or the difficulty of achieving 'tranquility' " (Brodey, *Ruined* 195). Nonetheless, courtesy is the duty of all to all, regardless of their unworthiness of it, from a worldview in which "[c]are for civility mean[s] care for civilisation" (Tanner 28). Austen credits her heroines for their civility under duress, but ultimately denies them heroic stature for fulfilling humanity's inherent obligation to live a moral life. Moreover, her dips into tragicomedy allow readers only transient glimpses of unalloyed grief or ecstasy before undercutting such emotional profligacies with intrusive comic realism—the exquisite always collapses into laughter at entrenched human imperfection. The author affectionately satirizes the asceticism of masochistic suffering, the laziness of any excuse for abdicating the duty of virtue, and the illusoriness of the very perfectibility toward which she insists that all aspire. Austen rejects the histrionic egocentrism of obsessive goodness, dogged apathy, or self-congratulatory sin with "no hope of a cure" (*MP* 68), as variations on a self-indulgence that mimics the polarity of literary conventionalism. The human tendency to extremes of skepticism and utopianism exposes an imagination cramped by renunciation of faith, of the redemption whose blend of fluidity with order is so well expressed through comic hope.

Thus, Austen imposes on her heroines' narrative landscapes the Chaucerian crude, the earthy banal. Noble Elinor and her beloved husband Edward "had . . . nothing to wish for, but the marriage of Colonel Brandon and Marianne, and rather better pasturage for their cows" (*SS* 374–375). Ethereal Fanny apparently proves fecund and more attached to material comfort than we supposed—"after they had been married long enough," she and Edmund "want an increase of income" (*MP* 473). Similarly, sacrificial Anne presumably enjoys driving around in her new, "very pretty landaulette" (*P* 250). As doyennes of a grander-scale social sphere, repentant Marianne, Elizabeth, and Emma must brook becoming even more important than they already considered themselves, while Catherine likely remains obtuse enough to keep Henry charmed. The novelist mocks our mistaken over-admiration of her heroines by inviting us to wonder how much they really learned and whether they deserve their apparently happy endings. Even in our quest for female heroism or "heroinism," we are turned out to pasture. Austen's women are not granted the luxury of frailty, despite their frailties, nor special accolades for rising to graciousness from the ashes of social, financial, educational, or experiential impoverishment. The sardonic narrator makes continual revelations at their expense that expose readers to the gaps between their apparent heights of beneficence and the mediocrity of their everyday concerns. Austen's finest heroine dreams of greener pastures for her cows.

Yet the heroines' unheroic nature makes possible the heroinism we discern in their enduring efforts to provide "what [is] due to every body, and what would be wisest for [themselves]" (*MP* 396) in accordance to a now unfashionably absolute truth that exists outside of time and space. Decorum—and the virtues of humility, forgiveness, and charity that enable and fuel it—is as difficult and essential today as ever. All self-discipline results from strength, and decorum can be as challenging as physical courage and as—or more—essential to the preservation of civilization; "[t]rue propriety can only spring from . . . sincere moral commitment to self and others in society" (Nardin 15).[5] When we reexamine the stories of Austen's women and their honing into sophisticated social ambassadors whose love of impossible neighbors seems to defy the odds and almost to violate probability, and consider these heroines' simultaneous comic exposure as mortals like us, our longing to connect with and even to become the author makes more sense.

Austen's "fans" cook and eat what she is believed to have cooked and eaten, don the style of garments she wore, play piano pieces found in her personal music collection, wear replicas of her jewelry, walk all the places she is presumed to have walked, and (in my case) hug a tree at Godmersham that existed when she visited there and under which she may have sat and thought the brilliantly witty thoughts that permeate the novels we love. At risk of dismissal as yet another stereotyped Janeite over-pleased with tea, playing dress-up, and idolizing her favorite writer, I refuse to apologize for hugging that tree. In imagining ourselves into the worlds of Austen and her heroines, we rehearse our authorial revision of ourselves. In playacting Austen herself, we endeavor to discover what goodness and light and conviction and forgiveness and persistent virtue and redemptive humor and benignly biting wit within ourselves responds to these elements in Austen's art. We conflate our assumed knowledge of the author with the reality of our awakening knowledge of pieces of ourselves that foretell our possibilities for newly becoming.

A T-shirt for sale online reads, "Jane Austen: Giving Women Unrealistic Expectations Since 1811." Unrealistic expectations of whom or what? Surely not of themselves. This view of the novels as fairytales completely misses the point. Jane Austen knows where the boundaries of realism lie. Much of her addictive, ironic humor emanates from play with those very boundaries. She would agree with today's most cynical of finger-wagging readers that the worthiest of women will not find a man who equals or exceeds her in love, devotion, chastity, intellect, wit, talent, looks, *and* wealth. "[B]ells r[i]ng and every body smile[s]" (*NA* 252) by the end of all her novels, but they are not about gaining a fictional ideal man or marriage, but a quest for the rebirth of self. In an unpredictable, messy, often hostile universe, the extension of grace to others through courtesy reflects and reinforces the underlying order of that universe. It also mirrors Austen's own visitation of miracles on her heroines after their most traumatic ego-tests, "when hope is gone" (*P* 235), which (though it does not generally take the form of romantic wish fulfillment) mirrors the miraculous mystery of divine Grace.

Like Edward Ferrars but with authorial intentionality, Austen "t[akes] up a pair of scissars . . . and spoil[s] both them and their sheath by cutting the latter to pieces" (*SS* 360). Despite the many cinematic reinterpretations to the contrary, Austen refuses sensibility. She does not allow readers to stay sheathed in self-serving delusions or to deny our own potentially destructive edges. Even though she gifts us and her heroines with pleasurable narrative closure, all along the way she cuts to pieces our efforts to cocoon ourselves in fictitious comforts. Her novels are not euphoric happily-ever-afters. Catherine will "make a sad heedless young housekeeper" (*NA* 249); Emma's wedding is "pitiful" in its dearth of lace (*E* 484); Anne "dread[s] . . . a future war" (*P* 252), and Elinor covets "rather better pasturage for [her] cows" (*SS* 375). With accuracy, we could say that through her heroines, Austen shows women and men how best to live in truth to their Creator by honoring body, mind, heart, soul, soil, sister, and brother. This is not only a duty but the key to our survival amid terror and strife. But we will all inevitably and perpetually fail in this vast undertaking. Comedy, with its cyclical seasons, like our daily falling and getting up, sinning and sorrowing and trying again, comprehends this reality and enables us, while forever hoping and striving, to laugh. Jane Austen's comedy reaches for heaven with its feet six inches deep in mud.

Notes

Preface

1. Richard Dawkins's reductive remark of *Pride and Prejudice* is typical of this usually masculine reactionism: "It must be my prejudice, and I am not proud of it, but I can't get excited about who is going to marry whom, and how rich they are" (Dawkins).

2. See such stories as "Hemingway Look-Alike Contest Is the Best Thing You'll See All Day" (*Huffington Post*, August 1, 2013, *huffingtonpost. com*); "Hemingway Days in Key West" (*610 WIOD News Radio*, July 25, 2015, *wiod.com*); and "Ernest Hemingway Look-Alikes Descend on the Hemingway Days Festival" (Jordan Riefe, *The Hollywood Reporter*, July 31, 2014, *hollywoodreporter.com*). The "Running of the Bulls" is generally described in brief as merely "offbeat," "whimsical," a "spoof." Riefe's piece does mention a bar employee's complaint of sexual harassment by event attendees and hints at but does not develop this observation into a critique of machismo. Stories routinely imply that the festival's literary aspects—writing competition and scholarship—are compatible with the other activities.

3. See such stories as "Jane Austen unveiled as face of new £10 note" (*The Telegraph*, July 24, 2013, *www.telegraph.co.uk*), "The Woman Who Got Jane Austen on British Money Wants to Change how Twitter Handles Abuse" (*The Wire: News from The Atlantic*, July 28, 2013, *www. thewire.com*), and "Jane Austen to be face of the Bank of England £10 note" (*BBC News*, July 24, 2013, *www.bbc.com*).

4. All quotes from Austen's novels are taken from the third Chapman edition of *The Novels of Jane Austen*, volumes 1–5, Oxford: Oxford UP, 1933–1966.

5. As Jo Alyson Parker articulates it, the author endeavors "to establish the legitimacy of the feminocentric novel" (40).

6. Austen famously stated in a letter to her closest niece, Fanny Knight, that "pictures of perfection as you know make me sick & wicked" (23-25 March 1817). This passage and all quotes from Austen's letters are from Deirdre Le Faye's third edition of *Jane Austen's Letters*.

7. Austen's nephew, James Edward Austen-Leigh, states in his memoir of his aunt that she may have harbored a "feeling of deference natural to a loving child towards a kind elder sister. Something of this feeling always remained; and even in the maturity of her powers, and in the enjoyment of increasing success, she would still speak of Cassandra as of one wiser and better than herself" (16). Biographer Carol Shields states, "The younger sister always sought the favor of the older, always thinking of Cassandra's entertainment and satisfaction" (*Jane* 126). Jon Spence agrees with this assessment of the sororal relationship, but qualifies it with the disclaimer that "in the world of art Jane Austen was free" (*Becoming* 193), citing as an example Austen's rejection of Cassandra's suggestion that Fanny Price be paired with Henry Crawford and Edmund Bertram be paired with Mary Crawford at the end of *Mansfield Park*.

8. Colleague Susan E. Jones and I contributed to this trend the book *Jane Austen's Guide to Thrift: An Independent Woman's Advice on Living Within One's Means* (Berkley Books, 2013).

9. This quote is from a letter Cassandra wrote to niece Fanny Knight, describing the author's passing and eulogizing her.

10. For example, whereas Marilyn Butler argues "that her manner as a novelist is broadly that of the conservative Christian moralist of the 1790s" (164), J. Russell Perkin asserts that "Austen's own theory of the novel is more aesthetic than moral or ideological" (150).

11. I treat Austen's work as a whole in this study, drawing comparisons among individual novels across drafting and publication dates and chronologies, in part because in Austen's case, as Kathryn Sutherland argues, "there is no seamless division into early, middle and late writing, but instead a vital and unexpected revision of material over a considerable period" (15). Sutherland also claims that apart from *Northanger Abbey*, the completed novels were "the products of the mature Chawton years," which were themselves "the culmination

of some twenty to thirty years of drafting, redrafting and continued experiment" (13).

12. In this chapter, I draw loosely on Howard Gardner's theory of "multiple intelligences."

Chapter 1

1. Lance Bertelsen, who emphasizes the importance of painting and drawing to Austen's literary aesthetic, offers a somewhat different view in that he perceives this minimalist technique as engaging readers' creative participation in textual interpretation (369). Anita Gorman makes a similar point, stating that "[d]escription . . . can provide part of the rhythm of anticipation and pleasure within narrative . . . and reveals also by what is left out" (130).

2. A number of scholars acknowledge the importance to Austen of regaling her letter-readers (especially Cassandra), as she endeavors to do her novel-readers: "Clearly Austen felt an aesthetic responsibility to render her letters entertaining performances. They were not entirely unstudied, spontaneous outpourings" (Bander 121). In addition, Austen employs in the subjects of "cooking and food" what one critic defines as "the ancient emblems of comedy" (Monteiro 81).

3. Austen asks her sister, "Have you any Tomatas?—Fanny & I regale on them every day" (11–12 October 1813).

4. This remark may be a humorous allusion both to Jane and her parents' time in Bath with her affluent brother and his family, and to the high living of the Regency court, but it also plays up women's entitlement to the comforts of life. Kaplan rightly concludes that, "far from being trivial, the gestures, habits, dress, and décor of daily life have the capacity to convey social and moral knowledge about persons or experiences. They thereby implicitly challenge the gentry view of the quotidian as insignificant" ("Representing" 223).

5. Venetia Murray describes the excessive consumption of steaks at men's clubs of the eighteenth century, at which "the size of the steaks on offer was an indication of status, or the generosity of the host, and the amount a man could consume a test of his virility" (167). While men who could afford it were urged to gorge themselves on red meat, women

were discouraged from eating much or well, and many considered the consumption of red meat to be unfeminine. Maggie Lane points out that in Austen's fiction, jolly Mrs. Jennings and Mrs. Musgrove aside, "all the fatness and certainly all the epicurism and gluttony . . . belong to men" (90) and are symptomatic of "the excesses of patriarchy" that often cause grief to the women in their families (93). Barbara Seeber similarly asserts that "[t]he ability to command food is linked to social hierarchy and to the domination of nature and women" (*Jane* 93), a dynamic Austen comically overturns in her food enthusiasms.

6. See the chapter "On the Female Form" in the anonymously authored 1811 conduct book, *The Mirror of the Graces; Or, The English Lady's Costume.* The supposed "Lady of Distinction" to whom the book is attributed is described on the title page as one "Who has witnessed and attentively studied what is esteemed truly graceful and elegant amongst the most refined Nations of Europe" ("Regency"). The anonymous author lists numerous foods that women should avoid as well as when and where they should walk, how they should bathe and care for their skin, and what they should think, thereby regurgitating a philosophy of female self-repression of which a prescriptive diet is symptomatic.

7. This bias in favor of "a higher body fat content arose from the persistence and threat of famine" (Heydt-Stevenson, *Unbecoming* 191) and disease.

8. Maggie Lane views women's inability or refusal to consume food in Austen's novels—the "eating disorders" of Marianne Dashwood, Fanny Price, and Jane Fairfax—as evidence of "social disorder" in an oppressive male-controlled existence. She also notes that although expressed enthusiasm for eating is shunned by the heroines and treated as "intrinsically anti-heroic" (86), Austen positively depicts Mrs. Jennings's hospitality and the ample repast served to the ladies at Pemberley and emphasizes a balanced, sociable existence in which food plays a critical role.

9. Pamela Steele describes Marianne's bodily movements on her fateful hike as a foreshadowing outline of her pending relationship with Willoughby and Louisa Musgrove's leap from the Cobb as emblematic of her impulsive, obdurate personality. The outcomes of these characters' rash actions exemplify "Austen's view of severe illness as a way to moral enlightenment" (Steele 156).

10. Susan E. Jones explains—in the context of historical background on specific breeds, Mrs. Austen's home dairy, and *Emma*'s cow refer-

ences—that Harriet Smith is associated with "cows of indeterminate background" ("Oysters").

11. Mrs. Smith's admirability is tainted by the sinister irony of her rise to "worldly prosperity" (*P* 252) through her pursuit and reclamation (with Captain Wentworth's help) of "her husband's property in the West Indies" (251), thus likely benefitting from slavery. In addition, Mrs. Smith suppresses her knowledge of Mr. Elliot's despicable character when she believes Anne plans to marry him and seems to encourage the match for self-serving reasons until Anne's allusion to caring for someone else liberates her to reveal her information. She implies that she felt honor-bound to withhold her knowledge of his corruption when she believed the marriage was inevitable: " 'I could no more speak the truth of him, than if he had been your husband. My heart bled for you, as I talked of happiness' " (211). This situation is reminiscent of Colonel Brandon's struggle over whether to inform Marianne of Willoughby's immoral character; he does so via Elinor only after Willoughby's engagement to Miss Grey.

12. Pamela Steele suggests that Fanny's body functions as a marker of others' moral states at Mansfield, "to express the pain that transgressors of her code of behavior inflict upon others. . . . Her reactions grow more severe as wrongdoing moves from thoughtlessness to actual vice" (158).

13. John Wiltshire and others view Fanny's sickliness as a manifestation of her powerlessness and an implied critique of her oppressed position: "Her distress is communicated in a physical mode, because . . . the overt expression of the instigating emotions is forbidden" ("Health" 128). Scholars tend to view female characters' illness in Austen's novels as a symptom of their subjugation to a patriarchal culture.

14. Amy Pawl asserts that Fanny Price "is no parody" (314) but manifests the influences and conventions of the sentimental novel tradition. Pam Perkins makes a similar point, claiming that Fanny Price and Mary Crawford represent contrasting tropes of comedic heroines: "Fanny is a Burneyesque heroine; her roots lie in the domestic and often sentimental comedy of female development" and "Mary . . . has her [older] roots in the witty, amoral temptresses of the Restoration and early eighteenth-century 'laughing' comedy" (3). On a related note, Michael Kramp explores Austen's depictions of her heroes' "disciplined masculinity" and sexual self-control as contributing to the stabilizing

"organization of the modernizing nation" in the aftermath of the French Revolution (149).

15. Mark Canuel explains, "The Mansfield household provides . . . a technology of classification. With her wealthier relations, she always knows where she stands" (128), and notes that Fanny's experience among her adopted family is characterized by a constant blend of painful embarrassments with the benefits of upper-class life.

16. This pattern also introduces potentially oppressive sexual implications relative to the male gaze's turn toward Fanny as she comes of age. John Wiltshire asserts that a woman's physical wellness "is in the first place a commodity" whose value is defined by "its appeal to the male gaze" ("Health" 126). Sir Thomas reinforces this when he remarks on Fanny's improved figure and her embarrassment suggests an awareness of his market-assessment of her body.

17. Alice Chandler characteristically observes, in relation to the sexual metaphor, that Fanny "is frightened of riding, as we imagine she would be at first, but riding Edmund's mare gives her great pleasure. When Mary Crawford, a born horsewoman, takes it away from her and starts riding with Edmund herself, Fanny, with almost clinical accuracy, develops a headache" (93–94).

18. I am indebted to former student Father Charles Browning for this insight. On a related note, by name affiliation, both of these young women also inherit the moral malaise of Lady Bertram—formerly Miss Maria Ward. Young Maria Bertram and Fanny Price share in common the ironic inheritance of the names of their emotionally absent, dysfunctional mothers.

19. Aunt Norris is a more complex character than she appears to be; while she seems consciously to wish Fanny ill, she may unconsciously act on compassionate motives or at least in reaction against male privilege and its consequences for women. She does prove herself capable of self-sacrifice (albeit for an undeserving object) when she retires from society to serve as companion to the outcast Maria, thereby giving up many opportunities for meddling and "spunging."

20. Akiko Takei explicates Austen's portrayal of women's physical activity in her novels in the context of contradictory eighteenth-century stereotypes of female weakness. Social, medical, and conduct-book discourse both encouraged and heavily circumscribed middle- and upper-class women's physical activity, thus contributing to the very

conditions that caused the feminine delicacy these sources presented as biologically predetermined. Austen goes beyond feminist thinkers of her age in her promotion of "women's right to be active and healthy for their own good, not for the sake of others" (84).

21. Mary may be exaggerating the length of their walk to magnify her achievement as well, as suggested by her succeeding debate with Edmund about the distance they have traveled. Takei quotes a male conduct-book author of the late eighteenth century in demonstrating the social expectation that "women should be modest in displaying their health. Gregory's advice says, 'But though good health be one of the greatest blessings of life, never make a boast of it, but enjoy it in grateful silence' " (72). Her source is John Gregory's *A Father's Legacy to His Daughters*, 3rd ed., 1774, in vol. 1 of *Female Education in the Age of Enlightenment*, edited by Janet Todd, 6 volumes, London: Pickering, 1 996.

22. See the article, " '. . . let him succeed at last, Fanny': Edmund Bertram as Henry Crawford's Double in Jane Austen's *Mansfield Park*," in which I and co-author and former student Christina E. Unkel describe in greater depth the unflattering parallels between Fanny's seeming hero and her would-be seducer.

23. Whereas Fanny represents the positive medium between her aunts, her mother represents the negative. Pauline Beard discusses the resemblance between Mrs. Price and Lady Bertram, remarking of Fanny's mother that "she seems in constant useless but languid motion."

24. Like Maria and Julia, Mary was raised in a destructive way; Fanny's secondary status as a dependent cousin at Mansfield may have been to her advantage in lessening the interest of dysfunctional adults in molding her into their image.

25. She "is variously and sometimes tediously astonished, shocked, agitated, amazed, startled, stunned, surprised, alarmed, overwhelmed, bewildered, and generally distressed throughout the novel" and finally, "the end of both right conduct and good etiquette is personal and social well-being" (Weinsheimer 194, 198).

26. Austen's presumption of women's right to a meaningful existence as a precondition of wellness resonates with the arguments of Wollstonecraft; a number of scholars have explored parallels between the two writers. Freedom to exercise both one's body and one's mind, thus benefiting both, represents the larger goal of social liberty for

women: "Equality in taking exercise is a paradigm of the women's rights Wollstonecraft has to vindicate" (Takei 74).

27. Carol Shields analyzes Austen's bodily references in her novels, and generalizes that "images of the body are relatively rare in her writing, unless those body parts have achieved a metaphorical or abstract sense" because of the author's emphasis on the transcendence of reason, her historical-cultural context, and her literary methodology as "a dramatic rather than a descriptive writer, concerned with morality and using speech as her medium" ("Images"). I agree with John Wiltshire's generalization that the novels "themselves represent, embody, sanity and healthiness" (*Body* 220).

Chapter 2

1. Two general trends in critical discourse on the sexual content in Austen's novels consist of either downplaying its existence or degree, or, as in recent years, over-reading it, particularly in interpretations of perceived erotic coding. Regarding the latter, a case in point is the debate over double-entendres. See Jill Heydt-Stevenson's " 'Slipping into the Ha-Ha': Bawdy Humor and Body Politics in Jane Austen's Novels" as contrasted with Brian Southam's " 'Rears' and 'Vices' in *Mansfield Park*," the latter of which critiques some of the former's sexualized interpretations of Austen's language, such as Heydt-Stevenson's confidence that Mary Crawford's "*Rears, and Vices*" joke is a reference to sodomy in the Navy ("Slipping" 314–315). Such debates underscore the importance of careful linguistic research to any interpretation that depends on specific word usages that could be misread by the superimposition of contemporary usages and connotations. Southam points out that Austen's work must be interpreted in the context of "the social and literary culture and conventions within which she was writing" (24), and identifies her genre as "the Woman's Novel: fiction written by women, primarily for women, about the woman's world, domestic in focus, its repeated story the heroine's path to marriage" (25). While I agree with Heydt-Stevenson that sexuality is an integral component of Austen's oeuvre ("Slipping" 339) and that the novelist conveys "hostility toward ideologies that dominate women" (337), I also agree with Southam's critique—it is easy to over-read and decontextualize particular refer-

ences, thus endowing Austen with a linguistic and conceptual obscenity that contradicts her literary and social milieu.

2. I argued for the sexually suggestive nature of Austen's fictional flirtations as an effective narrative technique, in a lecture at the 2001 Jane Austen Society of North America Annual General Meeting ("Uncorsetting Austen: Sexual Passion and Narrative Structure in the Novels"). A few ideas I explored in that talk are incorporated into this chapter.

3. See Hazel Jones, pp. 155–157. As Alison G. Sulloway explains, until 1857, "the law of femin[ine] *coverture*" still held, in which, as she quotes Sir William Blackstone's explanation, " 'the very being or legal existence of women is suspended during the marriage, and consolidated into that of the husband' " (36).

4. Josephine Ross points out that Austen's fiction reinforces the value of numerous social conventions of her time as "safeguards for the individual—and for vulnerable young women in particular" (193). These protective mores are especially critical in light of the prevailing pattern of the heroines' lack of effective father figures (see Tony Tanner's catalog of Austen's missing and weak fathers, p. 45).

5. Darryl Jones interprets Colonel Brandon's remark about his brother in *Sense and Sensibility* that "his pleasures were not what they ought to have been" as possibly a reference to "wife-beating or sexual abuse" ("Highest" 207).

6. Susan E. Jones convincingly argues that Willoughby is capable of murder, citing textual evidence that he contemplates doing away with both Mrs. Smith and his wife, Sophia Willoughby ("Death").

7. As one critic puts it, Austen's heroes possess "traces of arrogance, conceit and sadism . . . [t]hey teach, humiliate, punish, frustrate and tantalise the women they love but only to a degree which Jane Austen manages to disguise as acceptable behavior" (Beer 68).

8. One's marital decision "affects the family and the neighborhood" and even "the nation" (Erickson 207). Catherine Bristow claims that "Austen is less concerned for the general good of society than for the safety of each individual woman" that is achieved through their "regulation of passion" (31), but in a larger sense, these two concerns are interdependent.

9. As Celia Easton states, unlike the young Eliza, Marianne's "premature pleasurable indulgence is only metaphorically sexual—riding alone in a carriage with Willoughby and touring his aunt's prop-

erty—but it too was an accession to seduction, a willing abandonment of propriety and discretion" (122). Easton also rightly observes that Austen's "women do not need men to rescue them" but are agents of their own destinies who "have only themselves . . . to blame" when they make bad choices (133, 135). The fallen women include the two Elizas (*SS*), Maria Bertram (*MP*), and, although a little respectability was bought for her, Lydia Bennet (*PP*). Marie E. McAllister argues that the older Eliza, Colonel Brandon's first love, dies of venereal disease, and that " 'Consumption' is Austen's euphemism—and not only Austen's—for syphilis" (89).

10. Darryl Jones claims that the binaries of the Husband and the Lover, which respectively represent virtuous or "outrageously virile" men, are prevalent tropes in women's narratives of Austen's era that she "uses but also subverts" ("Highest" 213–215), citing Colonel Brandon as an example of Austen's complication of this typecasting: when he duels with Willoughby, both men prove "equal shots, equal sportsmen, equal phalluses—equal Lovers" (217).

11. Instead, Susan Morgan explains, the author "introduce[s] into British fiction the simple and endlessly influential point that women can grow, can be educated, can mature, without the catalyst of a penis. . . . She erases the physical basis of character" and "holds a heroine responsible for herself" ("Why" 352).

12. The antithesis to this approach is reflected in Austen's juvenilia, in which her heroines react to gender injustice the opposite way, reinforcing a limiting body-based female identity, ironically, by personifying a toxic male-identified physical excess-as-liberation. Jill Heydt-Stevenson analyzes female characters' lack of self-regulation in Austen's juvenilia, showing "how these young women tend either to internalize cultural violence by expressing their frustrations and needs in intoxication and food, a process itself that devours their willpower; or they externalize that violence in sexual escapades and adventures in thievery" as a way of compensating for the "larger social crimes against women themselves" ("Pleasure" sec. 2).

13. Glenda Hudson argues that Austen promotes "ideal egalitarian relationships based on fraternal qualities" (*Sibling* xiii) and that "Austen's concept of love is grounded more significantly in domestic rather than sexual instincts" (37). This reflects a common either-or approach to the subject in modern scholarship. Hudson, Darryl Jones, and oth-

ers also use the term "incestuous" loosely with respect to Austen's work, in a way that introduces aberrational sexual connotations that contradict Austen's hierarchy of values for courtship and the marriage relationship as well as her Anglican worldview and historical context, in which cousin-marriage was a legal practice. Thus, although the reader may consider cousin-marriage incestuous, Austen and her characters clearly do not. See Mary Jean Corbett, *Family Likeness*, pp. 35–37, for her discussion of the implications she sees in Austen's portrayals of marriages inside and outside the family and why she considers "incest" an inappropriate term for Austen's cousin-pairings, particularly with reference to the Fanny-Edmund relationship.

14. Jan Fergus avers that the misguidedness of first impressions constitutes a common pattern in Austen's works, in which "good looks and charm inevitably create favourable responses and biased judgement" ("Sex" 71).

15. Dennis Allen rightly asserts that Austen's "characters' final happiness is an indirect reward for their moral growth" and that "desire is not satisfied in spite of repression but because of it" (436), "after . . . any expectation of its fulfillment [has been] given up" (437), as he claims proves true for both Jane and Elizabeth Bennet.

16. Maaja Stewart interprets female sexuality and domesticity in *Sense and Sensibility*, *Mansfield Park*, and *Persuasion* in "an explicit imperial context" (72), claiming that Elinor Dashwood, Fanny Price, and Anne Elliot are "characterized by their ability to defend the integrity of the self against assaults from the outside" (73).

17. Eleanor Ty notes that Austen "shows her awareness of the unreliable and potentially haphazard nature of male protection," and "the ease with which a comic social encounter could turn into a kind of Gothic horror" (251).

18. As Claudia L. Johnson points out, even James "participates in abusive attempts to compel his sister to break her engagements" (*Jane* 47), a disturbing example of fraternal betrayal.

19. A "physically abusive partner often physically and socially isolates his victim, perhaps even prior to the use of any physical violence. Women are often discouraged by the batterer from . . . interactions with immediate family or friends. . . . Within this type of relationship, violence often escalates in severity and frequency over time" (Pagelow, 1981, 1997; cited in McHugh et al. 558).

20. By contrast, both Henry and his sister "share a tendency to avoid deep emotional involvement generally, and to form relationships in which they remain comparatively aloof while others become attached to them. . . . This is especially true of their sexual relationships . . . they enjoy a sense of power without running emotional risks"—in other words, they both possess "the desire for conquest, for a show of power over a particularly strong and challenging nature" (Moler 147).

21. As Maureen M. Martin expresses it, Mr. Knightley's dislike of Emma's relationship with Harriet stems from "Emma's encroachment on his patriarchal prerogatives. Emma is less willing than ever to submit to his guiding hand" (12) and her "love of power" reveals and directs her "self-assured sexuality" (10). I agree with this view to some extent, but would argue that Emma's primary goal in her interactions with men is not power as such, but the preservation of her selfhood by insisting on agency in a relationship; Harriet plays the critical role in her assessment of whether or not Mr. Knightley can and will honor her spunky individuality and enable her to thrive in marriage.

22. I am indebted to Hannah Menendez, a former student in my Austen course, for this last insight. She claimed that it reflects well on Mr. Knightley that he focuses on Emma's character and acknowledges her beauty only upon Mrs. Weston's persistently drawing his attention to it, as if he finally grudgingly admits, "All right! She's pretty!"

23. Claudia L. Johnson points out that in Emma's assumption of "power over the destinies of others . . . she poaches on what is felt to be male turf" (*Jane* 125). Yet even Mr. Knightley accepts "her right to preeminence" in Highbury society (126).

24. Frank amply proves himself an unworthy love interest for Emma. He objectifies Jane Fairfax, as evidenced when he anticipates resetting the family jewels to ornament her disembodied head: " 'The head'! . . . Frank seems to be thinking of Jane as an artefact to be decorated and enjoyed as a prestigious possession" (Wiltshire, *Body* 135).

25. My interpretation of the Emma-Knightley relationship has shifted significantly since the publication in 2000 of my more skeptical reading in the article, "Fathers and Lovers: The Gender Dynamics of Relational Influence in *Emma*."

26. She is "ward[ing] off what" Alice Chandler goes so far as to characterize as potentially "a verbal rape" (98).

27. Although this remark by Elizabeth to Colonel Fitzwilliam, on the surface, refers to her defense of Bingley's freedom to choose his own wife, it also applies to her beloved sister Jane (whose role in even subtly furthering her own love plot has been subverted by Darcy's interference) and to herself.

28. While acknowledging the difference in degree of the men's errors, Nancy Yousef makes a persuasive case for the parallels between Edward's deceit of Elinor and Willoughby's betrayal of Marianne, showing how the two characters make at least three disturbingly similar self-justifying remarks ("Emotions").

29. The critical misjudgment of marrying for looks is more rare for Austen's female characters, *Persuasion*'s Lady Elliot being one of the few examples (and she is already deceased by the timeframe of the novel).

30. Robyn Warhol claims that objectifiers of women like the two Elliot men who "look evaluatively at others' bodies" (11) are critiqued in *Persuasion*, whereas Wentworth and his brother-in-law "do not, without prompting, even see the body when they look at another person, men whose masculine worthiness is continually endorsed by the story" (9). I would argue that Wentworth grows into this perspective by a reform in his attitude toward Anne, but agree that it is critical that he not "make an object of Anne" (Warhol 11) if he is to earn her hand and make a worthy husband.

31. Christopher Nagle interprets these incidents as manifestations of Austen's adaptation of the hero and heroine of sensibility as influenced by Laurence Sterne, "establish[ing] both the worthiness of Wentworth, Austen's new Man of Feeling, as well as Anne's perfect fit as his feeling corollary, a tremblingly responsive yet socially responsible Woman of Feeling; or, borrowing from Sterne, a female 'SENSORIUM' " (105).

Chapter 3

1. Alison G. Sulloway describes the no-win situation that radical feminists of Austen's era decried, in which "Men of the middle and upper classes . . . posed as women's protectors by imprisoning them at home, then leaving them penniless and uneducated, and then refusing them any entry into work upon which they could survive without penury or

indignity" (72). Although Austen was fairly well educated and her family supported her writing endeavors, when her brother James took over their father's living, he and his wife descended on the Steventon rectory and scooped up most of its contents for as little as possible, while the retiring Mr. Austen and the female family members were ejected to scrape along at Bath, perhaps inspiring the author's depiction of John and Fanny Dashwood's vulture-like usurpation of Norland in *Sense and Sensibility* (Sulloway 18, 102–103).

2. See Marilyn Butler's incisive commentary on Austen's critique of the "sensibility" of "the worship of self" that threatens society with "the anarchy that follows the loss of all values but self-indulgence" (194).

3. Kathryn Davis avers that although Mrs. Dashwood is more closely affiliated with Marianne in her "emotional effusiveness," she gradually grows into a more Elinor-like sense in the course of the novel (70).

4. Charlotte Palmer and Mrs. Jennings are largely absent from *Sense and Sensibility* criticism, except for backhanded compliments or oversimplifications. Mrs. Jennings has been characterized as morally upright but "wonderfully deficient in both sense and sensibility" (apRoberts 357) and Charlotte as "all surface chatter, gossip and drollery" (Tauchert 66). Patricia Howell Michaelson convincingly views mother and daughter as the "most obvious" users of the stereotyped "woman's language" of Austen's time, with Mrs. Jennings recycling other people's dialogues and Charlotte employing "exclamation points and empty intensifiers" ("Woman's" 58). However, both characters possess acumen that their farcical feminine language betrays. Ian Watt does credit Mrs. Jennings for her role in awakening Elinor and Marianne from their "adolescent sensibility"—as someone who possesses "the essence of what really matters as regards" both elements the title highlights—but only briefly supports this claim by illustrating her prioritization of relationships over wealth and status (52, 53). P. Gila Reinstein similarly affirms the "mother-substitute" as "[p]erhaps an ideal combination of sense and sensibility" who "evaluates situations more justly than any other adult" (277), but does not offer an in-depth elaboration of this stance.

5. Some critics view *Sense and Sensibility* as "an antisentimental novel" (Tuite 56) and assume its "parody of the novel of sensibility" (95), and Inger Sigrun Brodey rightly generalizes that "Austen attacks only the sensibility which has become *in*sensible to others, to nature,

and even to oneself through excessive codification, elitism, or narcissism" ("Adventures" 114). Marianne does possess genuine feelings, but allows them to consume her, thus abandoning her responsibilities to family, society, and herself. Brodey argues that Elinor possesses "more poignant feelings than Marianne" (119).

6. Beth Lau perceptively argues that Austen's "depiction of Elinor's and Marianne's coping styles . . . anticipates current psychological theory and practice" (40). She explores how Marianne's obsessive grief "reflects the permanence and pervasive dimensions of pessimistic thinking" (42) while Elinor's engagement in "socializing with others and continuing her household duties" as well as "compartmentaliz[ing] her misfortune" (43) reflects her optimism. This is a fascinating and valid point, but Lau overstates the case in presenting Elinor as Marianne's opposite; by characterizing Elinor as "content" (49) and successful in avoiding depression, Lau downplays her analogous romantic grief.

7. Inger Sigrun Brodey remarks that "one cannot help but be astonished by the importance of female suffering in the late eighteenth century—the assumption that young, beautiful women are somehow particularly 'interesting' and attractive when they are in distress"; this attitude encourages female ruination as a kind of aestheticism (*Ruined* xix). Valerie Wainwright recognizes in Elinor, rather than the affective vulnerability I see, more of an authorially affirmed "tough-mindedness" and a combination of "remarkably selfless" behavior with a well-considered "self-concern" that resonates with Lockean rationalism ("Being"). Despite Elinor's tenacity of principle and reason, however, she proves herself to be nearly as emotionally fragile as Marianne.

8. It is telling that Austen's novels were considered " 'salubrious reading for the wounded' and prescribed as an aid to convalescence for the most severely shell-shocked soldiers" of World War I and inspired Rudyard Kipling's 1924 short story, "The Janeites" (Harman 146). In *Sense and Sensibility*, from being "near-mad with grief, paralysed by misery, the heroines are brought back from the brink to new lives of reasonable and harmonious happiness" (Tauchert 71). Austen reinforces that despite the sometimes chaotic fluctuations of earthly existence, it is housed within an ordered universe in which restoration is always possible.

9. A representative example is the claim that "Mrs. Jennings lacks the imagination necessary to see beyond the surface of her immediate circumstances" (Stohr 391–392).

10. Charlotte does show a natural concern for her child when the apothecary indicates the infectious nature of Marianne's illness, promptly leaving Cleveland with the child, but the novel briefly describes this one instance of her "alarm . . . on her baby's account" (*SS* 307) in third-person and does not characterize it as an over-reaction. (The 1995 film directed by Ang Lee and starring Emma Thompson lends comic relief to an otherwise painful segment of the film by imaginatively depicting Charlotte repeatedly shrieking for the nurse and whisking the baby away from danger.) Charlotte is clearly a devoted mother and daughter and a caring friend.

11. Claudia L. Johnson perceptively contends that *Sense and Sensibility* "urges the need to govern what we allow ourselves to hope and to believe" and dramatizes "the danger of hoping too intensely for so much, given a world that cannot be penetrated by our understandings, much less conjured by our wishes" ("Twilight" 172–173, 184).

Chapter 4

1. This remark appears in Austen's polite but self-assured response to a letter from Mr. Clarke, the librarian at Carlton House who communicated the Prince Regent's desire that Austen dedicate any of her novels to him (an obligation she reluctantly fulfilled in *Emma*). Austen employs the plea of ignorance to reject Clarke's suggestions for future novelistic themes, arguing that she must write what she knows. In the footnote to this letter in his memoir, Austen's nephew, James Edward Austen-Leigh, remarks that "It was her pleasure to boast of greater ignorance than she had any just claim to. She knew more than her mother-tongue, for she knew a good deal of French and a little of Italian." Quoted from "Letters of Jane Austen—Brabourne Edition," "Appendix 1: Correspondence with Mr. Clarke, from Austen-Leigh's Memoir," #iii, note 2, at pemberley.com.

2. According to Paula Byrne, Austen possessed admirable skill in dramatic reading and a thorough "knowledge of the world of the theatre" (x, xii). Penny Gay likewise considers the novelist to have been immersed in plays from her youth and describes various indicators of that influence in her juvenilia, mature fiction's theatrical narrator, and allusions to contemporary dramatic trends (1, 22, 24–25). For example,

Austen depicts Marianne Dashwood as a "tragedienne" like Sarah Siddons, performing in a "drama of sensibility" that ends as "the model of sentimental comedy" (35).

3. See David Selwyn, pp. 66–69 and Sandie Byrne, pp. 22, 45 for information on Austen's sewing ability, gifting of hand-stitched items, and attitude toward the skill as a lesser art.

4. Mary DeForest and Eric Johnson cite as evidence of the emphasis on women's intelligence in Austen's works that "[i]n most of the marriages that take place during the course of the novel, women have a higher density [of Latinate words] than the men they marry" (399). This pattern is especially striking, considering that women of Austen's time were prohibited from attending university or "enter[ing] the professions . . . [and] were considered unfitted to receive education in any classical language" (Lenta 27).

5. For example, the Stanford-Binet Intelligence Scale and its framing conception of "intelligence" have been critiqued as limited and biased. Roger W. Sperry originated the theory of "right" and "left" brain lateralization based on his work with epileptic patients in the 1960s. Despite the ongoing proliferation of systems for categorizing and identifying intelligences (which feature anywhere from a handful to several thousand competencies), gender- or otherwise bias-driven studies, results, and counterstudies continue to fuel controversy. Rather than seeking to determine a person's "intelligence" level as such, many assessment tools today are intended to enlighten those surveyed to their dominant traits, abilities, and interests, toward effective educational and vocational guidance. Jung-inspired methodologies and surveys of the Myers-Briggs and "StrengthsFinder" variety demonstrate the popularity of this trend. Thanks to Jessica Redman for providing her insights and expertise on these issues.

6. Psychologist Howard Gardner posits in his groundbreaking 1983 study that there are "several *relatively autonomous* human intellectual competences" (8), as supported by wide-ranging qualitative and quantitative data across multiple disciplines, "that . . . can be fashioned and combined in a multiplicity of adaptive ways by individuals and cultures" (9). His approach and the now nine "multiple intelligences" that he identifies resonate with Austen's implied view in her novels and have influenced my approach to her depiction of women's gifts or "competences" and their significance. Gardner advocates his theory

of the multiplicity of distinct human mental capacities with an eye to educational reform.

7. The centrality of piano-playing as a female activity in Austen's novels is characteristic of middle-class women's lives in the nineteenth century; women generally held exclusive reign over the piano, which provided them "a particular distinction within domestic culture" that explains why "the sacrifice of her piano is one of the harshest elements of the woman's share in the economic disasters portrayed in nineteenth-century fiction" (Burgan 51). In *Emma*, Frank Churchill's gift of a piano dramatically improves Jane Fairfax's limited life with her aunts, despite his obtrusive anonymity in giving it, which places Jane in a socially awkward position (*E* 51).

8. Lance Bertelsen argues that this style reflects the artistic precepts "that underlay the 'undetermined' manner of eighteenth-century portraiture and the verbal economy of literary pictorialism" (370). Janine Barchas discusses Austen's "playful and confident painterly allusions to the wide-ranging artistic styles of Sir Joshua Reynolds, George Morland, William Hodges, and Charles Hayter" through her choice of minor characters' names (159).

9. Gillen D'Arcy Wood makes the interesting point that "piano playing, in particular the regimen of practice, positioned British women such as Austen at the vanguard of a new, disciplined approach to time management and mechanical efficiency that was the domestic analogue of their male counterparts' education in the professions" (369–370). Wood views Jane Fairfax as an example of Austen's "participat[ion] in the imagined professionalization of female accomplishment" (366) that occurred during her time as part of "the debate over female education" (368).

10. Juliette Wells insightfully observes that this tactic enables Anne to maintain the appearance of proper sociability: "Piano-playing, especially to accompany dancing, allows Anne to yield to her emotions in a kind of protective cocoon that affords her privacy without actual withdrawal" ("In music" 107). This scene may also reinforce the argument that Austen participates in her era's "romantic reactions against" a trend toward "mechanical virtuosity" in the arts (Wood 366).

11. Susan Morgan points out that Elizabeth moves from a self-protective stance of critical detachment resembling her father's to "understand[ing] that a lively intelligence is personal and engaged" ("Intelligence" 67).

12. In his book-length study of Austen and Mozart, Robert K. Wallace compares Austen's "unexampled mastery of symmetry, balance, clarity, and restraint" in her novels with that of Mozart and claims that in addition to manifesting the key classical values, both artists also "anticipate the world of Romanticism in similar ways" (2).

13. Wells observes that "it is the harp's elegance, rather than its sound or tone, that matters here" and "the language of posing, not of actively playing" emphasizes this ("Harpist" 105).

14. Antonia Losano observes that Emma herself becomes the focus of Mr. Elton's attention while she paints, and the narratorial description focuses on her creative process rather than the portrait, possibly indicating Austen's identification with Emma and "the tribulations of the woman artist" caused by her "inherent desirability and gradually increasing power" (191).

15. Susan E. Jones emphasizes needlework's importance for women of the eighteenth and nineteenth century, during which women of the upper classes "learn sewing as ornamentation and as a social skill, useful in moments of emotion or ennui"; Mrs. Smith preserves her genteel status, despite her poverty, in creating decorative thread-cases as "part of a code that Austen uses to signal her readers that this item falls into the category of products that a woman of the gentility might make, but ordinarily only for family members and singular friends" ("Thread-cases").

16. David Selwyn indicates that although "drawing and painting were important accomplishments" (77), this visual art in Austen's time "was considered . . . [as] requiring skill in copying but little in the way of creativity" (85); I will show how Elinor's application of her ability to envision possibilities engages her creativity in a way similar to what many scholars denote Emma's "imaginism" but to more productive ends in the case of Elinor's protégée, Marianne.

17. Colonel Brandon has his faults as well, including that he seems preoccupied with his own sufferings over those of the dying Eliza. Darryl Jones claims that he is more disturbed by "her adultery and divorce, rather than her husband's evidently horrific brutality" (*Jane* 83) and expresses relief at the fatality of her illness due to her fallen state (84).

18. Moreland Perkins designates Elinor "one of the few intellectuals fully rendered in English-language fiction" (7), whose male-identified

"intellectual energy" contrasts with the "reticent domesticity" (54) of the man she loves and reflects a subversive gender-role reversal.

19. Devoney Looser argues that Eleanor Tilney "reads history to be entertained by human nature" and treats it "as fiction" in a way that reflects Austen's defense of the value of novels in an era in which histories were more respected (*British* 196).

20. As Kathi L. Groenendyk explains, "The picturesque movement paired the object with the viewer as people framed their view of landscape, or even used special glasses, to see scenery as landscape painting" (10).

21. Barbara Horwitz goes so far as to argue that "No other writer of her time asserted that men admired intelligent women or preferred to marry women of good sense, rather than those who were only pretty and good natured. Jane Austen was the only writer to insist that good nature was not enough to make a woman admirable" (127).

22. Austen benefited from a posse of "enthusiastic female support-ers" (Kaplan, *Jane* 99) who contributed to her thriving "creative voice and . . . professional writer's identity" (91). On a practical level, her sister, Cassandra, respected and protected her music and writing talents and the time she needed to cultivate them, and aside from Jane's minimal breakfast-making duties, "she was privileged with a general exemption from domestic chores when Cass and Martha were at home—almost as a man was privileged" (Tomalin 213).

23. David Selwyn identifies sewing as Fanny Price's only "accomplishment," pointing out that Mary Crawford is impressed by her sewing ability. She possesses significantly more important spiritual gifts, however, as will be discussed in the next chapter.

24. According to Jocelyn Harris, Austen chooses Henry as the mouthpiece for her "defense of fiction" as well as of "all women writers—including her own self" (*Revolution* 27).

25. Female community could be threatening to men, as Patricia Meyer Spacks's analysis of female gossip in the eighteenth century suggests. She argues that "the persistent association of 'curiosity' with gossip hints a more specific fear: that females, attentive to the minute, might uncover everything . . . and betray it to other females. The imagined assembly of only women . . . embodies uncharitable power" ("Talent" 3). Emma is a case in point, having "kept herself alive with the energies of gossip" as a resource that "supports the imaginative and improvisational" (13).

26. Some people thought the focus on elegant accomplishments neglected to "provide women with the sovereign subjectivity and intellectual resources thought necessary for their roles in family, society and nation, for independence when unmarried or widowed and for their individual spiritual salvation" (Kelly 258). Others were concerned that "unusual proficiency in the arts" would incite their rebellion against "accepted feminine roles" and encourage their taste for acclaim over the development of the virtues desirable for these roles (Wells, "In music" 101, 99).

27. In the case of Elizabeth Bennet, of course, the fact that Darcy pursues and ultimately marries her shows that he undercuts his own "explicit set of criteria for a mate" (Wells, "Fearsome").

28. Susan Morgan explains that Elizabeth's "impertinence" is the reason she is so beloved but also that this quality makes clear "that the major concern of [*Pride and Prejudice*] is with the possibilities and responsibility of free and lively thought" ("Intelligence" 54).

Chapter 5

1. For the relevant sections on the *History of England* in Moore's book, see pages 43-44, 52-56, and 60, and on the heroines' subjection to inhospitality in *Northanger Abbey* and *Mansfield Park*, see pages 85, 90-94, 109-112, 121-126, and 130. On a related note, similar to Moore and others, Misty Krueger designates Austen as one who "espouses the Stuart-Tory cause, much as her ancestors did" (246), citing as evidence the novelist's juvenilia and marginalia. Krueger gives no definitive reason for the young Austen's loyalty, but suggests that she was influenced in her expressions of it by "the genres of vindication as well as martyrology" (257).

2. See Ephesians 5:22-33. Note that all biblical references in this book are from the Authorized King James Version of the Bible from 1611.

3. As explained by Father Charles Browning, Austen would have participated in the general confession, with absolution, before the Eucharistic prayers, as articulated in the 1662 *Book of Common Prayer*, and private confessions would have been reserved for visitations to the sick; Holy Communion also would have been significantly less frequent in the Anglican Church of Austen's day. These factors would help to explain the sense of preciousness Austen infuses into her portrayals of female characters' confessions and sacramental food distributions.

4. Austen's epistolary pronouncement to Cassandra, "Now I will try to write of something else;—it shall be a complete change of subject—Ordination" is commonly misinterpreted as the author's forecasting of her next novel's subject. In fact, she was well into the composition of *Mansfield Park* by the writing of this letter; Deirdre LeFaye claims she is following up on information she sought from her cleric brother James via Cassandra about "the time necessary for the process of ordination" in order to be accurate respecting the duration of Edmund Bertram's ordination trip (411). However, Oliver MacDonagh suggests the common misinterpretation of Austen's remark "may also have been inspired" (1) because of the novel's exploration of median or "'middle' Anglicanism" and the religious and social issues surrounding it during Austen's era (2). He views the novel as concerned with "[t]he religion of the heart and act" (14).

5. Even when Sir Thomas discovers this circumstance, he is careful to avoid undermining Aunt Norris's authority or image with Fanny, imputing better intentions to her than likely motivated her unkind intervention. Though he overrules her mandate by ordering a fire for Fanny, he arguably does so more as part of his effort to manipulate Fanny's actions through her emotions than from true concern for her welfare.

6. Roberta Gilchrist explains that "the chapter house" where "daily meetings of the community" took place and "[t]he head of the house would occupy a raised seat at the east end" often occupied the "east range" of the cloister (111, 166). In addition, "It appears that English nunneries most often used galleries to accommodate women lodgers at the west or east end of the church, although eastern galleries may have been reserved additionally for novices" (109).

7. Gilchrist also discusses upper-class women's interiorized domestic habitation in castles and separation from men in social activities as influencing "nunneries of the highest social status" in which "medieval religious women" eschewed "communal dormitory and refectory in favour of separate households, or *familiae*" (168).

8. Fanny was on the brink of substituting for Mrs. Grant at one rehearsal when Sir Thomas returned; although one might interpret this willingness as a sign of her beginning to succumb to social pressure, it is important to note that she did not agree to take on the part or participate in the performance itself.

9. According to James Bond, "Many religious women chose to live solitary lives walled up in cells as anchoresses. A few nun-

neries . . . evolved directly out of anchoress settlements" while other anchoresses were "linked with established nunneries" (63). Fanny Price both enters an established house and builds (or rebuilds) a community around her, so both forms of anchoresses somewhat apply to her relationship to space and community at Mansfield.

10. The symbolism of the two gold chains and the cross Fanny wears at her coming-out ball suggests contrasting associations: Fanny's bondage to two exploitative men and also her marriage to Christ as best facilitated by clergyman Edmund, whose chain accommodates her cross (and who does reform his views of Mary Crawford). Fanny refuses participation in the home theater in part because it incites worship of the god of self, with Aunt Norris as head of the altar guild and usurper of the altar cloth.

11. A woman's vow of lifelong celibacy in marriage to Christ eliminated the expectation of motherhood as well, in which role her personal development would be largely or entirely displaced by consuming child-drearing, domestic, and other responsibilities. Social perception of this inherently subversive element becomes especially evident in the Victorian era, in which women's emphasis on intensive charitable work and especially devotions "could be controversial and lead to the perception of women's religious orders as a challenge to Victorian family values" (Fletcher 298). And yet, the mass appeal of the "Angel in the House" conception of women's moral purity and its rejuvenating influence would seem to support monastic life as especially fitting to the female gender.

12. Joyce Kerr Tarpley insightfully suggests that Fanny's living spaces at Mansfield and Portsmouth "may represent a kind of entering into the Christian's 'closet' " and interprets the upper and lower spheres she navigates as "the world of temporal action and 'sin' below" and the region "above this world" in which she strives "to work out her 'own salvation with fear and trembling' " (18), quoting Philippians 2:12 in this last phrase. Tarpley views Fanny and Mary as allegories, respectively, of "the growth and development of a Christian mind and . . . the secular mind with which it must contend in the modern world" (18). Sister M. Lucy Schneider recognizes a shift in the significance of Fanny's spaces that parallels her increasing influence, from "her inconsequence" in the tiny attic to "her acquisition of the east room . . . when she began to teach her callers values as well as to learn those values herself" (233).

13. Roger Sales draws parallels between the "Regency Crisis" when King George III becomes mentally incapacitated and Sir Thomas's

correlative disappearance to Antigua. *Mansfield Park*'s shifts in leadership suggest a "potentially subversive" response to the problem of an ineffectual sensualist as Prince Regent of England, in that "the younger son is a better regent than the legal heir and the poor female relation is superior to both of" Sir Thomas's sons (72).

14. As Sarah Emsley puts it, one heroine "possesses a firm knowledge of herself, but struggles to act with confidence," whereas the other "acts confidently but has to learn to think about the consequences of her actions" (129).

15. A few scholars discern medieval influences in Austen's work and offer developed explications of them. Susan Allen Ford reveals connections between Austen's *Emma* and neo-medieval Gothic novels, including Ann Radcliffe's *The Romance of the Forest* (1791) and Regina Maria Roche's *The Children of the Abbey* (1796), claiming that Austen both satirizes and affirms the Gothic genre. Emma faces "threats from within" and struggles to decode others' linguistic maneuvers while also herself playing "the Gothic villain" to Jane Fairfax as heroine, and the narrator both undercuts feminine victimhood and affirms Gothicism's narrative ambiguity (Ford 112, 117). Regarding *Persuasion*, Jocelyn Harris makes an argument for Anne Elliot's role as a reinterpretation of the "Loathly Lady" ("Anne" 275) in Chaucer's "Wife of Bath's Tale"—she journeys from physical degeneration to "restored . . . youth and beauty" (276) while earning her hero's deference and emblematizing "the real heroism of constancy" (288).

16. Jones also points out that the minced chicken, oysters, and sweetbread Emma distributes are all low-cost, considered palatable for the sick, and matched to "second circle" associates, indicating both her effort to choose foods her father will allow others to consume and her class-consciousness. This provides another example of Emma's mixed motives. On a related note, Sandie Byrne asserts that though diverse Austen characters "take pride in keeping a good table, it is only the bad characters for whom hospitality is showily competitive" (41).

17. Mr. Woodhouse clearly means well, but as several scholars have pointed out, he "can both tantalise and terrorise his neighbours" through "food allocation" in a way that "belittles them" (Hopkins 65), and they submit to his control over their meal because "they must be seen to show respect" (Moss 199).

18. See Matthew 19 and 20 for the significance of the biblical concept of "the last shall be first, and the first last" (Matthew 20:16).

19. Sandie Byrne points out that the Bateses also receive apples from Mr. Knightley, which they have baked at a local oven "and [Miss Bates] offers them to her own guests, so Mr. Woodhouse has not provided food which would be a novelty or luxury to his guests" (130). Note that Miss Bates has expressed enthusiastic appreciation for Mr. Knightley's apples well before the dinner at which her mother is fed the familiar fruit (likely baked thrice rather than twice—once more than Miss Bates prefers) and biscuits and prevented from eating the more substantial fricassee dish.

20. Scholars suggest that several characters in addition to Mr. Woodhouse abuse their power through consumables. Lisa Hopkins opines that Mr. Knightley "uses food as a means of currency . . . [giving] apples to the Bateses and strawberries to the picnic party" as part of his strategic preservation of his privileged status (68). Sarah Moss argues that "food in *Emma* . . . is a currency of both love and oppression" in the context of England's food riots of 1815 and the increase in poverty accentuated by land enclosure, and that it reflects Austen's view of the necessity of "accept[ing] caring and exploitation together" (196). Moss emphasizes Emma's and Mrs. Elton's abuses of food currency and Jane Fairfax's refusal of Emma's "luxury food" gifts and dominance (202). Although Mr. Woodhouse deprives his female guests "of meat[,] mak[ing] the meal inadequate" (Seeber, *Jane* 111), at least Mr. Knightley's provision of the elemental but filling protein of "cold meat" (*E* 355) suggests his greater liberality toward women than his fussy neighbor.

21. Peter Smith calls attention to Emma's "remarkably injurious slander of Jane Fairfax" as further evidence of her serious flaws of character, compared to which Mrs. Elton is relatively benign in her "harmless absurdity" (224). He also reminds us that Mrs. Bates "is the widow of a former vicar of Highbury" and the Bates women's identity as members of "a clerical family" (232) lends significance to their "genteel distress" as symbolic of the precarious state of the Anglican Church that privileged Emma must help to alleviate (235). Marilyn Butler observes that *Emma* displays "a pattern . . . of vulnerable single women, whom it is the social duty of the strong and rich to protect" (257). Austen suggests, more particularly, that it is the implicit duty of women to support women; Emma's strength and wealth magnify her violation of this code.

22. According to Felicia Bonaparte, Fanny follows "the eternal truths of religion[;] she is not tied to old or new . . . as the modern

world is threatened by the chaos of dissolution, it is Fanny who makes possible that ordination of the soul that constitutes the inner religion appropriate for the modern era" (59–60). By contrast, Bonaparte argues, Mary Crawford and her brother "embody the secular tendencies Austen perceives in the modern world . . . they arrive in the novel orphaned, cut off from the legacy of the past, cut off from its philosophic traditions, especially from metaphysics, even the benefits of reason, but most importantly, cut off from the spirit of religion" (55).

23. On a related note, Deborah J. Knuth emphasizes Elizabeth's "regret for the loss of" her close relationship with Charlotte Lucas, which draws her closer to Jane and her Aunt Gardiner, and accentuates the contrast between the two women's life paths: "Elizabeth's triumphant marital success . . . in distinction to Charlotte's fate, places her amid a circle of (largely) female friends and relations, in a careful disposition that unites friendship with appropriate marriage as joint prerequisites for happiness" ("Sisterhood"). I would argue that these "prerequisites" are not equally weighted in Austen's novels, which prioritize reconciliation among sisters as the condition or cause of the "reward" of union with good men. Glenda A. Hudson states that "[s]ororal loyalty and affection are seen as important for the advancement and vitality of the family and therefore of society . . . sisters with strong sororal bonds . . . owe their moral, social and emotional education to their sisters in some ways even more than to their suitors or husbands" ("Precious"). While I agree with most of this assertion, I would question the implications of the phrase "even more," since I would argue that the normative pattern is that other women, not men, are the main or only educators of Austen's heroines and when male influence enters in, it is usually only in the function of reinforcement of female mentors' lessons.

Chapter 6

1. In *The Improvement of the Estate*, Alistair Duckworth states that the eighteenth-century novelistic tradition prior to Austen "generally testif[ies] to a world that is divinely structured" (23).

2. As Robert Kern points out, even the beloved but less appealing "Jane's exposure to the natural world results in a bad cold, but Elizabeth's makes her radiant" (262).

3. Colin Jager and others interpret Fanny Price's appreciation for, and Mary Crawford's insensitivity to, nature as indicative of Fanny's moral superiority (57). Rachel Trickett emphasizes the significance of Fanny's isolation in the landscape, and her identity as "very much a romantic" (91).

4. Felicia Bonaparte notes that Edmund also sees her as his rock (60), and claims that the name Fanny stems from St. Francis of Assisi (52). Fanny's various associations with trees, rock, garden, roses, and shrubbery forecast her effectiveness as an environmental advocate who will positively influence her uncle and his heir as well as her future husband.

5. Seeber also claims Austen incorporates a scale of male enthusiasm for hunting (of animals and, by association, of women) as a moral litmus test, with disinterest in hunting as a symptom of merit (*Jane* 71). Multiple male characters are morally defined and evaluated for their husband potential based on their landscape aesthetics. The characters of Edmund Bertram, Henry Crawford, and Mr. Rushworth in *Mansfield Park* are clarified by their views of nature—Edmund seeks a harmonious co-inherence of buildings with nature that is somewhat akin to Darcy's management of Pemberley and possesses an authentic moral center, whereas Henry prefers artificial "improvements" that resonate with his devious persona and Mr. Rushworth desires change without possessing a clear vision of either his landscape aesthetic or his own identity. Rosemarie Bodenheimer summarizes the paradigm of heroines' assessment of the architecture of men's outward estates as a manifestation of their inward states: "Elizabeth recognizes Darcy's value at Pemberley; Emma validates her esteem for Mr. Knightley at Donwell Abbey, and begins to amend her view of Robert Martin as she looks at the view of Abbey-Mill Farm" (610).

6. See Matthew 25:14–46 and Luke 12:35–48 regarding the biblical concept of the faithful steward.

7. Sandie Byrne observes that "[t]he symmetrical position of the [lime] avenue, equidistant between the garden and the river, suggests planned and ordered nature" that provides sun protection and "medicinal blossom and sweet sap" that "enriched the still-room and hives of earlier Knightleys" (223), thus producing a beauty that sweetens their lives.

8. Sulloway also remarks that Austen's depictions of "gardens and pastoral scenes in her" work show that "[s]he simply loved them

for themselves, for their beauty and the invigorating support that they offered to people under stress" (186). Susan Morgan and others note "the interdependence of the rhythm of the seasons and the rhythm of characters' lives" in such novels as *Pride and Prejudice* and *Persuasion* (*Meantime* 170). The influence of Romanticism on Austen is well-covered ground. William Deresiewicz argues that characters' propounded enthusiasms for nature in the early novels (*SS, NA, PP*) follow forced, undercut scripts of picturesque and Romantic attitudes, whereas the latter three (*MP, P, E*) manifest their protagonists' authentic ties to landscape, such as "an attentiveness and spontaneous emotional responsiveness to nature" (20) reflective of "Wordsworthian-Coleridgian ideas" (21; 19–22).

9. Duckworth provides a similar description of the structure of Austen's works, in which "concern with the predicament of the dislocated individual" is manifest in "the movement from a condition of initial security to a period of isolation and then to a final reinstatement in society" (10). While I agree with him that in Austen's narratives, "each heroine . . . is finally located in a properly organized space for her social responsible activity" (8), I view this "location" of the female characters as one that they more actively determine and as ecofeminist in its implications.

10. In Joe Wright's film version of "Pride & Prejudice," the Bennet women are visually identified with nature in various ways, including as a flock of geese, and Elizabeth is also associated with a lone tree. During her walk to Netherfield, the camera cuts to a long shot of a grassy field dominated by an irregularly shaped, gnarly tree crowned with lush foliage that has a bonsai look. The subtext suggests that Elizabeth is the exotic tree that stands alone but is teetering a bit in its striving for isolated independence. See my essay, "The Offending Pig: Determinism in the Focus Features 'Pride & Prejudice.' "

11. Elizabeth resembles both Darcy and Lady Catherine in a negative way in her sometimes insensitively brusque self-assertion, superiority complex, and isolationism, but Lady Catherine tops heroine and hero in arrogant self-confidence by pronouncing on the unknowable, as when "[t]he party . . . gathered round the fire to hear Lady Catherine determine what weather they were to have on the morrow" (*PP* 166). Alison G. Sulloway identifies predictions of weather as a male-designated conversation topic, citing Chapman's remark on the subject in his edition of *Emma*, thus making Lady Catherine's commentary

gender-inappropriate. Lady Catherine is a hubristic steward whose emphasis on image and display exposes the imaginary, destructive nature of her relationship with all living things; her sickly daughter, Anne, emblematizes the mother's refusal to nurture human and non-human beings according to their own principles.

12. I disagree with William Galperin's interesting interpretation of Elizabeth's relationship to Pemberley and Darcy, according to which she passively submits to their circumscription of her. Galperin claims that she is "mastered by the scene" and "annexed in the act" of her "fantasies of control" (127) and "at the height of her imagined authority is no better than a mistress" (129). Although Elizabeth in a general sense embraces "the social order that Pemberley represents" (132), she has already amply challenged and rejected Darcy's play at authoritarianism and communicated unequivocally her insistence on egalitarianism in marriage. The text also foreshadows her continued sassiness toward Darcy that stuns Georgiana.

13. As noted earlier, all biblical references are from the Authorized King James Version from 1611.

14. William C. Snyder agrees that Elizabeth's increased self-knowledge occurs "through apprehensions complemented by picturesque landscape: as a viewer, as a woman, she gains perspective, and modulates her feelings accordingly" (150). He also notes that the picturesque is characterized by "the blending of opposing qualities in landscape, [and] thus prompts a new reading of the relation between nature and gender" (144).

15. Barbara Seeber views Marianne's as well as Fanny Price's "love of trees" as genuine and suggests that in her farewell to Norland's trees, Marianne "recognizes the alterity of nature, that the trees exist outside of human demands—whether utilitarian or aesthetic" (*Jane* 85).

16. Rosemarie Bodenheimer distinguishes between the language characters use when speaking of nature and their genuine experiences of it, and suggests distinct phases in their attitudes toward the environment in the novels. "In the early novels, the picturesque is created not as an idea, but as a vocabulary which can be well or badly used" (606). For example, Bodenheimer argues that the quieter experience of nature by characters like Elinor Dashwood (and later, Anne Elliot) suggests a greater appreciation for it than Marianne's loud but self-centered ebullience would seem to imply (which she views as sentimental parody and

"comic self-projection" [608–609]). Bodenheimer also critiques Fanny's nature speech to Mary Crawford as insincere, but sees the heroine as ultimately discovering a genuine passion for nature in which she loses her self-conscious language of appreciation. I see truth in these claims, but discern sincerity as well as exaggeration in the impassioned commentary of characters like Marianne and Fanny; diversification of their views and experiences does lead to less stagey talk and more absorbed admiration.

17. Alison G. Sulloway's interpretation of gardens as representing "androgynous spaces" is apropos to Austen's use of shrubberies, as "half-way between the man's absolute freedom to travel all over England at will, and the woman's small, restricted, domestic boundaries" (198). She provides interesting contextual background on how conduct-book writers exploited altered and mismatched "pastoral metaphors" for women from Renaissance verse and the chivalric tradition in absurdly contradictory as well as denigrating and subjugating ways that Austen undercuts. For example, these authors "loved pastoral metaphors of women as cattle or sheep and men as shepherds, or women as mute and decorative foliage on the 'fringe' of the central places tilled by male gardeners" (29). By contrast, Austen's heroines must take possession of and consciously define their spaces.

18. This pattern manifests a characteristic predicament of Austen's female protagonists, who "encounter pressures from within and without to conform and only from within to protect their sense of self. However, although men and women are vulnerable to shaping by external sources (Fanny Price moves towards accepting Henry Crawford), this plasticity also offers the possibility that they can affect the direction of their lives. They are not fixed by nature or nurture in a dichotomy of male supremacy and female inferiority" (L. Smith 29).

19. Jill Heydt-Stevenson asserts that Austen "suggests that not only the placement of trees, but also the management of women and of other nations will affect the health and future of Britain" (*Unbecoming* 152). I would qualify this assertion in that Austen depicts the critical importance of her heroines learning how to "manage" themselves in and through naturescapes.

20. Lisa Hopkins notes the importance of Mrs. Weston's pregnancy and birth of the female child for which Emma hopes, describing "the rhythms of the narrative structure as . . . encas[ing] the story of Emma within the understated framework of Mrs Weston's swelling womb" (66)

and, more apropos to my point here, Hopkins remarks that "the novel itself gives birth to a girl, a new Emma" who revises her plans for the future to embrace marriage and motherhood (62). However, the novel's "new Emma" is much more than a woman who has changed her mind about marrying and having her own family—she effects a moral and spiritual rebirth because this is what her conscience and self-respect demand in her effort to become her whole self.

21. Jessica Brown offers an insightful analysis of Anne as practicing an "aesthetic of restraint that yields a life-giving, elegant spaciousness" (179) that furthers her ability to understand and interact empathetically with others as well as to absorb natural beauty in a self-rejuvenating way (180, 184). According to Brown, Austen portrays Anne's "expansive restraint" as stemming from her prayerfulness and, thus, "as a spiritual discipline, one received and practiced through divine help" (189).

22. Adela Pinch offers the interesting view that "*Persuasion* explores what it feels like to be a reader" as compared to the sensation of "the presence of other people" and their impact on oneself (139). She analyzes Anne's suppression of or attentiveness to particular speeches and sounds surrounding her at the concert hall, such as her honing in on Wentworth's speech and allowance of a mental "rushing in of sensations" as she "reduce[s] the external [social] world to a blur" (155).

23. Celia Easton argues that the city is not evil in Austen's vision and that she "refuses to demonize urban life. She takes her heroines into the city but she trusts their merits to stand up against whatever vices the city has to offer" (121); Easton also argues that it is to the disadvantage of male characters such as Mr. Bennet to be ignorant of the city (his inexperience with London contributes to his failure to find Lydia and Wickham [127]). These are valid points, though a female preoccupation with town and its superficial pleasures does generally signal moral inferiority in Austen's fiction.

24. Although to some extent, Anne Elliot may benefit from a revision in "the definition of home . . . from a physical location to an emotional condition" that "seems to allow women greater movement and an expanded role, as in the case of Mrs. Croft" (Vorachek 38), the physical and emotional locations are not either/or—they coalesce in the water.

25. Jocelyn Harris claims that Anne's restoration of her former beauty resembles the transformation of the old woman into a beautiful

young wife in Chaucer's "The Wife of Bath's Prologue and Tale" ("Anne" 275). The Crofts' "equality of 'maistrie' is what Anne and Wentworth will seek" (288). Harris also discusses parallels between *Persuasion* and Samuel Richardson's *Sir Charles Grandison*, and between her novel and Shakespeare's *The Winter's Tale*. "Like Shakespeare in his last plays, [Austen] turns woe into joy, for her seasonal returns restore a fallen world in a renewal that looks biblical, even millennial" (*Revolution* 188). Anne experiences a rejuvenation that resembles the "renewal of the lost lady" in *The Winter's Tale* (190).

26. Jon Spence, among others, suggests that Anne is aware of Wentworth's proximity when delivering this speech ("Abiding" 630). Jill Heydt-Stevenson points out that Anne and Wentworth actively participate in the visual and picturesque in their second courtship; "they learn to see contextually, and in this process they become, metaphorically speaking, landscapes for each other to inspect and interpret . . . their visual exchanges become the sites of interpretation" ("Mourning" 55).

27. According to Deborah Kaplan, women on board ships experienced the benefits of being with their husbands and sometimes their children, but also had to face such problems as cramped quarters, social isolation, bad weather, outbreaks of diseases on-ship which could necessitate sending their children to relatives on land for extended stays, and so on, as Fanny Austen's experiences reveal. Austen's idealization of life on the sea is more symbolic than utopian; she "construct[s] a profound, ideological vision of cultural change. It champions a spirited professional and entrepreneurial social group" that "offer[s] women as well as men happier and more vital social roles" ("Domesticity" 120).

28. Although we do not know whether Anne will travel aboard ship with Captain Wentworth or await him from an onshore hearth, or a combination of both, Wentworth has adjusted to the current of Anne's character in the course of his reform and will likely be attentive to her judgment and wishes. His declaration in opposition to women living on ship in his debate with his sister Sophia Croft occurs before his reform. Regardless, his provision to Anne "of a very pretty landaulette" (250) demonstrates his recognition of the importance of his wife's mobility.

29. Fanny Price goes through a similar process as a star-gazing idealist that some critics consider artificial in her speeches about nature; she must adjust her vision from the distant observer of life from park

benches and windows, and from the correlative social and emotional anonymity of a self-obscuring servant, to directing her life as an acting subject. As explored in chapter 5, her astute insight as a contemplative person at the sidelines of the action becomes a fully realized social and spiritual boon only when applied to the enactment of her monastic vocation as a spiritual advisor. She must also necessarily assert and coordinate her authentic inhabitation of inner and outer spaces—her freedom of individual desire—to become whole as well as a genuine part of the larger whole she serves.

30. On the one hand, as Richard Handler states, "In addition to the personal qualities of human beings, aspects and attributes of the nonhuman natural world can be improved by human action" (21). Yet we must be cautious in acting upon this prerogative: "The example of Pemberley shows that the improvement of nature must follow nature itself, or else improvement misfires and creates the unnatural" (Handler 22).

Chapter 7

1. Margaret Kirkham asserts that Austen came of age at a time when, for women, "to become an author was, in itself, a feminist act" (33) and the "Feminist Controversy" was of prominent public concern (53). Kirkham suggests that Austen was influenced by the backlash that occurred after Wollstonecraft's husband published his scandalous memoir of her in 1798, which undermined the credibility of other women writers and caused a "clamp-down on feminism" that may have contributed to the gap in Austen's literary output (54).

2. Mary Waldron describes "the perfect conduct-book young woman" in these terms: "well-informed, but discreet; a responder rather than an initiator; scintillatingly accomplished, but at the same time modest and quiet" (151).

3. Mary Poovey praises Austen's skill in depicting contrasting female characters as foils to the heroines and "to play at different roles, to explore, often through the characters of servants or lower-class women, direct actions forbidden to the more proper lady" (43). Austen also often chooses as doubles women of the same class whose surface differences serve as a distraction from their shared ideological stance. Claudia L. Johnson gives a similar explanation for female authors' use of

typecasting: "Skeptical women novelists try to engage in incisive social criticism and at the same time to assure touchy readers that *they* are not uppity and insubordinate women, by creating a new and short-lived character type: the freakish feminist, or 'female philosopher,' as she was then called" (*Jane* 19). Austen creates other "feminist" character types as well; only Mary Bennet and perhaps Lady Catherine might be termed a "female philosopher" among the fools I will analyze. Johnson also claims that even some modern readers "expect heroines to be like Fanny Price, to disclaim power" (127).

4. Paula Byrne observes that the author's "fools are as distinctive and perfectly discriminated as are the heroines" (x). On the subject of male fools as literary types, Stephen Ahern remarks of Willoughby's question to Elinor—"do you think me most a knave or a fool?"—that "it identifies the two poles often inhabited by the hero of sensibility narrative" (204). Men are as prone to foolishness in diverse forms as women are in Austen's narratives.

5. Lauber characterizes Austen's fools as static performers of "an endless repetition" of "variations on a theme" ("Fools" 511) who caricature "a single trait" and create surmountable obstacles for the protagonists (512).

6. Maaja Stewart generalizes, "In comic works . . . the fools respond, often in extreme fashion, to the basic conflicts and expectations of their worlds while remaining quite unconscious of the deeper human realities underlying these conflicts" (72), and shows how Austen rewrites and enriches conventional literary types in *Emma*'s Miss Bates and Mr. Woodhouse.

7. Kate Fullbrook avers that Austen employs "a complex ironic mode . . . of the survivor who must speak the truth indirectly, and pay service to the very proprieties that evoke a hostile response" (45). Some characters proclaim their wrongs very openly, however, particularly to female auditors; the feminist discourse of Austen's fools and ingénues is more conspicuous than commonly acknowledged.

8. David Cowart interprets *Mansfield Park*'s female characters through the lens of the biblical parable of the wise and foolish virgins, viewing Fanny as the only wise virgin and the other women as distinguished by whether they "act" or "stand by patiently, quietly maintaining the status quo pending the return of Mansfield's moral arbiter, Sir Thomas" (78). Fanny is more complex and rebellious than

Cowart's interpretation suggests, however, and herself becomes the "moral arbiter" of Mansfield.

9. These negative feelings toward Edmund become more obvious in the narrator's quoting of Fanny's thoughts about his nearly suicidal stupidity regarding Mary—"He is blinded, and nothing will open his eyes. . . . Fix, commit, condemn yourself" (424).

10. Patricia Howell Michaelson points out that this controversial protagonist "assumes the authority of a Lady Catherine" without her status, displaying a "manly" directness and initiative in conversation that deviates from the era's social standards of middle-class feminine conduct and explains why "some readers felt that she was 'pert'" (*Speaking* 210). Michaelson further explains that "reading aloud was understood as a way of practicing speech" (128); performing fiction such as Austen's provided women readers with a means of developing a diverse "range of linguistic skills . . . [b]y personating young and old characters, male and female, silly and wise" (190). This enabled women to explore their own complexities of character while refining their rhetorical flexibility (215).

11. Sandie Byrne identifies Mrs. Croft as among Austen's dominant women who are not portrayed "as bullying harridans" and who "feel no need to feign ignorance or imbecility" (156).

12. Devoney Looser points out that although "Mrs. Elton's statements demonstrate recognition of women's uphill battle to exert power in a patriarchal world" and female unity's importance as a counterforce, she is self-serving and self-contradictory: "For every statement that invokes women's rights rhetoric, there is one that reinforces female submission in marriage" ("Always" 194, 195).

13. Lauber acknowledges that Emma "temporarily becomes a fool. Deceiving herself about her own nature and her own needs, she necessarily blinds herself to the reality of those about her" and "constantly misses the obvious" ("Fools" 523). However, he claims she "is unique" in this, whereas several other Austen heroines—including Elizabeth Bennet, Marianne Dashwood, and Catherine Morland—also evidence this pattern.

14. In her exploration of *Women Writers and Old Age in Great Britain, 1750–1850*, Devoney Looser claims that although Austen "generally indicts those who engage in the most exaggerated and harmful stereotyping of the old" (77) and is "a feminist" whose "heroines may

range beyond dominant ideologies for women . . . her old maids appear to have conformed to them" (95). Jean B. Kern, on the other hand, contrasts male and female novelists' portrayals of old maids and claims that Austen "treats old maids sensitively and delicately" (212).

15. In "'My sore throats, you know, are always worse than anybody's': Mary Musgrove and Jane Austen's Art of Whining," Jan Fergus identifies Mary Musgrove as Austen's most "accomplished whiner" ("Comedy" 44), who skillfully expresses "both deprivation and entitlement" (43). Fergus also acknowledges the importance of "whining" as "a way to protest against the way one's life is ordered" and contextualizes Mary Musgrove's whining as indicative of her "insecurity and unhappiness ("Sore"). Fergus theorizes that Mary was the third wheel in childhood and that Austen critiques the gender double-standard of a society that tolerates "the expression of suffering" by men but not by women.

16. This description is quoted from Austen's letter to Fanny Knight in which the author characterizes Anne Elliot as "almost too good for me" and makes her famous assertion that "pictures of perfection as you know make me sick & wicked" (23–25 March 1817).

17. Jan Fergus remarks on a related pattern in *Pride and Prejudice*, in which Elizabeth Bennet employs "female irony" that "repeats the terms of the dominant male discourse, but displaces them: it can be read 'straight' as repetition (Mr. Darcy has no faults) and ironically as displacement (Mr. Darcy has many faults)" ("Power" 106).

18. Poovey states of eighteenth-century women's novels that they "often echo conduct books almost verbatim, stressing self-control and self-denial to the exclusion of psychological complexity and attributing almost all initiative to the evil characters rather than to the heroines" (38). Austen playfully draws on that tradition in her depiction of Anne's flat recitation, while endowing her and the other heroines with substantial initiative.

19. Although I would not designate as "tricksters" Mary Musgrove or other "feminist fools" I identify in this chapter (with the possible exception of Mary Crawford), Audrey Bilger's description is apropos of the paradigm I elucidate: "Tricksters draw attention to themselves and force the heroines and the reader to take a look at what all the fuss is about. They embody a potent threat to the status quo by providing a foil for the heroines' discreet conduct and by acting out the heroines' transgressive desires" (98). Bilger also makes the insightful point that

"[b]y satirizing foolish and manipulative women . . . Austen criticize[s] the perversions of character that take place within a male-dominated culture" (187). Mary's character is at least partially poisoned by her husband's behavior and the prerogatives that enable his exploitative maneuvering.

Chapter 8

1. Cornel West aptly defines a "great book" as one that most effectively addresses "the challenge of trying to be a decent person in the world. There is no more fundamental question." One should strive to be, like *Persuasion*'s Anne Elliot, what West denotes "a subversive for sweetness." See my article, "Why Cornel West Loves Jane Austen," from which I borrow the quotes from West included in this note, along with some of my own words.

2. Susan Greenfield similarly attributes Emma's social anxiety and resistance to separation from Harriet and Miss Taylor to her mother-loss (147, 156).

3. Patricia Meyer Spacks explains that through Elinor's secrecy about Lucy and Edward's engagement and its devastating consequences to her, she both protects others' feelings and engages in "self-preservation" (*Privacy* 111) through protecting her "own as well as others' privacy" (112).

4. One of the few weaknesses of the Emma Thompson screen play for the Ang Lee *Sense and Sensibility* is that the daunting task of conversing with Edward about "Mrs. Edward Ferrars" is relegated entirely to Mrs. Dashwood, thus significantly lessening Elinor's heroism. In the novel, Mrs. Dashwood only opens the subject by "hop[ing] that he had left Mrs. Ferrars very well" (359).

5. Tony Tanner makes the related point that Austen effectively portrays "the problematics of good manners" within "a much larger drama: the drama of the salvation and regeneration—or damnation—of the social order of her time" (28).

Works Cited

Ahern, Stephen. *Affected Sensibilities: Romantic Excess and the Genealogy of the Novel, 1680–1810*. New York: AMS Press, Inc., 2007. Print.

Allen, Dennis W. "No Love for Lydia: The Fate of Desire in *Pride and Prejudice*." *Texas Studies in Literature and Language* 27.4 (1985): 425–443. Print.

Anderson, Kathleen. "Fathers and Lovers: The Gender Dynamics of Relational Influence in *Emma*." *Persuasions: The Jane Austen Journal On-Line* 21.2 (2000): n. pag. *jasna.org*. Web.

———. "The Jane Austen Diet: The Weight of Women in Austen's Letters." *Persuasions: The Jane Austen Journal* 27 (2005): 75–87. Print.

——— and Susan Jones. *Jane Austen's Guide to Thrift: An Independent Woman's Advice on Living Within One's Means*. New York: Berkley Books, 2013. Print.

———. "Jane's 'Wonder Women': Female Heroism the Austenian Way." *Sensibilities: The Journal of the Jane Austen Society of Australia* 33 (2006): 20–34. Print.

———. "'. . . let him succeed at last, Fanny': Edmund Bertram as Henry Crawford's Double in Jane Austen's *Mansfield Park*." Co-authored with Christina E. Unkel. *Sensibilities: The Journal of the Jane Austen Society of Australia* 46 (2013): 53–68. Print.

———. "Lounging Ladies and Galloping Girls: Physical Strength and Femininity in *Mansfield Park*." *Women's Studies: An Interdisciplinary Journal* 38.3 (2009): 342–358. Print.

———. "Mrs. Jennings and Mrs. Palmer: The Path to Female Self-Determination in Austen's *Sense and Sensibility*." Co-authored with Jordan Kidd. *Persuasions: The Jane Austen Journal* 30 (2008): 135–148. Print.

———. "The Offending Pig: Determinism in the Focus Features 'Pride and Prejudice.'" Special Issue of *Persuasions: The Jane Austen Journal On-Line* 27.2 (2007): n. pag. *jasna.org*. Web.

———. "The 'Ordination' of Fanny Price: Female Monasticism and Vocation in *Mansfield Park*." *Persuasions: The Jane Austen Journal On-Line* 35.1 (2014): n. pag. *jasna.org*. Web.

———. "Uncorsetting Austen: Passion and Narrative Structure in the Novels." Jane Austen Society of North America Annual General Meeting. Seattle, Washington. 5 Oct. 2001. Lecture.

———. "Why Cornel West Loves Jane Austen." *The Huffington Post*, "Books" category, "The Blog," November 12, 2014. N. pag. huffingtonpost.com. Web.

apRoberts, Ruth. "*Sense and Sensibility*, or Growing Up Dichotomous." *Nineteenth-Century Fiction* 30 (1975): 351–365. Print.

Austen, Jane. *The Novels of Jane Austen*. Vols. 1–5. Ed. R.W. Chapman. 3rd ed. Oxford: OUP, 1933–66. Print.

Austen-Leigh, James Edward. *A Memoir of Jane Austen*. 2nd Ed. London, UK: Richard Bentley and Son, 1871. *gutenberg.org*. Web. 3 Jan. 2016.

Bander, Elaine. "Jane Austen's Letters: Facts and Fictions." *Persuasions: The Jane Austen Journal* 27 (2005): 119–129. Print.

Barchas, Janine. "Artistic Names in Austen's Fiction: Cameo Appearances by Prominent Painters." *Persuasions: The Jane Austen Journal* 31 (2009): 145–162. Print.

Beard, Pauline. "Sex, Debility, and Lady Bertram: Lover or Loafer?" *Persuasions: The Jane Austen Journal On-Line* 27.1 (2006): n. pag. *jasna.org*. Web. 21 Jan. 2011.

Beer, Patricia. *Reader, I married him; a study of the women characters of Jane Austen, Charlotte Brontë, Elizabeth Gaskell and George Eliot*. New York: Barnes and Noble, 1974.

Bertelsen, Lance. "Jane Austen's Miniatures: Painting, Drawing, and the Novels." *Modern Language Quarterly* 45.4 (1984): 350–372. *MLA International Bibliography*. Web. 13 July 2005.

The Bible. Authorized King James Version (KJV), 1611. *kingjamesbible-online.org*. Web.

Bilger, Audrey. *Laughing Feminism: Subversive Comedy in Frances Burney, Maria Edgeworth, and Jane Austen*. Detroit, MI: Wayne State UP, 2002.

Bodenheimer, Rosemarie. "Looking at the Landscape in Jane Austen." *SEL* 21.4 (1981): 605–623. *MLA International Bibliography*. Web. 28 Jan. 2006.

Bonaparte, Felicia. "'Let Other Pens Dwell on Guilt and Misery': The Ordination of the Text and the Subversion of 'Religion' in Jane Austen's *Mansfield Park*." *Religion & Literature* 43.2 (2011): 45–67. Print.

Bond, James. "English Medieval Nunneries: Buildings, Precincts, and Estates." *Women and Religion in Medieval England*. Ed. Diana Wood. Oxford, England: Oxbow Books, 2003. Print.

Brann, Eva. "Whose Sense? Whose Sensibility? Jane Austen's Subtlest Novel." *Persuasions: The Jane Austen Journal* 12 (1990): 131–133. Print.

Bristow, Catherine. "Unlocking the Rape: An Analysis of Austen's Use of Pope's Symbolism in *Sense and Sensibility*." *Persuasions: The Jane Austen Journal* 20 (1998): 31–37. Print.

Brodey, Inger Sigrun. "Adventures of a Female Werther: Jane Austen's Revision of Sensibility." *Philosophy and Literature* 23 (1999): 110–126. Print.

———. *Ruined by Design: Shaping Novels and Gardens in the Culture of Sensibility*. New York: Routledge, 2008. Print.

Brown, Jessica. "'So Much Novelty and Beauty!': Persuasion and the Spacious Aesthetic of Restraint." *Jane Austen and the Arts: Elegance, Propriety, and Harmony*. Eds. Natasha Duquette and Elizabeth Lenckos. Bethlehem, PA: Lehigh UP, 2014. 179–192. Print.

Brown, Julia Prewitt. "Jane Austen's England." *Persuasions: Journal of the Jane Austen Society of North America* 10 (1988): 53–58. Print.

Brown, Lloyd W. "Jane Austen and the Feminist Tradition." *Nineteenth-Century Fiction* 28.3 (1973): 321–338. *JSTOR*. Web. 2 Oct. 2015.

Burgan, Mary. "Heroines at the Piano: Women and Music in Nineteenth-century Fiction." *Victorian Studies: An Interdisciplinary Journal of Social, Political, and Cultural Studies* 30.1 (1986): 51–76. Print.

Butler, Marilyn. *Jane Austen and the War of Ideas*. Oxford: Clarendon P, 1975. Print.

Byrne, Paula. *Jane Austen and the Theatre*. London, UK: Hambledon and London, 2002. Print.

Byrne, Sandie. *Jane Austen's Possessions and Dispossessions: The Significance of Objects*. New York: Palgrave, 2014. Print.

Canuel, Mark. "Jane Austen and the Importance of Being Wrong." *Studies in Romanticism* 44.2 (2005): 123–150. Print.

Capitani, Diane. "Augustinian Aesthetics in Jane Austen's World." *Jane Austen and the Arts: Elegance, Propriety, and Harmony*. Eds. Natasha Duquette and Elizabeth Lenckos. Bethlehem, PA: Lehigh UP, 2014. 193–204. Print.

Chandler, Alice. " 'A Pair of Fine Eyes': Jane Austen's Treatment of Sex." *Studies in the Novel* 7 (1975): 88–103. *MLA International Bibliography*. Web. 23 June 2012.

Cohenour, Gretchen. "Economic Motivation: Injured Bodies in Austen's *Northanger Abbey*." *MP: An Online Feminist Journal* 2.5 (2009): 14–26. *Academinist.org*. Web.

Corbett, Mary Jean. *Family Likeness: Sex, Marriage, and Incest from Jane Austen to Virginia Woolf*. Ithaca: Cornell UP, 2008. Print.

Cowart, David. "Wise and Foolish Virgins (and Matrons) in *Mansfield Park*." *South Atlantic Bulletin* 44.2 (1979): 76–82. Print.

Curry, Mary Jane. " 'Exquisite' Nature: Serious Pastoral in *Emma*." *Persuasions: The Jane Austen Journal* 38 (2016): 107–115. Print.

Dadlez, E.M. *Mirrors to One Another: Emotion and Value in Jane Austen and David Hume*. Chichester, UK: Wiley-Blackwell Publishing, 2009. Print.

Davis, Kathryn. "Exonerating Mrs. Dashwood." *Persuasions: The Jane Austen Journal* 33 (2011): 61–74. Print.

Dawkins, Richard. Interview. "Richard Dawkins: By the Book." *The New York Times*, 12 Sept. 2013. Web.

De Beauvoir, Simone. *The Second Sex*. Trans. and Ed. H.M. Parshley. New York: Vintage, 1989. Print.

DeForest, Mary, and Eric Johnson. "The Density of Latinate Words in the Speeches of Jane Austen's Characters." *Literary and Linguistic Computing: Journal of the Association for Literary and Linguistic Computing* 16.4 (2001): 389–401. Print.

Deresiewicz, William. *Jane Austen and the Romantic Poets*. New York: Columbia UP, 2004. Print.

Dinkler, Michal Beth. "Speaking of Silence: Speech and Silence as a Subversive means of Power in Jane Austen's *Sense and Sensibility*." *Persuasions: The Jane Austen Journal On-Line* 25.1 (2004): n. pag. *jasna.org*. Web.

Duckworth, Alistair. *The Improvement of the Estate*. 1971. Baltimore, MD: Johns Hopkins UP, 1994. Print.

Easton, Celia. "Austen's Urban Redemption: Rejecting Richardson's View of the City." *Persuasions: The Jane Austen Journal* 26 (2004): 121–135. Print.

Ehrenpreis, Irvin. "Jane Austen and Heroism." *New York Review of Books* (1979): 37–43. Print.

Emsley, Sarah. *Jane Austen's Philosophy of the Virtues*. New York: Palgrave Macmillan, 2005. Print.

Erickson, Joyce Quiring. "Public and Private in Jane Austen's Novels." *Midwest Quarterly: A Journal of Contemporary Thought* 25.2 (1984): 201–219. Print.

Fergus, Jan. "The Comedy of Gendered Whining in *Persuasion* and *Emma*." *New Windows on a Woman's World*. Eds. Colin Gibson and Lisa Marr. Vol. 2. Dunedin, New Zealand: U of Otago, 2005. 40–55. Print.

———. " 'My sore throats, you know, are always worse than anybody's': Mary Musgrove and Jane Austen's Art of Whining." *Persuasions: The Jane Austen Journal* 15 (1993): 139–143. Rpt. Online: n. pag. *jasna.org*. Web. 2 Oct. 2015.

———. "The Power of Women's Language and Laughter." *The Talk in Jane Austen*. Eds. Bruce Stovel and Lynn Weinlos Gregg. Edmonton, AB: U of Alberta P, 2002. 103–121. Print.

———. "Sex and Social Life in Jane Austen's Novels." *Jane Austen in a Social Context*. Ed. David Monaghan. Totowa, NJ: Barnes & Noble, 1981. 66–85. Print.

Flavin, Louise. "Free Indirect Discourse and the Clever Heroine of Emma." *Persuasions: The Jane Austen Journal* 13 (1991): 50–57. Rpt. online. N. pag. *jasna.org*. Web. 30 July 2016.

Fletcher, Robert P. " 'Convent Thoughts': Augusta Webster and the Body Politics of the Victorian Cloister." *Victorian Literature and Culture* 31.1 (2003): 295–313. Print.

Folsom, Marcia McClintock. "The Narrator's Voice and the Sense of *Sense and Sensibility*." *Persuasions: The Jane Austen Journal* 33 (2011): 29–39. Print.

Ford, Susan Allen. "How to Read and Why: *Emma*'s Gothic Mirrors." *Persuasions: The Jane Austen Journal* 25 (2003): 110–120. Print.

Fullbrook, Kate. "Jane Austen and the Comic Negative." *Women Reading Women's Writing*. Ed. Sue Roe. Brighton, UK: Harvester, 1987. 37–57. Print.

Galperin, William H. *The Historical Austen*. Philadelphia, PA: U of Pennsylvania P, 2003. Print.

Gardner, Howard. *Frames of Mind: The Theory of Multiple Intelligences*. New York: Basic Books, Inc., 1983. Print.

Gay, Penny. *Jane Austen and the Theatre*. Cambridge, UK: Cambridge UP, 2002. Print.

Giffin, Michael. *Jane Austen and Religion: Salvation and Society in Georgian England*. New York: Palgrave Macmillan, 2002. Print.

Gilchrist, Roberta. *The Archaeology of Religious Women*. New York: Routledge, 1994. Print.

Giuffre, Giulia. "Sex, Self and Society in *Mansfield Park*." *Sydney Studies in English* 9 (1983–1984): 76–93. Print.

Gorman, Anita G. *The Body in Illness and Health: Themes and Images in Jane Austen*. New York: Peter Lang, 1993. Print.

Greenfield, Susan C. *Mothering Daughters: Novels and the Politics of Family Romance, Frances Burney to Jane Austen*. Detroit, MI: Wayne State UP, 2002. Print.

Groenendyk, Kathi L. "The Importance of Vision: *Persuasion* and the Picturesque." *RSQ: Rhetoric Society Quarterly* 30.1 (2000): 9–28. Print.

Handler, Richard. *Jane Austen and the Fiction of Culture: An Essay on the Narration of Social Realities*. Tucson: U of Arizona P, 1990. Print.

Harbus, Antonina. "Reading Embodied Consciousness in Emma." *SEL: Studies in English Literature 1500–1900* 51.4 (2011): 765–782. *Project MUSE*. Web. 9 Oct. 2013.

Harman, Claire. *Jane's Fame: How Jane Austen Conquered the World*. New York: Henry Holt, 2009. Print.

Harris, Jocelyn. "Anne Elliot, the Wife of Bath, and Other Friends." *Women & Literature* 3 (1983): 273–293. Print.

———. *A Revolution Almost Beyond Expression: Jane Austen's* Persuasion. Newark, NJ: U of Delaware P, 2007. Print.

Heydt-Stevenson, Jill. " 'Pleasure is now, and ought to be, your business': Stealing Sexuality in Jane Austen's Juvenilia." *Historicizing Romantic Sexuality* (2006). *Romantic Circles Praxis Series*. Ed. Orrin N.C. Wang. Web. 4 Oct. 2013.

———. "'Slipping into the Ha-Ha': Bawdy Humor and Body Politics in Jane Austen's Novels." *Nineteenth-Century Literature* 55.3 (2000): 309–339. Print.

———. "'Unbecoming Conjunctions': Mourning the Loss of Landscape and Love in *Persuasion*." *Eighteenth-Century Fiction* 8.1 (1995): 51–71. Print.

———. *Unbecoming Conjunctions: Subversive Laughter, Embodied History.* New York: Palgrave Macmillan, 2005. Print.

Hopkins, Lisa. "Food and Growth in *Emma*." *Women's Writing* 5.1 (1998): 61–70. *tandfonline.com*. Web. 19 Aug. 2015.

Horwitz, Barbara. *Jane Austen and the Question of Women's Education.* New York: Peter Lang, 1991. Print.

Hudson, Glenda A. "'Precious Remains of the Earliest Attachment': Sibling Love in Jane Austen's *Pride and Prejudice*." *Persuasions: The Jane Austen Journal On-Line* 11 (1989): n. pag. *jasna.org*. Web. 13 Jan. 2010.

———. *Sibling Love & Incest in Jane Austen's Fiction.* 1992. New York: St. Martin's, 1999. Print.

Jager, Colin. "*Mansfield Park* and the End of Natural Theology." *Modern Language Quarterly* 63.1 (2002): 31–63. *MLA International Bibliography*. Web. 19 Jan. 2006.

Johnson, Claudia L. *Jane Austen: Women, Politics, and the Novel.* Chicago: U of Chicago P, 1988. Print.

———. "The 'Twilight of Probability': Uncertainty and Hope in *Sense and Sensibility*." *Philological Quarterly* 62 (1983): 171–186. Print.

Johnson, Judy Van Sickle. "The Bodily Frame: Learning Romance in *Persuasion*." *Nineteenth-Century Fiction* 38.1 (1983): 43–61. Print.

Jones, Darryl Richard. "'The Highest Point of Extasy': Sex and Sexuality in the Novels of Jane Austen and Her Predecessors." Diss. U of York, 1994. Print.

———. *Jane Austen.* New York: Palgrave Macmillan, 2004. Print.

Jones, Hazel. *Jane Austen and Marriage.* London: Continuum, 2009. Print.

Jones, Susan E. "Death and the Darling Daughters: The Grim Reaper in *Sense and Sensibility*." Jane Austen Society of North America Annual General Meeting. Fort Worth, Texas. 14 Oct. 2011. Lecture.

———. "Oysters and Alderneys: *Emma* and the Animal Economy." *Persuasions: The Jane Austen Journal On-Line* 37.1 (2016): n. pag. *jasna.org*. Web. 15 May 2017.

———. "Thread-cases, Pin-cushions, and Card-racks: Women's Work in the City in Jane Austen's *Persuasion*." *Persuasions: The Jane Austen Journal On-Line* 25.1 (2004): n. pag. *jasna.org*. Web. 21 Aug. 2015.

Kaplan, Deborah. "Domesticity at Sea: The Example of Charles and Fanny Austen." *Persuasions: Journal of the Jane Austen Society of North America* 14 (1992): 113-121. Print.

———. *Jane Austen Among Women*. 1992. Baltimore, MD: The Johns Hopkins UP, 1994. Print.

———. "Representing Two Cultures: Jane Austen's Letters." *The Private Self: Theory and Practice of Women's Autobiographical Writings*. Ed. Shari Benstock. Chapel Hill, NC: U of North Carolina P, 1988. Print.

Kelly, Gary. "Education and Accomplishments." *The Cambridge Edition of the Works of Jane Austen: Jane Austen in Context*. Ed. Janet Todd. Cambridge, England: Cambridge UP, 2005. 252-261. Print.

Kern, Jean B. "The Old Maid; Or, 'To Grow Old, and Be Poor, and Laughed At.' " *Fetter'd or Free? British Women Novelists, 1670-1815*. Athens, OH: Ohio UP; 1986. 201-214. Print.

Kern, Robert. "Ecocriticism: What Is It Good For?" *The ISLE Reader: Ecocriticism, 1993-2003*. Eds. Michael P. Branch and Scott Slovic. Athens, GA: U of Georgia P, 2003. 258-281. Print.

Kirkham, Margaret. *Jane Austen, Feminism and Fiction*. Totowa, NJ: Barnes & Noble Books, 1983. Print.

Knuth, Deborah J. "Sisterhood and Friendship in *Pride and Prejudice*: Need Happiness Be 'Entirely a Matter of Chance'?" *Persuasions On-Line* 11 (1989): n. pag. *jasna.org*. Web. 13 Jan. 2010.

Kramp, Michael. *Disciplining Love: Austen and the Modern Man*. Columbus, OH: The Ohio State UP, 2007. Print.

Krueger, Misty. "From Marginalia to Juvenilia: Jane Austen's Vindication of the Stuarts." *The Eighteenth Century* 56.2 (2015): 243-259. *Project MUSE*. Web. 1 Feb. 2016.

Lane, Maggie. *Jane Austen and Food*. London: The Hambledon Press, 1995. Print.

Lau, Beth. "Optimism and Pessimism: Approaching *Sense and Sensibility* through Cognitive Therapy." *Persuasions: The Jane Austen Journal* 33 (2011): 40-52. Print.

Lauber, John. *Jane Austen*. New York: Twayne, 1993. Print.

———. "Jane Austen's Fools." *Studies in English Literature, 1500-1900* 14.4 (1974): 511-524. Print.

Le Faye, Deirdre. *Jane Austen's Letters*. Third ed. Oxford: Oxford UP, 1995. Print.

Lehner, Ernst, and Johanna Lehner. *Folklore and Symbolism of Flowers, Plants and Trees*. New York: Tudor Publishing Co., 1960. Print.

Lenta, Margaret. "Androgyny and Authority in *Mansfield Park*." *Studies in the Novel* 15.3 (1983): 169-182. Print.

Libin, Kathryn. "Lifting the Heart to Rapture: Harmony, Nature, and the Unmusical Fanny Price." *Persuasions: The Jane Austen Journal* 28 (2006): 137-149. Print.

Looser, Devoney. *British Women Writers and the Writing of History, 1670-1820*. Baltimore, MD: Johns Hopkins UP, 2000. Print.

———. " 'I Always Take the Part of My Own Sex': *Emma*'s Mrs. Elton and the Rights of Women." *Persuasions: The Jane Austen Journal* 25 (2003): 192-196. Print.

———. *Women Writers and Old Age in Great Britain, 1750-1850*. Baltimore, MD: The Johns Hopkins UP, 2008. Print.

Losano, Antonia. " 'A Great Passion for Taking Likenesses': The Woman Painter in *Emma*." *Persuasions: The Jane Austen Journal* 27 (2005): 185-194. Print.

MacDonagh, Oliver. *Jane Austen: Real and Imagined Worlds*. New Haven, CT: Yale UP, 1991. Print.

Mansell, Darrel. *The Novels of Jane Austen: An Interpretation*. London, UK: Macmillan, 1973. Print.

Martin, Maureen M. "What Does Emma Want?: Sovereignty and Sexuality in Austen's *Emma*." *Nineteenth-Century Feminisms* 3 (2000): 10-24. Print.

McAllister, Marie E. " 'Only to Sink Deeper': Venereal Disease in *Sense and Sensibility*." *Eighteenth-Century Fiction* 17.1 (2004): 87-110. Print.

McDonald, Kelly M. " 'A Reputation for Accomplishment': Marianne Dashwood and Emma Woodhouse as Artistic Performers." *Jane Austen and the Arts: Elegance, Propriety, and Harmony*. Eds. Natasha Duquette and Elizabeth Lenckos. Bethlehem, PA: Lehigh UP, 2014. 21-36. Print.

McHugh, Maureen C., Nicole Livingston, and Irene H. Frieze. "Intimate Partner Violence: Perspectives on Research and Intervention." *Psychology of Women: A Handbook of Issues and Theories*. 2nd ed. Ed. Florence L. Denmark and Michele A. Paludi. Westport, CT: Praeger, 2008. *ebscohost*. Web. 17 Aug. 2015.

McMaster, Juliet. "Hospitality." *Persuasions: The Jane Austen Journal* 4 (1982): 26–33. Rpt. online: n. pag. *jasna.org.* Web. 1 Feb. 2016.

———. *Reading the Body in the Eighteenth-Century Novel.* New York: Palgrave Macmillan, 2004.

Michaelson, Patricia Howell. *Speaking Volumes: Women, Reading, and Speech in the Age of Austen.* Stanford, CA: Stanford UP, 2002. Print.

———. "Woman's Language; or, How to Speak like Mrs. Palmer (and Other Silly People)." *Persuasions: The Jane Austen Journal* 33 (2011): 53–59. Print.

Moler, Kenneth L. " 'Only Connect': Emotional Strength and Health in *Mansfield Park.*" *English Studies: A Journal of English Language and Literature* 64.2 (1983): 144–152. Print.

Monteiro, Belisa. "Jane Austen's Comic Heroines and the Controversial Pleasures of Wit." *Jane Austen and the Arts: Elegance, Propriety, and Harmony.* Eds. Natasha Duquette and Elisabeth Lenckos. Bethlehem, PA: LeHigh UP, 2014. Print.

Moore, Roger E. *Jane Austen and the Reformation: Remembering the Sacred Landscape.* Burlington, VT: Ashgate, 2016.

Morgan, Susan. *In the Meantime: Character and Perception in Jane Austen's Fiction.* Chicago: U of Chicago P, 1980. Print.

———. "Intelligence in *Pride and Prejudice.*" *Modern Philology: A Journal Devoted to Research in Medieval and Modern Literature* 73.1 (1975): 54–68. Print.

———. "Why There's No Sex in Jane Austen's Fiction." *Studies in the Novel* 19.3 (1987): 346–356. Print.

Moss, Sarah. "Fetching Broth from Hartfield: Sustaining the Body Politic in Jane Austen's *Emma.*" *Eating Culture: The Poetics and Politics of Food.* Ed. Tobias Döring, Heidi Marcus, and Susanne Mühleisen. Heidelberg, Germany: Universitätsverlag, 2003. 195–206. Print.

Murray, Venetia. *An Elegant Madness: High Society in Regency England.* New York: Viking, 1998. Print.

Nagle, Christopher C. *Sexuality and the Culture of Sensibility in the British Romantic Era.* New York: Palgrave Macmillan, 2007. Print.

Nardin, Jane. *Those Elegant Decorums: The Concept of Propriety in Jane Austen's Novels.* Albany, NY: State U of New York P, 1973. Print.

Nigro, Jeffrey. "Visualizing Jane Austen and Jane Austen Visualizing." *Persuasions: The Jane Austen Journal On-Line* 29.1 (2008): n. pag. *jasna.org.* Web. 16 Mar. 2011.

"Oh Mr. Darcy! Jane Austen Super Fans." Narr. David Wright. *Nightline*. ABC, 14 Nov. 2013. Television. *abcNEWS.com*. Web.

Parker, Jo Alyson. *The Author's Inheritance: Henry Fielding, Jane Austen, and the Establishment of the Novel*. DeKalb, IL: Northern Illinois UP, 1998. Print.

Pawl, Amy J. "Fanny Price and the Sentimental Genealogy of Mansfield Park." *Eighteenth-Century Fiction* 16.2 (2004): 287–315. *MLA International Bibliography*. Web. 19 Jan. 2006.

Perkin, J. Russell. "Aesthetics, Politics, and the Interpretation of *Mansfield Park*." *Jane Austen and the Arts: Elegance, Propriety, and Harmony*. Eds. Natasha Duquette and Elizabeth Lenckos. Bethlehem, PA: Lehigh UP, 2014. 149–162. Print.

Perkins, Moreland. *Reshaping the Sexes in* Sense and Sensibility. Charlottesville, VA: UP of Virginia, 1998. Print.

Perkins, Pam. "A Subdued Gaiety: The Comedy of *Mansfield Park*." *Nineteenth-Century Literature* 48.1 (1993): 1–25. Print.

Pinch, Adela. *Strange Fits of Passion: Epistemologies of Emotion, Hume to Austen*. Stanford, CA: Stanford UP, 1996. Print.

Poovey, Mary. *The Proper Lady and the Woman Writer: Ideology as Style in the Works of Mary Wollstonecraft, Mary Shelley, and Jane Austen*. Chicago, IL: U of Chicago P, 1984. Print.

Regency Etiquette: The Mirror of Graces (1811) by a Lady of Distinction. Enlarged ed. Mendocino, CA: R.L. Shep, 1997. Reprint of *The Mirror of the Graces; Or, The English Lady's Costume. . . . By A Lady of Distinction*. London: B. Crosby and Co., 1811. Print.

Reinstein, P. Gila. "Moral Priorities in *Sense and Sensibility*." *Renascence: Essays on Values in Literature* 35.4 (1983): 269–283. Print.

Riefe, Jordan. "Ernest Hemingway Look-Alikes Descend on the Hemingway Days Festival." *hollywoodreporter.com*. *The Hollywood Reporter*, 31 July 2014. Web.

Sabine, Maureen. "With My Body I Thee Worship: Joe Wright's Erotic Vision in Pride & Prejudice (2005)." *Journal of Religion and Popular Culture* 20 (2008): n. pag. *MLA International Bibliography*. Web. 3 Dec. 2013.

Sales, Roger. *Jane Austen and Representations of Regency England*. 1994. New York: Routledge, 1996. Print.

Schneider, Sister M. Lucy, C.S.J. "The Little White Attic and the East Room: Their Function in *Mansfield Park*." *Modern Philology* 63.3 (1966): 227–235. *JSTOR*. Web. 1 Feb. 2016.

Schuessler, Jennifer. "Lots of Pride, a Little Prejudice." *nytimes.com*. *The New York Times*, 8 Oct. 2012. Web.

Seeber, Barbara K. *Jane Austen and Animals*. Burlington, VT: Ashgate, 2013. Print.

———. "Nature, Animals, and Gender in Jane Austen's *Mansfield Park* and *Emma*." *Lit: Literature Interpretation Theory* 13.4 (2002): 269-85. *MLA International Bibliography*. Web. 28 Jan. 2006.

Selwyn, David. *Jane Austen and Leisure*. London, England: The Hambledon Press, 1999. Print.

Shields, Carol. *Jane Austen: A Life*. New York: Penguin, 2001. Print.

———. "Jane Austen Images of the Body: No Fingers, No Toes." *Persuasions: The Jane Austen Journal* 13 (1991): 132-137. Rpt. online: n. pag. *jasna.org*. Web. 6 Sept. 2013.

Smith, LeRoy W. *Jane Austen and the Drama of Woman*. New York: St. Martin's P, 1983. Print.

Smith, Peter. "Politics and Religion in Jane Austen's *Emma*." *The Cambridge Quarterly* 26.3 (1997): 219-241. Print.

Snyder, William C. "Mother Nature's Other Natures: Landscape in Women's Writing, 1770-1830." *Women's Studies: An Interdisciplinary Journal* 21.2 (1992): 143-162. Print.

Southam, Brian. " 'Rears' and 'Vices' in *Mansfield Park*." *Essays in Criticism: A Quarterly Journal of Literary Criticism* 52.1 (2002): 23-35. Print.

Spacks, Patricia Meyer. *Privacy: Concealing the Eighteenth-Century Self*. Chicago, IL: U of Chicago P, 2003. Print.

———. "The Talent of Ready Utterance: Eighteenth-Century Female Gossip." *Women and Society in the Eighteenth Century*. Ed. Ian Duffy. Bethlehem, PA: Lawrence Henry Gipson Institute, 1983. 1-14. Print.

Spence, Jon. "The Abiding Possibilities of Nature in *Persuasion*." *Studies in English Literature* 21.4 (1981): 625-636. *MLA International Bibliography*. Web. 28 Jan. 2006.

———. *Becoming Jane Austen*. London, UK: Hambledon Continuum, 2003. Print.

Spratt, Danielle. "Denaturalizing Lady Bountiful: Speaking the Silence of Poverty in Mary Brunton's *Discipline* and Jane Austen's *Emma*." *The Eighteenth Century* 56.2 (2015): 193-208. Print.

Steele, Pamela. "In Sickness and in Health: Jane Austen's Metaphor." *Studies in the Novel* 14.2 (1982): 152–160. *MLA International Bibliography*. Web. 20 Jan. 2006.

Stewart, Maaja A. "The Fools in Austen's *Emma*." *Nineteenth-Century Literature* 41.1 (1986): 72–86. Print.

Stohr, Karen. "Practical Wisdom and Moral Imagination in *Sense and Sensibility*." *Philosophy and Literature* 30 (2006): 378–394. Print.

Sulloway, Alison G. *Jane Austen and the Province of Womanhood*. Philadelphia: U of Pennsylvania P, 1989. Print.

Sutherland, Kathryn. "Chronology of composition and publication." *The Cambridge Edition of the Works of Jane Austen: Jane Austen in Context*. Ed. Janet Todd. New York: Cambridge UP, 2005. 12–22. Print.

Swords, Barbara W. " 'Woman's Place' in Jane Austen's England 1770–1820." *Persuasions: Journal of the Jane Austen Society of North America* 10 (1988): 76–82. Print.

Takei, Akiko. " 'We Live at Home, Quiet, Confined': Jane Austen's 'Vindication' of Women's Right to be Active and Healthy." *Studies in English Literature* 47 (2006): 65–86. Print.

Tanner, Tony. *Jane Austen*. Cambridge, MA: Harvard UP, 1986. Print.

Tarpley, Joyce Kerr. *Constancy and the Ethics of Jane Austen's* Mansfield Park. Washington, DC: Catholic U of America P, 2010. Print.

Tauchert, Ashley. *Romancing Jane Austen: Narrative, Realism, and the Possibility of an Ending*. Basingstoke: Palgrave, 2005. Print.

Tomalin, Claire. *Jane Austen: A Life*. 1997. New York: Vintage, 1999. Print.

Trickett, Rachel. "Mansfield Park." *Wordsworth Circle* 17.2 (1986): 87–95. Print.

Tuite, Clara. *Romantic Austen: Sexual Politics and the Literary Canon*. Cambridge: Cambridge UP, 2002. Print.

Ty, Eleanor. "Catherine's Real and Imagined Fears: What Happens to Female Bodies in Gothic Castles." *Persuasions: The Jane Austen Journal* 20 (1998): 248–260. Print.

Vorachek, Laura. "Crossing Boundaries: Land and Sea in Jane Austen's *Persuasion*." *Persuasions: Journal of the Jane Austen Society of North America* 19 (1997): 36–40.

Wainwright, Valerie. "On Being Tough-Minded: *Sense and Sensibility* and the Moral Psychology of 'Helping.' " *Philosophy and Literature* 39.1A (2015). *Proquest*. Web.

Waldron, Mary. "Men of Sense and Silly Wives: The Confusions of Mr. Knightley." *Studies in the Novel* 28.2 (1996): 141–157. Print.

Wallace, Robert K. *Jane Austen and Mozart: Classical Equilibrium in Fiction and Music*. Athens, GA: U of Georgia P, 1983. Print.

Warhol, Robyn. "The Look, the Body, and the Heroine: A Feminist-Narratological Reading of *Persuasion*." *NOVEL: A Forum on Fiction* 26.1 (1992): 5–19. Print.

Watt, Ian. "On *Sense and Sensibility*." *Jane Austen: A Collection of Critical Essays*. New York: Prentice-Hall, 1963. Rpt. in *A Truth Universally Acknowledged: 33 Great Writers on Why We Read Jane Austen*. Ed. Susannah Carson. New York: Random House, 2009. 45–56. Print.

Weinsheimer, Joel C. "Mansfield Park: Three Problems." *Nineteenth-Century Fiction* 29.2 (1974): 185–205. Print.

Wells, Juliette. " 'A Fearsome Thing to Behold'? The Accomplished Woman in Joe Wright's Pride & Prejudice." *Persuasions: The Jane Austen Journal On-Line* 27.2 (2007): n. pag. *jasna.org*. Web. 25 July 2011.

———. "A Harpist Arrives at Mansfield Park: Music and the Moral Ambiguity of Mary Crawford." *Persuasions: The Jane Austen Journal* 28 (2006): 101–114. Print.

———. " 'In music she had always used to feel alone in the world': Jane Austen, Solitude, and the Artistic Woman." *Persuasions: The Jane Austen Journal* 26 (2004): 98–110. Print.

Wenner, Barbara Britton. *Prospect and Refuge in the Landscape of Jane Austen*. Burlington, VT: Ashgate, 2006. Print.

White, Laura Mooneyham. *Jane Austen's Anglicanism*. Burlington, VT: Ashgate, 2011. Print.

———. "Traveling to the Self: Comic and Spatial Openness in Jane Austen's Novels." *Critical Essays on Jane Austen*. Ed. Laura Mooneyham White. New York: G.K. Hall, 1998. 98–213. Print.

Wiltshire, John. *Jane Austen and the Body*. 1992. New York: Cambridge UP, 2006. Print.

———. "Jane Austen, Health, and the Body." *Critical Review* 31 (1991): 122–134. Print.

Wollstonecraft, Mary. *A Vindication of the Rights of Woman* and *The Wrongs of Woman, or Maria*. Ed. Anne K. Mellor and Noelle Chao. New York: Longman, 2007. Print.

Wood, Gillen D'Arcy. "Austen's Accomplishment: Music and the Modern Heroine." *A Companion to Jane Austen*. Ed. Claudia L. Johnson and Clara Tuite. 2009. Chichester, UK: Blackwell, 2012. 366–376. Print.

Woolf, Virginia. *A Room of One's Own*. 1929. New York: Harcourt Brace, 1981. Print.

Yousef, Nancy. " 'Emotions that reason deepens': Second Thoughts About Affect." *Nineteenth-Century Gender Studies* 11.3 (2015). Web.

Index

Art, artistry, xxiii, 89–110 passim, 113, 178, 248n8, 249n14, 249n16, 251n26

Austen, Jane

  authorship, xviii, xx, 28, 82, 85–86, 91, 135, 228, 250n21, 250n22, 250n24, 263n1

  literary technique, xx, xxv, 224, 233n1

    body/materiality of craft, 3–4, 6, 8, 9, 27–28, 33, 198, 238n27

    comedy, satire, xvi, xix–xx, xxv, 4–5, 10, 47, 72, 76, 81, 83, 112, 116, 143, 158, 186–190, 194, 203–206, 213, 221–222, 226–229, 233n2, 235n14, 245n8, 247n2, 259–260n16, 265n10, 266n17

    drama, 182–183, 224, 238n27

    narrative technique, 175–176, 181, 185, 224

    realism, 65, 70–71, 76–80, 82–83, 102, 112, 146, 154, 166, 183, 186, 191, 198, 210, 214, 218, 219, 226, 228–229, 245n7, 246n11, 265n13

  readers, xv–xvii, xix–xxi, xxv, 185, 195, 200–201, 225, 227–228

  relationship with Cassandra, xix–xx, 232n7, 233n2, 250n22

  supportive female community, 110, 250n22

  talents, 86, 247n3

beauty

  of art or object, 12, 91, 98, 136, 140–142

  of nature, 102, 151, 153–154, 160–161, 169–170, 178, 257n7, 257–258n8, 261n21

  of quality or effect, 6, 27, 89, 98, 100, 147, 151

  of women, 3–4, 6, 11, 21, 27, 45–46, 48–49, 56–57, 79, 87–88, 94, 141, 180, 189, 198, 242n22, 245n7, 261–262n25

bildungsroman, development, 4, 6, 9, 12, 27–28, 30, 67–68, 102, 117, 135, 146, 152, 160–162, 166, 168, 170–171, 173, 175, 183, 253n12

167, 171, 196, 197, 220–221,
234–235n10, 242n21, 267n2
Weston, Mr., 195
Weston, Mrs., 6, 8, 49, 221,
242n22, 260n20
Woodhouse, Emma
artistry, xxiii, 90–91, 96, 103–
106, 110, 249n14, 250n25
confidence and self-worth,
6, 27, 47, 50, 53, 90, 110,
197–198, 214, 226
relationship to Harriet,
47–49, 51–52, 118, 120,
134, 139, 141, 171, 196–
197, 220–221, 242n21
health, 4, 6, 8
hospitality, 118, 133–146,
168–169, 254n16, 255n20
intelligence, 87, 90–91, 103,
109–110, 112, 154, 169
leadership, 97, 118, 134, 136,
197, 242n21, 242n23
moral growth, xxiv, 8, 118,
120, 133–148, 168–174,
183, 196, 218, 220–221,
255n21, 261n20
relationship to nature, xxiv,
151, 153–154, 167–174, 183
sexuality and courtship
journey, 31, 47–53, 134
virtues, 105–106, 110,
220–221, 223
Woodhouse, Mr., 104, 135,
137, 139–142, 167, 168, 186,
254n17, 255n19, 255n20,
264n6
emotion, 8, 54, 82, 176–178, 182,
188, 214, 222

family roles and relationships
brothers, brotherhood, 25, 41,
86, 98, 100, 102, 104, 109, 111,
155, 208, 220, 239n5, 241n18
children, childhood, childcare,
9–10, 12, 48, 72, 77, 121,
125, 132, 164, 176, 198–202,
204, 206–213, 221, 246n10,
253n11, 266n15
fathers, father figures,
fatherhood, 167–168, 199,
200–202, 207–208, 210–212
mothers, mother figures,
maternity, 24, 57, 59, 96,
122, 130, 132, 147, 167,
176, 199, 202, 205–214, 221,
236n18, 246n10, 260–261n20,
267n2
sisters, sisterhood, sorority,
90, 100–102, 109–111, 115,
118–119, 123–124, 128–138
passim, 143, 145–148, 151,
155, 168–171, 173–174,
196, 215, 222–223, 255n21,
256n23
feminism, gender roles, 50, 53–54,
58, 66, 86, 108, 117, 157–159,
175, 179, 181–182, 185–206
passim, 209–215, 254n15,
260n18, 261n24, 261–262n25,
262n28, 263–264n3
friendship, 25, 55, 60, 100, 109,
134, 144–145, 147, 179, 214,
256n23

heroinism, heroism, 8, 82, 108,
215, 218, 219, 221–227,
254n15, 264n4, 267n4

hospitality, food and drink, 5, 9,
28, 77, 116–117, 127, 133–
145, 147, 165, 170, 178–179,
181, 255n20

identity, selfhood, 33, 46–47,
55, 59–61, 70, 72, 75, 80–82,
86–94 passim, 112–114,
128, 130, 148, 154–155, 157,
160–164, 166–167, 172–176,
179, 183–184, 190, 192, 195,
214, 215, 222, 259n14
intelligence, reason, talent, 35,
87, 95, 108, 112, 120, 189,
265n9

Mansfield Park, characters
Bertram, Edmund, 9, 10,
12–26, 45–47, 59, 109, 117,
120–127, 146, 153, 187–189,
196, 225, 236n17, 237n22,
241n13, 252n4, 253n10,
257n4, 257n5, 265n9
Bertram, Julia, xxii, 7, 10, 12,
15, 16, 18, 23–25, 126, 127,
147, 237n24
Bertram, Lady, xxii, 7, 10,
12–13, 18, 19, 22–27, 31, 122,
131, 132, 168, 186, 236n18,
237n23
Bertram, Maria, xxii, 7, 10–16
passim, 21, 23–25, 31,
60, 127, 236n18, 236n19,
237n24, 240n9
Bertram, Sir Thomas, 21–22,
26, 44, 122, 126, 131–133,
168, 213, 222, 236n16, 252n5,
253–254n13, 264n8

Crawford, Henry, 16, 20–22,
31, 43–47, 128, 221, 232n7,
237n22, 242n20, 257n5,
260n18
Crawford, Mary, xxii, xxiv, 7,
10, 14–15, 23, 25, 66, 87, 94,
95, 110, 111, 122, 148, 152–
153, 187–190, 194, 214–215,
222, 235n14, 236n17, 238n1,
250n23, 256n22, 257n3,
266n19
Norris, Aunt, xxii, xxiv, 7,
10, 17–19, 22–24, 27, 93,
122–126, 128, 136, 196, 213,
236n19, 252n5, 253n10
Price, Fanny
body and character
development, 9, 11–14,
22, 24–25, 27
exercise, 14, 17–19, 22, 23
frailty, 7–11, 17, 24
helpfulness, 13, 18, 25,
124–129 passim
relationship to Mary
Crawford, 16, 19, 23, 110,
187–189, 222, 225
men's attempts to control,
19–22, 25, 31, 43–45,
252n5, 260n18
mentor role, 118–133
passim, 146–147
relationship to nature,
152–153, 257n3, 257n4,
259n15, 260n16,
262–263n29
neglect and abuse of,
9–12, 16, 17, 19, 97, 116,
121–128 passim

166, 173, 256n2, 258n10,
259n14
mediocre piano-playing,
92–93, 95, 109, 112
self-respect, 37, 53–55, 59,
159, 193–194, 259n12
sexuality, 31, 34–36, 54
Bennet, Jane, 34–35, 37, 66,
70, 82, 110, 119–120, 147,
156, 159, 161, 191–194, 219,
241n15, 243n27, 256n23,
256n2
Bennet, Kitty, 7, 147, 156
Bennet, Lydia, 7, 34–37, 54, 60,
136, 156, 191, 193, 194, 219,
220, 240
Bennet, Mary, 31, 92–93, 95, 110,
111, 186, 194, 214, 264n3
Bennet, Mr., 55, 61, 198, 261n23
Bennet, Mrs., 7, 31, 34, 35, 136,
186, 198
Bingley, Caroline, 86, 87, 95,
111, 112, 152, 156, 157
Bingley, Charles, 34, 35, 37,
109, 159, 192, 243n27
Collins, Mr., 47, 146, 186, 191,
192
Darcy, Fitzwilliam, xix, 31, 35,
37, 52–55, 56, 57, 82, 87, 109,
119, 158–162, 163, 173, 191,
192, 193, 243n27, 251n27,
257n5, 258n11, 259n12
Darcy, Georgiana, 93, 136, 147,
259n12
de Bourgh, Anne, 7, 259n11
de Bourgh, Lady Catherine,
xxiv, 87, 109, 136, 157, 158,
159, 190–195, 214, 258–
259n11, 263–264n3, 265n10

Gardiner, Aunt, 8, 31, 35, 87,
160, 256n23
Gardiner, Uncle, 31, 160
Hurst, Louisa, 152, 156, 157
Lucas, Charlotte, xxiv, 54, 60, 66,
87, 110, 136, 152, 186, 191–194,
195, 198, 214, 256n23
Wickham, George, 31, 35, 37,
55, 119, 191, 219, 220

religion, 255–256n22
Anglicanism, 33, 122, 146,
253n10, 255n21
biblical references, 128, 136,
153, 161, 224, 254n18, 257n6,
264–265n8
Christianity, 65, 116–117, 119–
120, 124–125, 129, 136–139,
144–146, 151, 219, 223–224,
226, 228–229, 253n12, 257n4,
261n21
monasticism, 115–117, 124–
125, 127–133, 146–148, 151,
164, 253n11
sacramentalism, 40, 61, 117,
135–136, 138–141, 143,
145–146, 151, 184, 227
service, 106, 115–117, 120,
125–126, 128–130, 134, 141,
143, 145–146, 168, 175, 224,
262–263n29
vocation, 33, 115, 117–118,
120–121, 128, 130, 133, 136,
144–145, 147
Romanticism, sensibility, 10,
14, 32, 67–70, 81, 95–96,
99, 163, 178, 219, 221, 228,
229, 235n14, 243n31, 244n2,
244n4, 244–245n5, 245n6,

Romanticism, sensibility
(continued)
245n7, 247n2, 249n12,
259-260n16, 264n4